DATA ANALYSIS

MICROSOFT®
WITH ACCESS® 2010

From Si... ...telligence

Course Techn...
A part of Ceng...

FF

D1456729

 COURSE TECH...
CENGAGE Learnin...

Australia • Brazil • Ja...

COURSE TECHNOLOGY
CENGAGE Learning

**Data Analysis with Microsoft®
Access® 2010**
Larry Rockoff

Publisher and General Manager,
Course Technology PTR:
Stacy L. Hiquet

Associate Director of Marketing:
Sarah Panella

Manager of Editorial Services:
Heather Talbot

Marketing Manager: Mark Hughes

Senior Acquisitions Editor:
Mitzi Koontz

Project and Copy Editor: Dan Foster,
Scribe Tribe

Technical Reviewer: Laxmi Dash

Interior Layout Tech: MPS Limited,
a Macmillan Company

Cover Designer: Luke Fletcher

Indexer: Valerie Haynes Perry

Proofreader: Sandi Wilson

For product information and technology assistance, contact us at
Cengage Learning Customer & Sales Support, 1-800-354-9706

For permission to use material from this text or product,
submit all requests online at
www.cengage.com/permissions

Further permissions questions can be emailed to
permissionrequest@cengage.com

Microsoft, Windows, Access, SQL Server, and Excel are either
registered trademarks or trademarks of Microsoft Corporation in
the United States and/or other countries.

All other trademarks are the property of their respective owners.

All images © Cengage Learning unless otherwise noted.

Library of Congress Control Number: 2011936038

ISBN-13: 978-1-4354-6010-2

ISBN-10: 1-4354-6010-3

Course Technology, a part of Cengage Learning
20 Channel Center Street
Boston, MA 02210
USA

Cengage Learning is a leading provider of customized learning
solutions with office locations around the globe, including Singapore,
the United Kingdom, Australia, Mexico, Brazil, and Japan. Locate
your local office at: **international.cengage.com/region**

Cengage Learning products are represented in Canada by Nelson
Education, Ltd.

For your lifelong learning solutions, visit **courseptr.com**

Visit our corporate website at **cengage.com**

Printed in the United States of America
1 2 3 4 5 6 7 13 12 11

For Lisa

ACKNOWLEDGMENTS

Although the writing of this book was initially an individual effort, it took many people to bring the project to fruition. A general thanks goes to all at Cengage Learning who had anything to do with the book, from the cover designer to the proofreader and indexer. As with my first book, I'd especially like to thank Mitzi Koontz, my acquisitions editor, for giving me the opportunity to proceed with a second project. Laxmi Dash, my technical reviewer, did an outstanding job in his review. I thank him for the numerous suggestions he provided. Lastly, Dan Foster, my project editor, was superb in pulling it all together and adding a professional touch to the entire project.

Finally, and most especially, I would like to thank everyone in my immediate family for their general encouragement as I've dedicated myself to this project. Thank you... Kyle, Emily, Dan, Steve, and Lisa.

About the Author

Larry Rockoff has been involved with Access, SQL, and business intelligence development for many years. His main area of expertise is with data warehouse and reporting tools. He currently works with data warehouse applications at a major international financial institution. He holds an MBA from the University of Chicago, with a specialization in Management Science.

His prior book, *The Language of SQL*, was published by Cengage Learning in June 2010, and is available worldwide, in both paper and electronic form.

He also maintains a website with occasional commentary on computing issues at:

- larryrockoff.com

Please feel free to visit that site to contact the author with any comments or questions. You are also encouraged to follow his Facebook author page or Twitter site at:

- facebook.com/larryrockoff
- twitter.com/larryrockoff

CONTENTS

INTRODUCTION

The title of this book is quite a mouthful but hopefully provides a reasonable idea of the topics to be covered. *Data Analysis with Microsoft Access 2010* tells you that the book is about both data analysis and Microsoft Access. The emphasis, however, is on data analysis. There are already many fine books that cover the nuts and bolts of Access from A to Z, but very few discuss Access with the goal of learning what it can accomplish as a data analysis tool. This is such a book.

If you're wondering what *data analysis* actually means, you're not alone. It's certainly an overused and somewhat trite term, and one that can be interpreted in many different ways. As a result, before we even begin looking at Access, we'll devote most of Chapter 1 to a general discussion of data analysis and how it relates to Access.

This book covers the latest version of Access. All screenshots are taken from Microsoft Access 2010.

Now for the subtitle: *From Simple Queries to Business Intelligence*. As you'll learn in Chapter 2, Access is comprised of five major components: tables, queries, forms, reports, and macros. As indicated by the phrase *simple queries*, the emphasis in this book is on queries. To a lesser extent, we will also cover tables. Forms, reports, and macros—although useful aspects of Access for the general user—are of limited importance for the data analyst and are therefore covered only marginally in this book.

The book's subtitle also mentions *business intelligence*. Coverage of this topic is a unique feature of the book, and one that you won't find in other Access texts. Like data analysis, business intelligence (BI) is a term that has many different meanings and implications, but as discussed in this book, business intelligence is a natural extension of the analytic process. What many don't realize is that Microsoft Access offers many of the basic capabilities required for a BI solution. While larger organizations will no doubt choose powerful server-based tools over Access for business intelligence development, it is nevertheless true that Access can be used as a first step for prototyping and development. At the very least, Access can serve as a tool for learning what BI is all about, even if it's not used in a final solution.

TOPICS AND FEATURES

The topics in this book are many and varied, but in essence, we'll focus on one main objective:

- How to use Access queries to analyze data

We will also cover numerous related topics, including:

- How to utilize business intelligence concepts in data analysis
- How to create tables and links to data in external data sources
- How to create and utilize pivot tables in both Access and Excel
- Strategies for using Excel in conjunction with Access

We assume no prior knowledge of Microsoft Access. In other words, this is an introductory book on Access, but one that focuses its content on those topics that will be useful for the data analyst.

A number of features make this book unique among introductory Access books:

- **The emphasis is on data analysis.**
  Access contains many components and can be used in multiple ways in an organization. We focus on its data analysis features, and spend relatively little time on Access's ability to create self-contained applications for data input and maintenance. Additionally, to handle relatively advanced data analysis issues, we intersperse the text with "Focus on Analysis" sidebars to explore those topics in detail.

- **Business intelligence concepts are explored in conjunction with data analysis.**
  Business intelligence is both a process and a specific way of organizing data to put it in a more intuitive format for the business analyst. As such, it can prove

useful for many data analysis tasks. We'll show you how to organize your data along those lines.

- **You will not be required to sit with a computer as you read the text.**
  It will not be necessary to download data or run through exercises as you read the text. The text includes small data samples that allow you to understand how Access queries work simply by reading the book.

- **You'll learn how Access queries relate to SQL.**
  SQL is the language that underlies access to data in Access. Many Access analysts may already know something about SQL or have a desire to learn a little SQL as they learn Access. Through the use of special "See the SQL" sidebars, we'll show you how the Access query concepts you're learning relate to SQL code. This material is purely optional, so if you have no need or desire to learn SQL, that won't affect your understanding of anything else.

With this book's emphasis on data analysis, several topics will receive little or no mention. These topics include:

- Installation
- Security Features
- Database Documenter
- Visual Basic
- SharePoint Links
- Database Repair and Administration
- Pass-Through and Data Definition Queries

In addition, we will not cover Access forms, reports, and macros in the main text. However, we provide an appendix with a brief tutorial on those topics.

PLAN OF THE BOOK

This book presents its material in a unique sequence. The majority of Access books run through their topics as if the reader were a systems programmer who needs to create and design an Access database from scratch, then create some forms to allow users to enter some data into the database, and then finally start to retrieve that data. In this book, we start with the assumption that the data you want to access and analyze is most often in external databases and spreadsheets. Our motivation is the data itself and the desire to learn more about what it means.

The 16 chapters in the book are broken down into three main parts:

- **Part I: Getting Started**

  This first section, comprised of two chapters, gets us going with some essential introductory material. The first chapter covers the meaning and purpose of data analysis, and provides a framework for the tools at our disposal. The second chapter presents an overview of Access, with an emphasis on its user interface and various ways to navigate through the software. We also provide some background information on how Access relates to other relational databases.

- **Part II: Access Queries**

  This second section contains the main material of the book. The chapters in this section can be divided into four main groups:

  Chapters 3 through 5 cover the basics of tables, queries, and joins. This explains how to use tables to import and link to data, and how to design tables with the necessary keys and proper data types. We then get into the various components of the *Select query*. This provides a way to retrieve data from various sources and is at the heart of the data analysis process. Finally, the chapter on joins discusses ways to retrieve data from multiple tables or queries.

  Chapter 6 steps aside from Access to explore the topic of relational database design. This provides the theoretical framework necessary for our subsequent efforts to organize and analyze data.

  Chapters 7 through 10 delve into various ways to design Select queries to retrieve precisely the data that is needed. These topics include expressions, functions, selection criteria, summarization, and subqueries.

  Chapters 11 and 12 cover a variety of other query types. Chapter 11 explains how Select queries can be converted into *Action queries*. These queries allow you to update, delete, or insert data rather than simply retrieve it. Chapter 12 covers the important topics of *Crosstab queries* and *pivot tables*. These topics lead directly to the third section of this book, the material on business intelligence.

- **Part III: Creating Business Intelligence**

  The four chapters in this final section explain how to extend data analysis into business intelligence. Chapter 13 provides a theoretical framework for the subject, with a survey of BI software and a discussion of its purpose and features.

  Chapters 14 and 15 move into the details of designing Access queries that can accomplish business intelligence objectives. In these chapters, you'll learn how to create queries and processes that can model the *dimensions* and *facts* of a BI solution.

Finally, Chapter 16 explains how to utilize the analysis capabilities of Excel pivot tables to explore the business intelligence structure you've created. Although Access provides a pivot table view of queries, Excel is usually the better tool for this type of analysis. We'll also touch on a new Excel tool, PowerPivot, which was introduced with Office 2010.

The two appendices to the book provide supplemental information. Appendix A covers the three main Access topics not discussed in the main part of this book: Forms, Macros, and Reports. With this tutorial, you'll be up and running with the basics of these other Access features.

Appendix B describes a sample business intelligence database that has been created in Access. This database is available on the book's companion website.

COMPANION WEBSITE DOWNLOADS

You may download companion website files from **www.courseptr.com/downloads**. Please note that you will be redirected to our Cengage Learning site. Two Access database files are available for download: SalesDatabase.accdb and DataWarehouse.accdb. These files are described in Appendices A and B.

TYPOGRAPHIC CONVENTIONS

In an effort to keep the book as readable as possible, special typography has been kept to a minimum. Nevertheless, in dealing with software and computer languages, certain conventions must be employed to aid in understanding.

First, we use *italics* to denote any type of special emphasis. Italics are generally employed when introducing a new term or concept for the first time, to indicate that the word has a special meaning.

We print Access functions, operators, and constants in ALL CAPS. Note that Access itself doesn't display these items as such. It generally just capitalizes the first one or two letters. For example, we display the function LTrim as LTRIM and the operator And as AND. This helps these words stand out and be recognized as special keywords.

Finally, we apply a number of conventions to the SQL statements that appear in our "See the SQL" sidebars. These are explained when the first sidebar is introduced in Chapter 4.

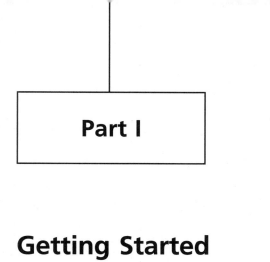

Part I

Getting Started

Chapter 1

What Is Data Analysis?

Data analysis means different things to different people. At face value, data analysis means nothing other than the fact that some sort of analysis is being performed on data. The first question one might ask is: What does analysis really mean, and what is the intended result?

Data comes in many forms and formats. One might want to look at data in a spreadsheet, or perhaps dozens of tables in a complex database. The data might be in an easy to understand format, or it might be a convoluted mess. The individual data elements might be text, numbers, or dates. Even something as simple as a date might be in one of dozens of different formats—for example: Sept 25, 2011; 9/25/11; 09/25/2011; 20110925; or 11238 (the 238th day of 2011).

Analysis is a more difficult concept to pinpoint. The dictionary definition indicates that analysis is primarily about discovering the essential features or meaning of something. Typical synonyms for analyze are *study, view, survey, compare, investigate,* and *examine.* All of these words tell us that analysis involves some sort of study and judgment made by human beings. Analysis isn't like processing an order or issuing a refund to a customer. There's no definite outcome. Ultimately, it represents a quest for greater understanding.

But even the notion that analysis involves greater understanding begs the question: greater understanding of what? Is the goal simply to understand the data, or does it involve something more than mere data?

In addition to these questions about data and analysis, we must also consider the software tools at our disposal. While it's true that we'll focus on the capabilities of Microsoft Access in this book, Access is far from the only available tool for data analysis. So, we'll look at what types of data analysis are best done with Access, and what is more easily accomplished with other software.

Excel Basics

If you were to do a search on book titles with the words "Data Analysis," you would probably find more books involving Excel than Access. This doesn't mean that you've picked up the wrong book to learn about data analysis. However, it is true that Access and Excel each have their particular strengths and weaknesses. The good news, though, is that they can often be used in tandem, so before we get into a closer examination of data analysis, we'll want to understand some of the essential capabilities of these tools.

Microsoft Excel is an amazingly functional and flexible piece of software that does just about everything a spreadsheet can offer. When the first microcomputer spreadsheet, VisiCalc, appeared in 1978, it was immediately recognized as a breakthrough tool for anyone working with data. The capabilities of spreadsheets continued to grow as Lotus 1-2-3 and then Excel were developed.

What is the essence of a spreadsheet? In physical terms, an Excel spreadsheet is a single file that is logically divided into any number of worksheets. These worksheets can be viewed via tabs at the bottom of the screen. Each worksheet is a grid of rows and columns, the rows being referred to by numbers and the columns by letters. Each cell in the grid is thus referred to by a letter and column. For example, cell C4 refers to a location in the third column (C being the third letter in the alphabet) and the fourth row.

In essence, spreadsheets consist of three overlapping layers: a data layer, a formula layer, and a presentation layer. The data layer allows users to enter any desired value into any cell. For example, if you enter the value 33 in a cell, that cell will normally display that number. Data might consist of numbers to be used in formulas, but data can also be simply a text value that's only present to provide descriptive information.

The formula layer gives Excel its unique abilities. The real power of formulas comes from the fact that a formula can contain a reference to another cell. At its simplest, a formula for cell D4 might contain the value:

$$= D1$$

This means that the value of cell D1 is automatically copied to cell D4. The remarkable aspect of this is that this reference to another cell is *relative*. This means that as new rows or columns are inserted into a spreadsheet, the references you already have in place continue to be valid.

An example of a more complex formula, with relative references, would be:

$$= (A2 * B2) + 50$$

This formula says to multiply the value of cell A2 by the value of cell B2, and add 50 to the result. In addition to relative references, formulas can also invoke built-in functions to yield complex calculations. A formula that utilizes one of the built-in functions might look like:

$$= SUM (B1...B25)$$

This function means to sum up the values of cells B1 through B25.

Finally, the presentation layer takes the end result of the data and formulas you've entered and adds visual elements to your cells. For example, you can specify that a cell be light green with a red border. More significantly, you can also define the format for numeric and date values. For example, you can specify that the numeric values in a particular cell should display with one decimal place, regardless of the underlying value.

Access Basics

We'll go over the Access user interface in detail in Chapter 2, but for now let's examine some of its essential characteristics, with an eye toward seeing how it compares to Excel. Like Excel, Access consists of a number of components. In physical terms, an Access database is a single file that can be logically divided into different objects. The primary objects are *tables*, *queries*, *forms*, *reports*, and *macros*. The specific objects in a database are listed in a Navigator pane on the left side of the screen.

The most significant objects in an Access database are tables and queries. Tables are distinct sets of data comprised of rows and columns, much like an Excel worksheet. Unlike Excel, however, rows are not numbered. Columns are referred to by field names rather than letters. Tables can be either internal or external. The data in internal tables is contained within the Access database. In contrast, external tables are merely links to data outside of the database.

Tables contain or point to essential data, but the real heart of an Access database is the query. Access queries are analogous to formulas in Excel, but they are quite a bit broader in scope. In a nutshell, queries specify *virtual tables*. Taking data from one or more tables or queries, queries create a separate set of data. Like tables, the data in queries appears as a grid of rows and columns. However, queries don't actually contain physical data. Through use of a *SQL statement*, queries merely define the data they are said to contain. The SQL statement is a definition of data in a query.

For purposes of data analysis, the less significant components of Access are forms, reports, and macros. Forms provide a way for users to enter data into tables. Reports allow for the viewing of data in a paper-based format. Macros provide a way of automating and executing commands.

Comparing Access and Excel

Let's now turn to some of the broad similarities and differences between Access and Excel. The main difference between the two is that the layers and worksheets of an Excel spreadsheet are far more interrelated than the objects in an Access database. This is what gives Excel its great flexibility. You can change a formula in one spreadsheet cell and immediately have that new formula affect hundreds of other cells through a multitude of direct and indirect relationships.

However, it should also be noted that this flexibility also has a distinct downside. Since formulas can be entered in any cell, the relationships and functionality of a spreadsheet are often difficult to discern. Functions and formulas aren't listed in one central location. They can be hidden in dozens or hundreds of individual cells. Borrowing a phrase from politics, one would say that Excel spreadsheets lack transparency. In other words, the flexibility of Excel comes with a price. The price is the inability to easily determine how a complex spreadsheet functions.

In contrast, Access databases have a more rigid structure. Tables hold your data, and queries contain your formulas. There is no overlap between the two.

Another aspect of Excel's flexibility is due to its presentation layer. As mentioned, a cell in Excel can contain data, a formula, or merely specifications as to how that data will be displayed. In contrast, presentation possibilities in Access are more limited.

To make the differences between Access and Excel more concrete, let's take an example of an analyst who wishes to examine orders from the past year and analyze the profitability of each month, comparing each month to prior months. To accomplish this type of analysis in Excel, one would typically copy the required data into the first worksheet in a spreadsheet. One would then add rows or columns with appropriate formulas to produce the desired statistics. As new months of data become available, the prior month's worksheet would be copied to a new worksheet and then updated with data for the new month. After 12 months have elapsed, one might also add a thirteenth worksheet that copies key statistics from the prior 12 worksheets in a different format for easy comparison of key values. One might also add another worksheet with a chart to display the same data in a graphical format. After doing all this, you have a spreadsheet with over a dozen worksheets with interweaving formulas and presentation components.

Now let's say one wanted to do a similar analysis using Access. In Access, you need to first layout and organize your data before you can do any kind of analysis. You would typically start with a connection to your company database to bring that data into tables in your Access database. You need not actually copy the data. Access allows you to establish links to external data. Now that you have the raw data available in a number of tables, you'll probably create a few queries to clean up and reorganize that data into new virtual tables to select just the data you need to work with. Whereas Excel may have required you to create separate worksheets for each month, in Access you would probably utilize date fields that allow you to distinguish between data in the different months. Finally, you can create a query that selects data from your tables or queries to capture the final statistics you need. You also have the ability to transform any query in Access into something called a PivotChart, allowing you to view the same data in graphic form.

The lesson to be drawn from this example is that Excel is quite a bit simpler when starting out. You can quickly get your data into a worksheet, add some formulas, and see results. But as the data becomes more complex, the interrelationships inherent in an Excel spreadsheet become more difficult to maintain and understand. In contrast, Access requires more upfront work to organize and transform data into a workable format. But once that is done, new queries can be easily written, since the structure of the data is more apparent.

The Purpose of Analysis

With some of the basics of Access and Excel in hand, let's now return to our initial question: What is Data Analysis?

To answer that question, we might start with some general goals and objectives, such as:

- To find meaning in our data
- To understand relationships in our data
- To make specific decisions
- To validate decisions we have already made
- To be able to easily retrieve detailed information

This is all true, but the problem with these types of platitudes is that they are too broad to be meaningful. Let's narrow it down to some more specific objectives. We want to deal with the reality that we have some data and a number of software tools that allow us to examine that data in certain ways. We may want to accomplish specific tasks, such as:

- Combine detailed data into groups, with summary descriptions and statistics
- Apply financial formulas to data
- Drill down from broad groups to the underlying detail
- Compare data in different datasets to find similarities and patterns
- Reorganize a database so relationships between tables are more meaningful
- Combine or split text data to put it in a standard format
- Use statistical inference to obtain meaningful correlations
- Present data in a graph so others can grasp the big picture through visual means
- Use mathematical optimization to determine ways to maximize profit

We still can't draw any conclusions about what data analysis really is, but we're getting a bit closer. Looking at it from the broadest possible perspective, we see three different types of transformations in the above tasks:

- Data transformations
- Mathematical transformations
- Visual transformations

In other words, we can say that data analysis is about the raw data involved, its visual presentation, and any mathematics used in the transformation. At the start of this chapter, it was stated that data analysis means different things to different people. To some, data analysis is all about the *data*. To others, data analysis really means *analysis*, with the assumption that analysis is mathematical in nature. Putting these words together, it appears that the term *data analysis* is a meaningful way to describe the process. And to these twin components of data and mathematics, we're adding the possibility of visual transformation.

In many ways, the data, mathematical, and visual transformations we're talking about correspond to the data, formula, and presentation layers of Excel spreadsheets discussed earlier. This is why Excel is such an intuitive tool, since it allows you to work simultaneously with all three types of transformations.

These three transformations are often related and intertwined. In some cases, they're three different ways of looking at the same process. For example, let's imagine that someone is creating a graph to summarize prior year sales. In this process, the data itself may need to be reorganized to get into the proper form for further analysis. Individual data fields may need to be cleaned up, plus the level of detail may require modification so that it's summarized by month. Also, mathematics may be employed to calculate various statistics that will be used in the presentation. Finally, charts are utilized to create the final visualization of the data for the viewer.

To obtain a better understanding of what's involved in data analysis, let's examine these three transformation types more closely. Hopefully, this will provide some greater insight into the entire task of data analysis before we get down to details. But first let's simplify our terms a bit. Using more conventional terminology, we'll refer to the three transformations as:

- Data transformation
- Quantitative analysis
- Visualization

Data Transformation

Data transformation indicates any way in which raw data is modified or organized. It may be something as simple as combining a first name and last name field together to create a field that shows a person's full name. It may be slightly more complex, perhaps involving applying some sort of formula to a number of data elements. It might mean reducing detail by creating summary rows for sets of data. Or, it can involve a complex process whereby an entire database is reorganized to create a completely different structure for the data.

Let's talk for a moment about the general nature of data. The usual custom is to store data in *databases*, which are said to contain all the data needed for an enterprise or application. Within databases, data is logically organized into any number of *tables*. Each table stores information about a specific entity, and consists of any number of *columns* and *rows*. Each row in the table stores information about a specific occurrence of the entity. Each column in the table stores information about a different attribute pertaining to the entity. For example, one might have a table named Customers that contains information about an organization's customers. Customers are the entity. Each attribute of a customer, such as name and phone number, would be stored in a different column. Each row in the table stores information about a specific customer.

Let's look at these different data structures and talk about what types of data transformations can occur with each type of structure.

The simplest data structure is an individual cell in a table. This is referred to as a *data item* or sometimes a *field*. You can combine data items in various ways. If the field contains a numeric quantity, we might apply some simple arithmetic operation or formula. Data items with text data can be concatenated or split into separate words. Another common possibility is to apply a built-in function to the data in one or more fields to yield some result.

Next, a number of data transformations apply to entire *rows* of data. A row is simply a collection of all the attributes for a single occurrence of the entity in a given table. We might, for example, apply aggregation to a set of rows. This allows us to summarize the values in those rows, combining those rows into larger groups of data. We might apply special *aggregate functions* to these groups so summary statistics can be seen. Another possibility is to *sort* a set of rows, so the rows are presented in a meaningful order.

When we add *columns* to the mix, we find certain data transformations that work on both rows and columns simultaneously. For example, we might want to group together not only values in our rows, but also values in our columns. The end result is a *matrix* of numbers that presents data in highly summarized and dynamic fashion. Excel pivot tables are a typical example of this type of presentation.

Rows and columns combine to form tables, and some data transformations work on the various tables that might exist in a database. We may want to establish explicit *relationships* between these tables. More broadly, a database designer may desire to *normalize* the design of the various tables so the data fits the *relational model*. The process of normalization will be covered in detail in Chapter 6, "Relational Database Design." Additionally, an analyst may want to create additional views of one or more tables, allowing the data to be seen in new ways.

Moving beyond traditional databases, there is also the possibility for even greater complexity in the form of specialized data structures. For example, you might want to maintain a system of mathematical equations in a special structure so that you can solve optimization problems. Or, you may want to create a *cube* structure for a set of data so that you can retrieve data in a multidimensional way.

As you'll see, Access is particularly strong in the realm of data transformation. Unlike Excel, Access offers specific means for handling most database data structures. Additionally, like Excel, Access allows for the creation of pivot tables, which provide a powerful way to transform data into a matrix structure.

Quantitative Analysis

Quantitative analysis relates to processes that are mathematical in nature. There's a full range of possibilities for how simple or complex such transformations might be.

In the simplest case, we may be just adding or subtracting two numbers, such as a calculation of profit as revenue minus cost. A more complex quantitative transformation might involve the calculation of an average or standard deviation of a group of numbers. Even greater complexity can occur with more advanced mathematical procedures, such as statistical regression analysis.

Perhaps the simplest type of quantitative transformation is the *calculation*. Using basic mathematical operators, such as addition, subtraction, multiplication, and division, we can combine numeric quantities to create any desired calculation or formula. Mathematical operators extend to the more complex, such as exponents, logarithms, absolute values, and square roots. In devising formulas, operators such as AND, OR, and NOT often come into play to add logic to the purely mathematical.

Moving beyond the simple calculation, the next level of quantitative transformation is the *function*. The defining characteristic of a function is that it is something that allows a formula to be applied to any number of input values to yield a single output value. The built-in functions found in both Access and Excel allow more complex mathematical formulas to be applied to numeric data. For example, built-in financial functions allow formulas to be utilized without requiring the user to know the exact details of the formula or how it works.

Both Access and Excel offer many possibilities for calculations and functions. It should be noted, however, that Excel provides a fuller range of choices when it comes to mathematical and financial functions.

Beyond calculations and functions, data analysis can involve more complex quantitative systems. Generally speaking, there are two types of quantitative analysis that are not possible in Access but are available in Excel through special add-ins. Since data in Access can be easily exported to Excel for further analysis, it's worth mentioning these possibilities. The two Excel add-ins you should be aware of are:

- Analysis ToolPak
- Solver

Once installed, the Analysis ToolPak appears on the Data tab of the Ribbon as *Data Analysis*. As used in this book, the term data analysis extends beyond statistics, but to many the term *data analysis* is synonymous with statistics. The Analysis ToolPak (or *Data Analysis*) add-in provides over a dozen specific tools for statistical analysis, ranging from descriptive statistics to regression analysis. The topic of statistics is beyond the scope of this book, but we can take a quick stab at summarizing the salient aspects of statistical analysis.

Roughly speaking, there are two main components to statistical analysis, *descriptive statistics* and *inferential statistics*. Descriptive statistics refers to ways to summarize a set of numeric data with simple statistics, such as mean (average) and standard deviation. These numbers provide clues as to the central tendency and level of variability of the data. Descriptive statistics can extend into such things as percentiles and visual tools like histograms.

Inferential statistics is more the heart of what statistics is all about, and deals with ways to make informed statements about the population from which a data sample is taken. The Data Analysis add-in contains over a dozen techniques, such as correlation and regression. To give one example, regression allows the user to explore data in order to determine the variables which can be used to predict the values of some outcome. For example, this type of analysis can be used to determine those variables that can best predict the customers who will purchase a specific product.

A second notable quantitative add-in available for Excel is the Solver. This add-in allows users to find an optimal solution for a set of equations through a mathematical procedure known as *linear programming*. This type of analysis is well beyond the scope of this book and generally requires a great deal of knowledge as to how to formulate a model with mathematical equations. Basically, this type of analysis allows a user to find either an optimal maximum or minimum for an objective equation, subject to various constraint equations. As one example, this can be used to determine an optimal mix of components to produce a product at a maximum profit, given current material and labor constraints.

Visualization

The final type of transformation we'll discuss is visualization. *Visualization* describes processes that are primarily about the presentation of data. Data is often manipulated for reasons pertaining to how it is perceived through visual means. In a basic sense, even the fact that we often view data in a grid of rows and columns helps us to quickly view and understand that data. Obviously, it's much easier to understand a mass of data if it's been organized into a grid. Subtotals can be added in various formats, which have differing effects on how it helps us to understand the data quickly. In more complex situations, summarized data can be transformed into a variety of charts and graphs for a more purely visual presentation of data.

Let's first talk about the basic visualization technique whereby data is placed in a rectangular grid. We tend to take the *spreadsheet* view of data as obvious, but that way of viewing data has not always been a given. Going back a few centuries to a time when Italian bookkeepers first devised a system of debits and credits as a way to organize accounting data, we have always looked for ways to present raw data in a more understandable fashion. In our current spreadsheet-driven view of data, rows represent specific instances of an entity, and columns represent attributes. We like to keep things in two dimensions, since that's the limit of what we can easily view at once. But what do we do if we encounter data with more than two dimensions?

To illustrate some of the dilemmas involved even in a basic presentation of data in a grid, let's take a situation in which we have information about customers and products. In the simplest case, we may want to sum up order amounts by customer and product. To accomplish this, we can put customer information in rows, product information in columns, and summarized order amounts in the intersecting cells, as shown in Figure 1.1.

	Blue Pen	Green Pen	Lamp	Red Chair
Susan Smith	8	0	0	328
Karen Castle	4	55	0	0
Tony Granite	0	0	28	0

Figure 1.1
Matrix of data with customers in rows and products in columns.

Alternatively, we can switch the columns and rows so that customers are in columns and products are in rows, as in Figure 1.2.

	Karen Castle	Susan Smith	Tony Granite
Blue Pen	4	8	0
Green Pen	55	0	0
Lamp	0	0	28
Red Chair	0	328	0

Figure 1.2
Matrix of data with customers in columns and products in rows.

This data in this example is easy to display since we have two entities (customers and products) that we are viewing in a two-dimensional grid of numbers. But what happens when we want to add one more entity to our analysis? Let's say we want to add in information about the date that each sale took place. This is completely independent of customer and product, so it's not obvious how this should be indicated. One possibility, which organizes sales by date first and then customers in the rows, and products in the columns is shown in Figure 1.3.

		Blue Pen	Green Pen	Lamp	Red Chair
5/2/2012	Karen Castle		55		
	Susan Smith				328
5/9/2012	Tony Granite			28	
5/10/2012	Susan Smith	8			
5/11/2012	Karen Castle	4			

Figure 1.3
Matrix of data with dates and customers in rows and products in columns.

Another possibility, shown in Figure 1.4, is to place dates in the columns and customers and products in the rows.

		5/2/2012	5/9/2012	5/10/2012	5/11/2012
Karen Castle	Blue Pen				4
	Green Pen	55			
Susan Smith	Blue Pen			8	
	Red Chair	328			
Tony Granite	Lamp		28		

Figure 1.4
Matrix of data with dates in columns and customers and products in rows.

As you might guess, there are numerous other possibilities. Plus, we haven't yet thought about how we might include any desired totals and subtotals. The main point is that the way we present data does definitely influence how that data is comprehended.

Aside from the representation of data in a grid, charts and graphs allow for even more sophisticated ways to present data through purely visual means. Both Access and Excel allow for the creation of over a dozen different types of charts. Some of the more popular chart types include columns, bar, line, pie, scatter, and area. Although charts are only briefly covered in this book, it's important that you be generally aware of the advantages that charts can bring to your analysis of data. In effect, charts can be seen as the final step in the process, by which information is expressed in purely visual means to the end user.

In summary, visualization is an often-overlooked aspect of data analysis. Our understanding of data sometimes comes more from how it is presented than from the data itself. The expression "a picture is worth a thousand words" does often have truth in it. However, no matter how many pictures and graphs are created, there still must be some underlying meaning and value to the analysis itself. Graphs must be interpreted correctly and must be based on relevant data. As is commonly stressed in statistics, it's very easy to draw incorrect conclusions if the underlying assumptions are false.

The Advantage of Access

Now that we've discussed the various types of transformations in greater detail, let's return, once again, to our initial question, "What is data analysis?" Data analysis is about both data and analysis. To many, analysis means quantitative analysis, but analysis can also mean the human endeavor that allows one to look at data and make meaningful decisions based on that data. And to all this, we add various visualization techniques that allow for more intuitive comprehension of that data.

When one compares the features of Access to those of Excel, one observes that the great strength of Access is its ability to transform data. While Access also provides for quantitative and visual transformation, the heart of Access is data transformation. In essence, Access is a database with loads of additional tools that extend its capabilities into analysis. In contrast, Excel is more a purely analytical tool.

From this, we need to stress that Access is a terrific tool with which to begin your data analysis journey. With Access, you'll be able to get your data into proper shape to allow subsequent analysis with Access, Excel, or other software tools. In fact, Microsoft provides numerous ways to move data quickly back and forth between Access and Excel. Excel can accomplish much of what Access can do but is limited when it comes to the data itself. In summary, Access has the upper hand over Excel when it comes to data transformation. Excel, however, has the upper hand when it comes to quantitative or visual transformation. Excel is particularly powerful when it comes to quantitative analysis.

One additional advantage of Access over Excel is that it allows for the creation of a complete software application. Although Access forms are only briefly covered in this book, the use of forms allows the software developer to create a complete application that can accomplish more than pure data analysis.

Looking Ahead

Although this book is all about Microsoft Access, we've held off on getting into details of Access in this first chapter. Data analysis is a somewhat nebulous topic, and we wanted to present some insight into the nature of this task before we discuss the available software tools. Although it's true that the software often dictates the analysis that can be done, it's also nice to step back from the software to get a feel for what exactly is desired.

In our summary of data analysis, we focused on the differences between Access and Excel and explored three basic types of transformations: data transformation, quantitative analysis, and visualization. Exploring these transformations in detail, we then remarked on the strengths and weaknesses of Access with regard to these transformation types. Data analysis remains a difficult concept to define precisely, but this survey hopefully provided some insight into some of the possibilities.

In the next chapter, we'll talk about how Access relates to other relational databases, and then present an introduction to Access itself, focusing on its user interface and a summary of its components. After reading the next chapter, you'll have a much clearer idea of what Access is all about, and how it functions.

Chapter 2

An Overview of Access

Microsoft Access was first introduced by Microsoft in 1992 and has since gone through eight major revisions. The current version is called Microsoft Access 2010.

Access is categorized as a desktop database and is by far the most popular software title in this category. Exactly what is a desktop database? In physical terms, one defining feature of desktop databases is that they usually consist of a single file. As such, they can be easily maintained on a single desktop (or laptop) computer.

In contrast, *server databases* are much more complex pieces of software and can easily consist of dozens or hundreds of files. Some of the more popular server databases include Microsoft SQL Server, MySQL, Oracle Database, and IBM DB2. With their more powerful features, server databases are typically employed to hold and maintain data for an entire organization. These databases are robust enough to handle the varied tasks associated with complex databases, such as performing backups and replication across multiple servers. With these additional capabilities, server databases are much more flexible than desktop databases.

However, Microsoft Access has many unique and useful features that server databases simply cannot touch. The great virtue of Access is its simplicity and ease of use. As such, Access is a great tool for data analysis, which, after all, typically takes place on the desktop. Whereas server databases are great at storing and organizing raw data, Access is optimized for the more focused task of data analysis.

We'll talk about the various components of Access shortly, but let's start with one key point. Access allows you to create two types of tables. First, it can create tables that hold data within Access itself. But more significantly, Access can also create *linked tables* that merely point to data that resides outside of Access. This external data can be in server databases, Excel spreadsheets, or even Word documents. The ability to create linked tables means that you can use Access as way to organize and then analyze any data that resides anywhere in your organization.

With this in mind, we can conclude that Microsoft Access has two main uses. First, as a standalone database, it can be used to create a database, allow users to enter and maintain data in that database, and then generate whatever reports and queries are desired from that data. This was its primary use in the early days of the software. Back when Access was first published, many of the server databases that we now have available were much more difficult to obtain and use. Just as spreadsheets have always been used at the department level to circumvent the organizational difficulties of obtaining data from a centralized systems department, Access was often used to set up small departmental databases to allow quick access to data.

However, as time has passed, server databases have become more available and easy to use. Without much effort, end users can download a server database such as MySQL or SQL Server to store data. This brings us to the second main use of Access: as a tool for data analysis of data that is typically stored outside of Access itself. With its ability to connect to external data via linked tables, Access turns out to be a great tool for viewing such data, even if the data resides in multiple databases maintained by different people or organizational units. In today's systems world, it's a relatively simple task to obtain access to any desired data. There is less of a need for business analysts to maintain data themselves.

Access and SQL

Although there are important differences between Access and the more complex server databases, there is one important similarity: Both Access and server databases rely on the underlying language of SQL. SQL (structured query language) is a standard database language used by all relational databases to access data. While it's true that Access isn't nearly as full featured a database as a server database such as Microsoft SQL Server, both Access and server databases use SQL to retrieve and access data. The difference is that most users of server databases write code directly in SQL to maintain their databases. Most users of Access use the graphical interface that Access provides. Server databases such as Microsoft SQL Server do have some elements of a graphical interface, but those interfaces are not as developed or user friendly as in Access.

The key distinguishing characteristic of Access is that it features a highly usable graphical interface, but at the same time works by using the same SQL found in more complex databases. In essence, it's important to understand that, in terms of how it accesses data, Microsoft Access is basically just a graphical interface for SQL. The primary component of Access we'll be talking about in this book is the *query*. Queries in Access allow you retrieve or update data in internal Access tables or in external tables outside of Access. Access queries are visible through both a *Design View* and a *SQL View* (and a few other views which we'll talk about later). You'll normally use the Design View when creating queries, but you should keep in mind that it's the SQL View that's really driving the process.

Since Access is based on SQL, experienced SQL developers can utilize Access as a quick tool for retrieving or updating data. A SQL developer can easily copy some SQL code into the SQL View of a query, and then quickly switch to Design View to further modify the query through graphical means. Alternatively, a SQL developer might design a query entirely in the Access Design View, and then switch to the SQL View to obtain the corresponding SQL code.

As mentioned in the Introduction, this book will occasionally display special "See the SQL" sidebars that show the SQL code for queries we're creating in the Design View. Although our emphasis in this book is on the Access graphical user interface, it's often helpful to see the underlying SQL code behind the queries you'll be creating. If you're interested in learning a little SQL, this will definitely help in your conceptual understanding of how Access really works. The goal of the "See the SQL" sidebars is not to turn you into a SQL developer but rather to assist in your appreciation of the benefits of using Access.

Relational Databases

Before we move on to a discussion of the Access user interface, let's take a step back and review a bit of history as to how relational databases developed.

In the early days of computing, there was no such thing as a database. Most data was physically maintained on devices such as magnetic tape, which only allowed for sequential access to data. To write data to a tape, one generally needed to write one *record* of data at a time in a sequential fashion. Each record was said to contain any number of data *fields,* which contained the values of some particular entity. The entire set of records on a magnetic tape was called a *file*. To read that information on the tape, one needed to read the file in a forward sequence. In reading data, one could either keep track of the information in the fields as they were being read, or else temporarily store that data in *tables*, which could then be later evaluated. However, these tables were never permanent in any sense. They existed only while the computer program doing the processing was reading data.

As hard-drive disk storage became available, the sequential files stored on magnetic tape were often moved to disk. This allowed quick access to multiple files on a single physical disk drive. However, these disk files were merely faster in the sense that they no longer required someone to manually mount a tape on a tape drive. The data contained in these files was still organized in a sequential manner.

The next advance in data storage came with indexed sequential disk files. These were often referred to as ISAM (Indexed Sequential Access Method) or VSAM (Virtual Storage Access Method) files. These types of files allowed direct access to specific records. One no longer needed to read an entire file sequentially just to retrieve data in a single record.

However, even with the advent of indexed sequential files, there was still no coherency to the data. Data might be stored in any number of files which had no relationship to each other. There was no larger structure to impose some meaning on the various files that contained an organization's data.

All of these limitations eventually led to the creation of true databases, which were introduced to organize data into a meaningful structure. In the continual drive to derive information from data, databases were devices that allowed data in multiple tables to be related to each other.

The earliest databases were called *hierarchical* databases. The IBM System/360 database was typical of this type. Hierarchical databases were followed by *network* databases. A prime example of the network database was the HP Image database.

The salient feature of both hierarchical and network databases was that they utilized a complex system of internal pointers to allow a record in one table to be linked to records in another table. For example, one might be reading a Customers table and also want to view the orders associated with each customer. There would be a pointer in each record in the Customers table pointing to the first record in the Orders table for that customer. That record in the Orders table would then contain a pointer to the next order for that customer. The last order in the chain of orders for that customer would have an indicator that the last order had been reached.

Coupled with the complex pointer-based systems of hierarchical and network databases were computer programs that relied on sequential processing to read the data in these databases one record at a time. Computer programs would typically read a record for a customer, and then use the pointers to retrieve all orders for that customer, and then all details for each order. This allowed all data to be obtained, but it required complex programming logic. Essentially, the data still needed to be processed one record at a time. The process to obtain all the data was complex and involved many loops as the various pointers were evaluated.

The development of relational databases in the early 1980s represented a real break-through in this logjam of data retrieval. The main problem with data storage prior to relational databases was not how the data was stored, but how it was accessed. Along with relational databases, the development of the language of SQL allowed for an entirely new method of accessing data.

Unlike earlier data retrieval methods, SQL permitted the user to access a large set of data at one time. With one single statement, a SQL command could retrieve or update thousands of records from multiple tables. This eliminated a great deal of complexity. Computer programs no longer needed to read one record at a time in a special sequence, while deciding what to do with each record. What used to require hundreds of lines of programming code could now be accomplished with just a few lines of logic.

The simplified processes for retrieval possible with SQL meant that databases no longer needed to contain pointers to relate tables to one another. Rather than use explicit pointers, SQL relies on common fields to link tables together. For example, an Orders table might contain a CustomerID field, indicating the customer to whom the order belongs. The Customers table would contain the same CustomerID field with corresponding values. SQL is then able to *join* the Customers and Orders tables to retrieve all necessary customer and order information at once. It was no longer necessary to use a convoluted process to retrieve each order for each customer, one at a time.

The Access User Interface

We'll begin our examination of Microsoft Access with a whirlwind tour of its user interface. There are four main components to the interface:

- The Backstage View
- The Ribbon
- The Navigation Pane
- Tabbed Documents

The Backstage View, a new feature of Access 2010, is unique in the sense that it fills the entire screen when it's present. The other three components share the screen when they're visible. Let's start with the Backstage View. When you open Microsoft Access for the first time, you're presented with the screen shown in Figure 2.1.

This is the Backstage View. Notice that the top of the screen displays five tabs: File, Home, Create, External Data, and Database Tools. The current focus is on the File tab. Although the File tab is always visible and available, the Backstage View appears

Figure 2.1
Backstage View.

only when the File tab has been selected. Additionally, the File tab is unique in the sense that this is the only tab that does not display the full Ribbon that's used in Microsoft Office 2010 applications. No matter what you are doing in Access, these five tabs will always be present and available.

The Backstage View allows you to create new databases, obtain help, and modify configuration options.

When using Access for the first time, the first thing you need to do is to create a new database to work with. In physical terms, the database will be a new file with an ACCDB suffix. This is much like creating a Word or Excel file.

Let's start by selecting the Blank database template and then clicking the Create button on the right. You then see a new database as shown in Figure 2.2.

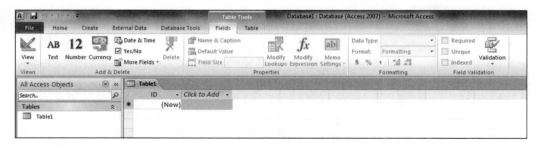

Figure 2.2
A new database.

Now that a new database has been created, Access automatically takes you out of the Backstage View and displays the other three components mentioned previously: the Ribbon, the Navigation Pane and the Tabbed Documents sections. This is the normal arrangement you'll see when working in Access.

The Ribbon consists of the original five tabs (File, Home, Create, External Data, and Database Tools), plus two additional *contextual tabs*: Fields and Table. Contextual tabs pop up in different ways, depending on what you are currently doing. After having created a new database, Access assumes that we now want to create some tables, so they've provided these two tabs related to table creation. Notice that the label Table Tools appears above the contextual tabs, to tell us what type of tabs they are.

As each tab is selected, the Ribbon shows commands appropriate for that tab. For example, since the focus is now on the Fields tab, we see commands appropriate for creating new fields. From the left, these appear as: View, Text, Number, Currency, and so on. These commands have been organized into five different groups: Views, Add & Delete, Properties, Formatting, and Field Validation.

As with other Microsoft Office products, the Ribbon can be hidden if desired. This is accomplished by clicking the Minimize the Ribbon icon, which is found just above the Ribbon at the far right. After minimizing the Ribbon, you can either toggle on the Expand the Ribbon icon in the same location, or simply click on any Ribbon tab to view the Ribbon again.

The next component of the user interface is the Navigation Pane. This appears on the left side of the screen, under the label All Access Objects. We see a Tables section, with one table listed, called Table1.

An Access database can contain five different object types: Tables, Queries, Forms, Reports, and Macros. In brief, tables hold data, or point to data in other databases. Queries correspond to SQL statements, and organize or take action upon the data in one or more tables in various ways. Forms are a mechanism for displaying information about one row in a table (or query) at a time, typically for data entry. Reports provide a tool for organizing data for display on paper. Finally, macros are a set of commands that can be used to automate Access processes.

The Navigation Pane displays all objects in the current database, organized by these five object types. There are actually many different ways to organize the objects in the Navigation Pane. For instance, rather than display objects alphabetically by object type, one can display them by the date created or modified. If you want to apply your own preferences as to how the Navigation Pane is organized, simply select the small down arrow at the top of the Navigation Pane.

Like the Ribbon, the Navigation Pane can also be minimized. To do this, simply click the Shutter Bar Open/Close icon in the upper right corner of the Navigation Pane. The same icon can be used to reopen the pane.

The final component of the user interface is the Tabbed Documents area. This large area in the center of the screen (below the Ribbon and to the right of the Navigation Pane) allows you to see all objects you are currently working on. However, you can only view one object at a time. In this example, we see the tab labeled Table1 for the open table. We could actually have any number of tables, queries, forms, or any other object open at the same time, in which case we would see multiple tabs, one for each object. You can select one tab at a time, to work on that corresponding object. As you select each tab, the appropriate information is displayed to allow you to work with that object.

Another aspect of the Access user interface is the concept of views. Once an object is opened in the Tabbed Documents area, that object can be seen via several views. For example, table objects can be seen in any of these four views:

- Design View
- Datasheet View
- PivotTable View
- PivotChart View

For tables, the Design View allows you to directly view and edit the design of the table. The Datasheet View allows you to view or update the data in the table. The PivotTable and PivotChart views let you create pivot tables or charts based on the data in that table. Other object types, such as queries, have different views that pertain to that object. We'll cover the various views and what they mean later in the book.

In addition to the five object types that can appear in the Navigation Pane, there are a number of objects that can appear as tabs in the Tabbed Documents area but don't appear in the Navigation Pane. For example, when you work with the Relationships tool (which will be seen later in Chapter 5), that will cause a Relationships tab to open in the Tabbed Documents area.

As a final illustration of the user interface, let's look at a screenshot for a database that has multiple objects open at once (Figure 2.3).

Notice that six objects appear in the Navigation Pane. There are two tables, one query, one form, one report, and one macro. The Tabbed Documents area shows three objects currently open: CustomersTable, CustomersQuery, and Relationships. As

Figure 2.3
A database with multiple objects.

seen in the Navigation Pane, CustomersTable is a table, and CustomersQuery is a query. The Relationships object is another open object, but it isn't listed in the Navigation Pane. Of the three open objects, the tab for the CustomersTable object is selected, so that is the object with which we're currently working. The CustomersTable is shown in the Design View. As for the Ribbon, notice that the Create tab is currently selected, so we only see commands for creating objects.

The Backstage View

Let's now explore the various options of the Backstage View in greater detail. Figure 2.1 showed the options that appear when the a new database is initiated under the Backstage View. Again, this occurs when you select the New command under the File tab. Let's take a look at some of the other options under the Backstage View.

As seen in Figure 2.1, the main commands are listed on the left side under the File tab. At the top, you'll see these basic file commands:

- Save Object As
- Save Database As
- Open
- Close Database

The Save Object As command lets you copy whatever object you have highlighted in the Navigation Pane and save it with a different name. In some cases, you can also transform it into a different type of object. For example, if you're doing a Save Object

As on a table, you can save it as another table, a query, a form, or a report. Similarly, queries can be saved as a query, form, or report. Forms can be saved as a form or report. Reports can only be saved as a report.

Note that objects can also be saved and copied by simply doing a copy and paste of the object directly in the Navigation Pane. When you copy and paste, you can only copy the object to the same type of object. However, when copying and pasting a table, you're given two options that aren't available with the Save Object As command. When you copy and paste a table, you have these three options when you do the paste:

- Structure Only
- Structure and Data
- Append Data to Existing Table

The Structure Only option copies the design of the table without copying any data. The Structure and Data option is the equivalent of the Save Object As command, copying both structure and data. The Append Data to Existing Table option allows you to copy the data of one table to another.

Below these four commands, you'll find a list of any recently opened access files. Below the list of those files, you'll see an Info command. When you select this command, your screen will appear as in Figure 2.4.

Figure 2.4
Info command in the Backstage View.

As seen, three main options are presented under the Info command:

- Enable Content
- Compact & Repair Database
- Encrypt with Password

The Enable Content option is of particular interest. When working with Access, you'll sometimes see a security warning such as appears in Figure 2.5.

Figure 2.5
Security warning.

Selecting the Enable Content button prevents this warning from appearing.

The Compact & Repair Database button is also noteworthy. This procedure allows you to shrink the physical size of your Access file and is particularly useful if you've recently added large amounts of data to your database tables.

The Encrypt with Password button is useful if you'd like to restrict access to your database.

The Save & Publish command allows you to save your Access database in one of several different formats, or publish your database to a Microsoft SharePoint site. If saving your database, you will normally want to save it in the default format with an ACCDB suffix.

The final command we want to examine is the Options command. When this command is selected, a new window will pop up, such as shown in Figure 2.6.

This window has 11 tabs on the left, each of which allows you to specify numerous settings. Of the dozens of available settings, a few are of particular interest.

Figure 2.6
Options command in Backstage View.

First, under the General tab, you'll see a Default File Format for Blank Database drop-down menu. This allows you to select the file format. In most cases, unless you need to maintain compatibility with an earlier version of Access, you should choose Access 2007. Note that even if you are using Access 2010, Access 2007 is the most current file type. Basically, this means that your files will be saved with an ACCDB suffix.

Next, under the Current Database tab, you'll see an Application Title text box. This allows you to change the text that appears in the title bar at the very top of the Access window. If you don't enter anything in this text box, the title bar will display the name and format of the physical file you're currently working with. Figure 2.2 shows how the title appears if you don't enter a value in the Application Title text box. The title in Figure 2.2 is:

Database1: Database (Access 2007) – Microsoft Access

In most cases, this is more information than the average user needs. By entering the value "Chapter 2" in the Application Title text box, we were able to change the title to the shorter title seen in Figures 2.3 and 2.4.

Another useful option under the Current Database tab is the Compact on Close checkbox. If you check that option, the database will automatically do a Compact and Repair Database every time you close the database.

Next, the Customize Ribbon tab allows you to completely customize and rearrange the commands you see in the Ribbon.

Finally, the Quick Access Toolbar tab allows you to modify the Quick Access Toolbar. Like Word and Excel, Microsoft Access has a Quick Access Toolbar that appears in the upper left corner of the screen, above the Ribbon. This toolbar allows you to assemble your most frequently used commands in one place for quick access. This is actually quite a useful tool. Since the Ribbon is a dynamic structure that frequently changes appearance, it's sometimes difficult to locate commands, even when you think you know where they are. By placing a command in the Quick Access Toolbar, you'll always have immediate access to that command.

Looking Ahead

We began this chapter with an examination of the salient features of Access as a database. Access uses the same SQL language used in more complex server databases as a means of accessing data. On top of this base functionality, Access adds a user-friendly graphical interface that simplifies the task of communicating with data.

A review of some earlier data storage and databases illustrated the tremendous advance of relational databases over prior methods of data storage retrieval. With the modern relational database, combined with the language of SQL, it was no longer necessary to read sequentially through data files or use an elaborate system of pointers to retrieve data.

We then moved on to a presentation of the Access user interface. There are four main components: the Ribbon, the Navigation Pane, Tabbed Documents, and the Backstage View. Whereas the Ribbon is common to all Microsoft Office products, the Navigation Pane is unique to Access and is key to understanding how to navigate the interface. Most objects in Access are directly accessible via the Navigation Pane: Tables, Queries, Forms, Reports, and Macros.

In our next chapter, we move on to the second part of the book, which covers Access queries. This section begins with an exploration of Access tables and how data external to Access can be utilized in an Access database.

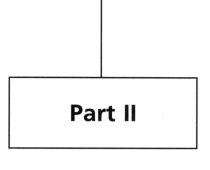

Part II

Access Queries

Chapter 3

Tables and External Data

Our first two chapters provided some background information on the basics of Access and the task of data analysis. We now move on to the main topic of this book: Access queries. Simply put, a query is a process that retrieves or updates data from some data source. Before that query can take place, however, that data source must be clearly defined. In most cases, data sources are defined via an Access table.

An Access table can either hold data itself or merely point to data in another location. Tables can be created in Access or have their design imported from another location. In essence, there are three general possibilities for initiating the use of a table in Access:

- Create a table in Access
- Import a table from an external location
- Link to a table in an external location

In the first scenario, creating the table in Access, one creates the table definition in Access. After the table is created, data can be added to the table as desired.

In the second scenario, importing a table, one specifies the location of the table to be imported. The design of that table, along with all of its data, is then brought into a new table in your Access database.

In the third scenario, linking to a table, one specifies the location of the table to link to. The design of that table is then brought into a new table in your Access database. By linking to the table, the data in that table is available to your Access database. However, the data itself is not moved into Access; it remains in the external location.

Let's begin with the first scenario, creating the table in Access. As we go through this process, we'll learn about some of the key features of tables in Access, such as Primary and Foreign Keys, Data Types, and NULL values. We'll then show how to import tables and link to tables in an external location. Finally, we'll cover the process of exporting data out of Access into an external location.

Creating Tables

In our last chapter, we briefly introduced relational databases and discussed the history of how relational databases evolved from simpler forms of data storage. As we now begin to discuss database tables, we'll focus a bit more on what relational databases mean, with reference to tables.

A relational database is a collection of data, stored in any number of tables. In common usage, the term *relational* is used to indicate that the tables are related to each other. Database purists, however, will point out that the term *relational* has nothing to do with relationships, but has more to do with the mathematics of relation theory.

Even before we look at tables in Access, let's take the case of a database that consists of just two tables: Customers and Orders. The Customers table contains one record for each customer who ever ordered. The Orders table has one record for each order placed. Each table can contain any number of fields, which are used to store the various attributes associated with each record. For example, a Customer table might contain fields such as FirstName and LastName.

At this point, it's useful to visualize some tables and the data they contain. The common custom is to display a table as a grid of rows and columns. Each row represents a record in the table. Each column represents a field in the table. The top header row normally has the field names. The remaining rows show the actual data.

In modern relational database terminology, records and fields are usually referred to as *rows* and *columns*, corresponding to the visual representation. However, Access persists in using the older terms of records and fields.

Let's look at an example of the simplest possible relational database. In this database, there are only two tables, Customers and Orders. Here's how they might appear:

Customers Table

CustomerID	FirstName	LastName
1	William	Smith
2	Natalie	Lopez
3	Brenda	Harper

Orders Table		
OrderID	**CustomerID**	**OrderAmount**
1	1	50.00
2	1	60.00
3	2	33.50
4	3	20.00

In this example, the Customers table contains three columns (or fields): CustomerID, FirstName, and LastName. There are currently three rows (records) in the table, representing William Smith, Natalie Lopez, and Brenda Harper. Each row represents a different customer, and each column represents a different piece of information about the customer. Similarly, the Orders table has three columns and four rows. This indicates that there are four orders in the database and three attributes for those orders.

Of course, this example is highly simplistic and only hints at the type of data that could be stored in a real database. For example, a Customers table would normally contain many additional columns describing other customer attributes such as city, state, zip code, and phone number. Similarly, an Orders table would ordinarily have columns describing additional attributes of the order, such as order date, sales tax, and the salesperson who took the order.

Notice that the first column in each table, CustomerID and OrderID, consists of an integer in an ascending numeric sequence. This is referred to as a *primary key*, which we'll discuss later in this chapter. Primary keys serve as a means of uniquely identifying each record. Also notice that the second column in the Orders table also contains the CustomerID. This is known as a *foreign key*. Foreign keys assist in relating a row in one table to a row in another table. For example, if a row in the Orders table has a CustomerID value of 1, that means that the order was placed by the customer with a CustomerID of 1 in the Customers table.

Let's now look at the process for creating tables in Access. The procedure is simple and straightforward. You begin by selecting the Create tab on the Ribbon. You can then either click the Table or Table Design command to begin the process of creating a table.

We mentioned in the last chapter that each object can be seen in multiple views. Tables can be seen in any of these four views: Design View, Datasheet View, Pivot-Table View, PivotChart View.

The Table Design command opens a new table in Design View. In contrast, the Table command opens a new table in Datasheet View. The Design View allows you to easily view and modify the design of the table but doesn't show the data in the table. The Datasheet View allows you to view the data in the table and, to a limited extent, modify the design. To illustrate the process, let's first click the Table Design command. The top portion of the screen looks like Figure 3.1.

Figure 3.1
Creating a table with the Table Design command.

The main Tabbed Documents area of the screen now shows a tab called Table1, with three columns that allow us to specify the fields of a new table. The columns are named Field Name, Data Type, and Description. You can enter information for any desired fields. The Data Type column will require you to select one of the available Data Types in Access. Examples include Text, Memo, Number, and Date/Time. After entering a few fields, your screen may look like Figure 3.2.

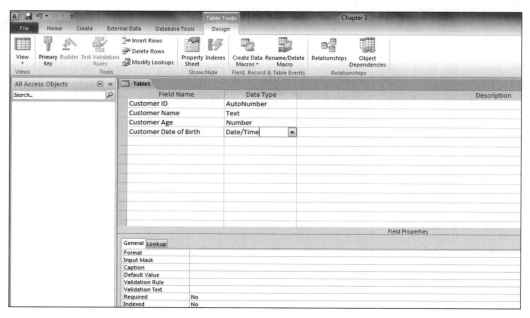

Figure 3.2
Table design in progress.

We'll discuss the specifics of the various Data Types later in the chapter. For now, simply accept that we have the ability to create each field with a desired Data Type to indicate the type of data the field can contain. Also notice that there is a *Field Properties* section at the bottom of the screen. This section provides additional detail about each field, specific to its Data Type. As each field is selected in the upper section, the properties for that field are shown and can be modified in the Field Properties area.

We mentioned that the Table Design command opens a table in Design View. This leads to the question as to how you can change the View type. On the very left side of the Ribbon, you see a View command. When you select the command, you're presented with a drop-down menu that lets you select between Datasheet View, Design View, PivotTable View, and PivotChart View. The Design View is what we're in now. When in Design View, you'll see a Design tab under Table Tools in the Ribbon.

Let's say we decide to switch to Datasheet View. When this change is initiated, we're first asked whether we want to save the table. After responding positively, a dialog box appears asking whether we want to define a primary key. In general, it's a good idea to create a primary key for any table you create. The topic of primary keys will be covered in the next section in this chapter, but for now, we'll reply that we want to create a primary key. Since this table happens to contain an AutoNumber field, Access will use that field as the primary key.

After the table is saved with the name MyFirstTable, the screen appears as in Figure 3.3.

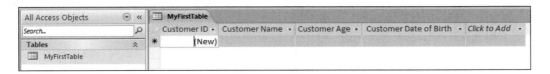

Figure 3.3
Datasheet View of a table.

Notice that the field names now appear as the first row in the grid. We have not yet entered any data. After entering a few rows of data, the data portion of the screen might look like Figure 3.4.

Customer ID	Customer Name	Customer Age	Customer Date of Birth	Click to Add
1	Jonathan Swift	44	5/5/1967	
2	Julio Taylor	32	6/2/1979	
3	Anne Tanning	31	9/28/1980	
(New)				

Figure 3.4
Datasheet View of a table with data.

We started the table creation process with the Table Design command. What if we had chosen the Table command instead? The Table command takes us directly into the Datasheet View, allowing us to enter both field names and data at once. It looks like Figure 3.5.

Figure 3.5
Creating a table with the Table command.

The Click to Add cell can be clicked to provide a new field name and Data Type for the field. As before, data can be entered in the rows below. In essence, this allows you to create a portion of the table design and enter data at the same time. Through this process, one can create a table much as was done in the Design View. However, we recommend sticking to the Table Design button and the Design View to create new tables. Although less flexible, The Design View allows you to more easily specify the design of a table before commencing with the task of putting data into a table. The Datasheet View allows you to add fields to a table, while specifying the Data Type for each field, but it doesn't let you set all available properties.

We've seen that the Datasheet View of tables allows you to add new fields to a table and add or modify data. The Datasheet View also allows you to do some basic data filtering in a table. If you click on any of the small triangles next to each field name, you'll see a drop-down menu that lets you sort or filter data based on data in that field.

Notice that the Ribbon shows different contextual tabs depending on the view you're in. While in Design View, the Ribbon shows a Design tab under Table Tools. In Datasheet View, the Ribbon shows Fields and Table tabs under Table Tools. Again, contextual tabs are sensitive to what you are doing at the moment.

You might be wondering about the available PivotTable and PivotChart Views. These views convert whatever data is present in the table into a pivot table or chart. They have nothing to do with table creation.

Data Types

While creating tables, we skimmed over the many properties that can be associated with each field as the table is created. Perhaps the most important property associated with each field is its Data Type. Figure 3.2 illustrated the process of entering fields in a table. In this example, we created four fields with four different Data Types: AutoNumber, Text, Number, and Data/Time. These are probably the most commonly used Data Types, but there are more.

However, before we discuss the characteristics of the various Data Types, let's talk about why they are so significant. Data Types are critical in that they determine not only the type of data each field can contain, but also the types of operations that can be performed on that data once it exists. When we look at functions and expressions in Chapter 7, we'll see that the Data Type has a direct relationship with the types of calculations that can be performed on data. Let's take a common example. Since they consist entirely of numbers, zip codes can be stored as either a numeric or a text field. However, the common practice is to store zip code fields as a text field for the simple reason that we would rarely need to utilize a numeric computation with that data. On the other hand, we may want to employ text operations on zip codes, such as selecting only the first 5 digits of a 9-digit zip code. Similarly, dates can certainly be stored as text, or even as numeric data. However, dates are better stored as a Date/Time field, because that Data Type allows you to employ all sorts of special functions that can perform calculations on dates. For example, a built-in Access Date/Time function can be used to calculate the number of days between any two dates.

The Data Type of a field dictates most of the available properties pertaining to the field. As seen in Figure 3.2, the Data Type is given its own column to indicate the value for that property. There is also a separate Field Properties window below the table field listing, which lists additional properties for the field, based on the selected Data Type. We're not going to go into detail for every property for every Data Type; instead, we'll just focus on the most useful properties.

Let's now look at the characteristics of some of the more commonly used Data Types. Here's a complete list of available Data Types:

Data Type	Brief Description
AutoNumber	Automatically generated integers in an ascending sequence
Text	Any alphabetic, numeric, or symbol string up to 255 characters in length
Number	Any numeric value used for mathematical calculations
Date/Time	Any date and/or time

Data Type	Brief Description
Memo	Long memos or notes up to 64,000 characters in length
Currency	Numeric values displayed in the local currency
Yes/No	Specifies only two values: True or False
OLE Object	Contains a link to a Microsoft OLE object
Hyperlink	Contains a web link, such as a URL
Attachment	Contains an attachment to another file
Calculated	Specifies a calculation based on other fields in the same table

Of all these Data Types, AutoNumber, Text, Number, and Date/Time are by far the most important. The others apply only in unusual situations.

The AutoNumber Data Type is used to automatically place an integer value in a field in an ascending numeric sequence, as each record is added to a table. This Data Type is most commonly used in association with indexes and primary keys, and will be discussed in detail in the next section of this chapter. Essentially, AutoNumber fields ensure that each record in a table has some unique value, which can then be used to specifically identify each record in the table.

Text Data Types can hold any type of data, whether it be character, numeric, or a symbol such as a period or comma. Text data can be parsed down to its individual characters, or combined with other text data to form longer strings of data. When sorted, text data is displayed in an alphabetic sequence, where A comes before Z and numbers appear before letters.

One important property of Text Data Types is Field Size. By default, when new text fields are created, they are given a field size of 255, which is the maximum size of a text field. If you'd like to ensure that data in a field doesn't exceed a certain length, then a lower value can be entered. Access doesn't store unused spaces in a text field, so entering a lower value doesn't affect the storage requirements of a database.

Number fields can hold any numeric values and are critical to data analysis. The most important property of a Number Data Type is the Field Size, which in computer lingo refers to the number of bytes available to store the number. In reality, the Field Size specifies the type of numeric value that the field can contain. This property is important enough to discuss in some detail. The available values for the Field Size property for Number fields are:

- Byte
- Integer

- Long Integer
- Decimal
- Single
- Double
- Replication ID

When new number fields are created, the default Field Size is Long Integer. Bytes, Integers, and Long Integer Field Types can only contain integer values. They cannot hold any fractional numbers with decimal places. Bytes can hold a value from 0 to 255. Integers can hold a value from -32768 to 32767. Long Integers can hold a value from -2,147,483,648 to 2,147,483,647. That's a range of over four billion numbers, which is certainly adequate for most purposes. An important caveat is that Long Integers must be used if you have a field in a table that will be used to link to an AutoNumber field in another table. That is because AutoNumber fields are Long Integers by default.

Decimals are similar to integers, except that they can hold a decimal point. They can hold up to 28 decimal places. It's generally recommended to use Decimal numbers for data pertaining to financial calculations.

Unlike Bytes, Integers, Long Integers, and Decimals, Single and Double numbers are *real* numbers. Like Decimals, they can hold decimal numbers, but unlike Decimals, the values of Single and Double numbers are stored using scientific notation. This means that for very large numbers, the exact value of the number may be only approximate. Single numbers can hold numbers from $1.4e^{-45}$ to $3.4e^{38}$, with up to seven decimal places. Double numbers can hold numbers from $4.9e^{-324}$ to $1.8e^{308}$, with up to fifteen decimal places.

The Replication ID type of number can be safely ignored. This is a special Data Type that generates a long GUID (Globally Unique Identifier).

A few other properties of Number fields are worth mentioning. Decimal numbers offer special Precision and Scale properties that allow you to set the total number of digits that can be stored as well as the number of digits to the right of the decimal point that can be stored. The Decimal Places property pertains to Single, Double, and Decimal types, and allows you to specify how many decimal places will be displayed for a number. This is different from the number of decimals that are stored. Finally, the Format property allows you to specify how the number will generally be displayed, irrespective of how it is stored.

The available Formats for Number fields are:

Format	Example
General Number	1222.567
Currency	$1,222.57
Euro	€1,222.57
Fixed	1222.57
Standard	1,222.57
Percent	122256.70%
Scientific	1.22E+03

The Date/Time Data Type allows a field to hold date and time information. These fields can hold a date, a time, or both. An important property for Date/Time fields is the Format. This property, like the Number Format property, specifies how a Date/Time field displays its data. The available Formats for Date/Time fields are:

Format	Example
General Date	6/23/2011 2:20:44 PM
Long Date	Monday, June 6, 2011
Medium Date	06-Jun-11
Short Date	6/19/2011
Long Time	2:20:44 PM
Medium Time	2:20 PM
Short Time	14:20

The four Data Types we've discussed cover the vast majority of situations. AutoNumber Data Types are frequently used for Primary Keys. Text, Number, and Date/Time Data Types provide ways to separate out these three basic types of data. The remaining Data Types shown in Figure 3.7 are much less commonly used. The Memo Data Type is similar to Text, except that it allows for entries up to 64,000 characters in length. It exists primarily to store longer notes and documents. The Currency Data Type is similar to the Decimal type of Number Data Type, except that it displays in local currency. The Yes/No Data Type appears as a checkbox in Access and allows for only two values: True or False. The OLE Object Data Type can contain a link to a Microsoft OLE object. The Hyperlink Data Type can contain a link to a web page URL or file share. The Attachment Data Type can contain an attachment to any file.

The final Data Type, Calculated, merits a few extra words of explanation. This Data Type, which is new with Access 2010, allows you to specify a calculation based on other fields in the same table. For example, if you have QuantitySold and PricePerItem fields in a table, you can create a Calculated field in the same table called TotalSales, calculated as QuantitySold times PricePerItem. In most cases, however, it's not necessary to create these types of calculated fields in your tables. As will be seen in Chapter 7, it's just as easy to put these calculations in the queries you will be creating to view data in your tables. We recommend putting calculations in Queries rather than Tables, since that allows for greater flexibility in your data design.

Indexes and Primary Keys

In our discussion of Data Types, we glossed over one very important property: the Indexed property. This property applies to all Data Types except OLE Object, Attachment, and Calculated.

The Indexed property of a field encompasses two distinct but related concepts: indexes and primary keys. Indexes are a mechanism for speeding up access to data, based on a particular field. Primary keys are a type of index that ensures that each record can be uniquely identified. A field with a primary key will not contain any duplicate values in that field. There can be only one field in a table identified as a primary key.

There are three possible values for the Indexed property:

- No
- Yes (No Duplicates)
- Yes (Duplicates OK)

The *No* value means that the field is not indexed. Since it's not indexed, it also cannot be a primary key. The *Yes (No Duplicates)* value means that the field is indexed and does not allow duplicate values in that field. Such a field might also be a primary key. The *Yes (Duplicates OK)* value means that the field is indexed but does allow duplicates. Since it allows duplicates, it cannot also be a primary key. Note that it isn't possible for a field to be a primary key and not be indexed.

Let's illustrate the meaning and mechanics of indexes and primary keys by looking at two tables that have been set up to hold customers and their orders. Figure 3.6 shows a Customers table, with focus set on the first field, CustomerID.

If you look at the Field Properties window, you'll see that the Indexed property of the CustomerID field is set to *Yes (No Duplicates)*. This is an index that does not allow duplicates, and so can potentially also be a primary key. To actually create the primary

Figure 3.6
Indexed property.

key, one additional step is needed. A field can be designated as a primary key by either 1) clicking the Primary Key command in the Tools section of the Table Tools Design tab on the Ribbon, or 2) right-clicking on the field name and selecting Primary Key. Once the Primary Key property has been set for a field, you'll see a small key icon to the left of the field name. The Primary Key icon in the Ribbon will also be highlighted.

The procedure for creating indexes and a primary key is easy enough, but let's now talk about what this accomplishes. The easier concept to discuss is indexes. Indexes are a hidden structure that speeds up the process of accessing data. When a field is indexed, every time a record is added to a table an added process stores a pointer to that record's physical location for the value in the indexed field. The next time a search is done involving that value, the index already knows exactly where to find that record. Indexes on a field speed up retrieval but can slow down updates or deletions since there is an added step of adjusting the pointer.

Primary keys are useful and necessary for two reasons. First, since primary keys are indexes that do not allow duplicates, they enable you to uniquely identify a single row in a table. Also, since there can be only one primary key in a table, this designation identifies the preferred way of identifying unique rows in that table. Let's say you have a customer named William Smith. You could certainly attempt to retrieve his record by specifying his first and last name and selecting on those fields. However, there might very well be more than one William Smith in the table. However, if there is a CustomerID field set up in the table as a primary key, one can use that number to obtain the correct record. This guarantees uniqueness. For this reason, primary keys are often defined as an AutoNumber Data Type. As mentioned, the AutoNumber Data Type automatically generates unique integers in an ascending sequence.

Primary keys also allow you to easily relate one table to another. To illustrate this point, let's look at an Orders table that contains orders for our customers. This is shown in Figure 3.7.

Field Name	Data Type
OrderID	AutoNumber
CustomerID	Number
OrderDate	Date/Time
OrderAmount	Number

Field Properties

General Lookup

Field Size	Long Integer
Format	
Decimal Places	Auto
Input Mask	
Caption	
Default Value	
Validation Rule	
Validation Text	
Required	No
Indexed	Yes (Duplicates OK)
Smart Tags	
Text Align	General

Figure 3.7
Orders table.

The OrderID is the primary key for this table, as indicated by the small key icon to the left of the OrderID field. Since this table contains orders, it makes sense that an OrderID would be the primary key. However, notice that this table also contains a CustomerID field. This illustrates how primary keys allow tables to be related to each other. Since the CustomerID is a primary key in the Customers table, and therefore given a unique value, we can be certain that the value of CustomerID in the Orders table points to one and only one customer. In other words, when we're looking at an order, we know exactly who the customer is for that order.

In Figure 3.7, the focus is on the CustomerID field, allowing us to see that the Indexed property for this field has a value of Yes (Duplicates OK). This means that the field is indexed but is not a primary key. Indexing allows for quick access for queries against this table that select by CustomerID. However, since there may be numerous records with the same CustomerID value, we have to allow for duplicates.

One final point about the CustomerID field: In SQL terminology, this field is a candidate for something called a *foreign key*. A foreign key is a field in a table that points to a primary key in another table. More specifically, a foreign key enforces the fact that the value in the foreign key field must already exist as a corresponding primary key in the other table. In our example, this would mean that the CustomerID in the Orders table must actually exist in the Customers table for that order to be added to the database. Essentially, foreign key relationships add structure and data integrity to a database, by enforcing this type of restriction. Fields set up as foreign keys do not have to be indexed, but they generally are.

Higher-end server-based SQL databases such as Microsoft SQL Server allow you to explicitly specify foreign keys as a property of a field. Access, however, handles foreign key relationships in a different manner. In Access, the equivalent of foreign keys can be specified in something called the Relationships Tool. This topic is covered in Chapter 5, "Joins and Relationships."

One final note about indexes: In addition to being able to specify the index type via the Indexed property of a field, Access also permits you to view and edit all the indexes for a table in a single window. If one clicks the Indexes command in the Show/Hide section of the Ribbon under the Table Tools Design tab, a window pops up, such as the one shown in Figure 3.8.

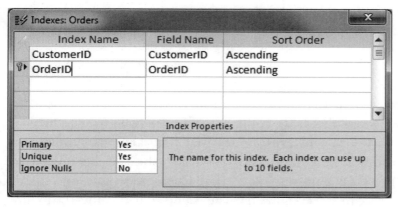

Figure 3.8
Orders table.

This window lists all the indexes for the Orders table previously seen in Figure 3.7. Since the focus is currently on the OrderID index, we can see the properties for that index in the lower left corner of the window. The properties show that this is a primary key with unique values. If we were to change focus to the CustomerID index, it would indicate that the index is not a primary key and does not require unique values. Note also that the Indexes window permits you to set up indexes based on more than one field. This may be useful if, for example, one normally searches names by both the FirstName and LastName fields. In such a case, a single index can be created that considers the values of both fields simultaneously.

NULL Values

Another important property of table fields is the Required property. This specifies whether that field is required to contain data when a row is added to the table. Possible values for this property are Yes and No. This seems obvious enough, but there are important considerations to understand in situations when a field is not required to contain data.

As a desktop implementation of SQL, Microsoft Access fails to make one important aspect of SQL clear: the ability for data to contain NULL values. In SQL terminology, a field that does not contain data is said to contain a *NULL value*. A NULL value is not the same as spaces. Spaces have a value. NULLs do not. To clarify the difference, most high-end SQL databases such as Microsoft SQL Server display the word NULL in capital letters when one encounters a field with no data present. This allows the user to distinguish a NULL value from spaces.

However, Access does not display the word NULL in such a manner. This makes it somewhat more difficult to distinguish NULLs from spaces in Access.

It's reasonable to ask why all this matters. In the language of SQL, the underlying language behind all Access data retrieval, NULL values have a specific meaning. To illustrate, let's say you have a Customers table with four records with these values in a LastName field: Jones, Garcia, spaces, and NULL. If you formulate a query that retrieves all records with a last name of Jones, you'll get one record back. However, if you formulate a query that retrieves all records with a last name not equal to Jones, you'll get only two records back—the one with Garcia and the one with spaces. What happened to the fourth record? The record with a value of NULL is not selected in either case. In SQL, NULL values are indeterminate. Since they have no value, one can't say if they equal or don't equal any particular value.

In future chapters, we'll see ways to test for NULL values, and we'll discuss functions that allow you to view NULL values. But for now, just be aware that if the Required property is set to No, then you must deal with these types of data issues.

Note also that even if you are linking to data in external databases, Access will not automatically display NULL values, even if the underlying database contains NULLs. Let's say, for example, that you're linking to data in Microsoft SQL Server. If you view the data in SQL Server, you'll see NULL values where appropriate. However, if you view that same data in Access, you'll just see spaces where NULLs occur.

One final point about NULL values: Primary keys in a table can never contain NULL values. That is because primary keys, by definition, must contain unique values, and NULLs are not considered to be values.

Importing Data

Up to this point, this chapter has been concerned with the creation of tables and various table field properties. We now want to turn to situations in which Access tables can contain or point to data external to the Access database. In most data analysis situations, you'll be confronted with data from a variety of sources. Your first problem will be to make that data available so that Access can be used for analysis.

Two basic methods allow you to access external data: 1) import the data into Access tables, and 2) establish links to data residing outside of the Access database. We'll discuss the import option in this section and linking in the following section.

When you import data into Access, it goes into Access tables. You can create tables first, and then do the import, or you can utilize an Access wizard to create any needed tables as you're doing the import. For simplicity, we'll demonstrate the second possibility—that of invoking an Access wizard to import data.

We'll start with a scenario in which the external data is in an Excel spreadsheet. The first step is to select the Excel command in the Import and Link group under the External Data tab. This initiates a wizard that allows you to import data from an existing Excel spreadsheet. The wizard then runs through a number of questions. The first screen asks for the source and destination of the data. The source is selected by browsing to the desired Excel file. There are three choices for the destination: 1) import the data into a new table, 2) append the data to an existing Access table, or 3) link to the data source by creating a linked table. We'll select the first option (to import into a new table). The wizard then turns to the screen shown in Figure 3.9.

Figure 3.9
Import Spreadsheet Wizard.

The spreadsheet we're attempting to import happens to have two worksheets: Teachers and Students. After selecting the Teachers worksheet, we see the three columns on the worksheet—TeacherID, FirstName, and LastName—along with the data. The next screen asks whether the first row contains columns headings. In our case, it does. The following screen allows you to specify specific Data Types or indexes for each of the columns. The next screen lets you choose a primary key. In our example, we'll choose TeacherID as the primary key. The final screen asks for a name for the new table. We'll use the name Teachers.

At the completion of the wizard, the new Teachers table appears in the Navigation Pane. If we right-click on the table name and select Open, we see the data shown in Figure 3.10. The data imported from Excel is now ready to use.

Figure 3.10
Datasheet View of the Teachers table.

This example illustrated how to import data from an Excel file, but there are several other file types from which data can be imported. These include Access databases, ODBC databases, XML files, SharePoint lists, HTML documents, Outlook folders, and dBase files. ODBC stands for *open database connectivity* and refers to server databases such as Microsoft SQL Server. We'll show how to link to data in ODBC databases in the following section.

One of the file types available for import is Access. This means that you can import data from tables in other Access databases into your current Access database. In fact, not only can you import tables, but you can also import any other object type: Queries, Forms, Reports, Macros, and Modules. When you first select the Access icon in the Import and Link section of the Ribbon on the External Data tab, you'll first be asked for the source and destination of the data. The source is selected by browsing to the desired Access file. There are two choices for the destination: 1) import the object (tables, queries, forms, etc.) into the current database, and 2) link to the data source (this applies only to tables). After specifying the source and desti-nation type, you see a window such as shown in Figure 3.11.

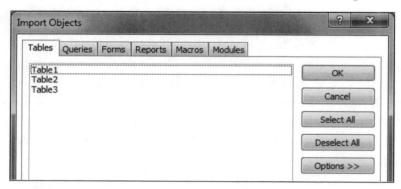

Figure 3.11
Import Objects window.

You can click on any tab or tabs and select any number of objects from the other database. Additionally, you can select the Options button for additional choices. For example, you can choose to import only the design of your specified tables rather than all data in the tables.

Linking to Data

The preceding example of importing from Excel provided options of either importing data or linking to it. If we had chosen to link to the data, we would have gone through the same sequence of screens, except for those that let you select Data Types and specify a primary key. Those steps aren't necessary for linked tables, since the structure is defined in the external data. The result of creating a linked table based on the same Teachers worksheet in the Excel spreadsheet is shown in Figure 3.12, which shows the Datasheet View of the table.

Figure 3.12
Datasheet View of a linked table.

The new linked table was given a name of TeachersLinked. Notice that this linked table has a different icon in the Navigation Pane. The icon displays an arrow next to the Excel symbol. The arrow indicates that this is a linked table. The data in the Tabbed Documents section appears the same as before. However, there's a distinct difference between imported and linked data. Imported data resides in tables in the Access database. Linked tables merely point to external data. The data is not held within the Access database. In a way, this gives you far greater flexibility. When you change the data in the Excel file, the same change shows up in your linked Access table.

Linking to Excel data isn't terribly difficult. But now we want to take up a slightly greater challenge—that of linking to data in external databases. This is a far more useful scenario, in that it allows you to connect to your corporate data, which presumably resides in server databases such as SQL Server, MySQL, or Oracle. Access refers to these types of databases as ODBC databases. The act of linking to ODBC databases involves two steps: 1) creating an ODBC connection in the Data Sources Control Panel, and 2) linking to the database in Access using the ODBC connection.

The first step, creating the ODBC connection, will typically require the assistance of your database administrator. He or she will first need to grant you access to specific tables in one or more databases on a specific server. The details of this procedure are beyond the scope of this book, but it involves setting up a DSN (data source name) entry in the Data Sources (ODBC) item, which is found in the Administrative Tools section of the Control Panel. In setting up the DSN, three basic types of connections can be created: 1) a user DSN, 2) a system DSN, or 3) a file DSN. The user DSN creates an entry that can be accessed only by the current user on the machine. A system DSN can be used by any user on the machine. File DSNs are standalone files that can reside anywhere on the machine.

After the DSN is created, you can easily link to the desired data by clicking the ODBC Database command under the External Data tab in the Ribbon. The process is similar to what has already been seen for importing data. You'll first be asked if you want to import or link to data in the data source. Regardless of whether you choose to import or link, your next step will be to choose data in the Select Data Source window that pops up. An example of this window is shown in Figure 3.13.

Figure 3.13
Select Data Source window.

If the DSN you previously created was a File DSN, you'll stay on the File Data Source tab and select that file. If the DSN was a User or System DSN, you'll go to the Machine Data Source tab, and select the DSN name from the list. After doing this, you'll see a list of tables to which you've been given access. You then merely select the tables you'd like to link to (or import). If you're linking in tables, the tables will be presented to you one by one, and you'll be asked to select a primary key for each table. If you're importing tables, Access will create new tables with data for all the tables you select.

When accessing tables in ODBC databases, you'll usually want to link to tables rather than import data, since this allows you to see current data without having to do another import. Once a link is created, it remains valid as long as the underlying data is available.

Once tables are linked to Access, they can be managed via the Linked Table Manager, which is accessed via the Linked Table Manager command in the Import & Link section of the Ribbon under the External Data tab. When you click on this icon, you'll see a window such as that shown in Figure 3.14.

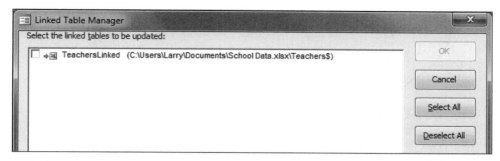

Figure 3.14
Linked Table Manager.

This window lists all linked tables in your database and allows you to refresh any of those tables. This procedure is necessary only if the underlying design of those data sources has been modified. It's not needed merely to get new data. For example, let's say that the spreadsheet referenced in the TeachersLinked table has been modified to include an additional column. When you use the Linked Table Manager to update the link to that spreadsheet, it will retrieve the new design for the corresponding Access table.

Exporting Data

Before leaving the subject of importing and linking to external data, let's briefly cover the reverse task: exporting data out of Access. There are numerous possibilities for moving data out of Access and into another application. You can export data to all file types that can be imported, except for Outlook. Additionally, you can export to PDF, email, and Word merge files.

We'll illustrate the process by exporting the TeachersLinked table that we previously obtained from Excel. To keep things simple, we'll export the same data back to Excel. The process begins by highlighting the TeachersLinked table in the Navigation Pane. To initiate the export, we click the Excel command in the Export section of the Ribbon, under the External Data tab. You'll then see the window shown in Figure 3.15.

In this window, we'll select the destination file, which may or may not already exist, and check the box to export data with formatting and layout. The data is then exported to the designated Excel file. Exporting to file types other than Excel is very similar. The export process is simply the reverse of the import process.

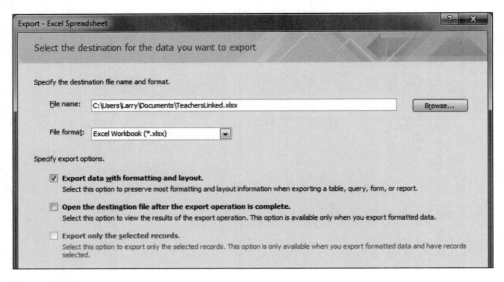

Figure 3.15
Export to Excel Wizard.

Looking Ahead

This chapter covered quite a bit of material—all of it related to Access tables. We began by showing how to create tables in either the Design View or Datasheet View. After illustrating this process, we discussed a number of important properties pertaining to tables, such as Data Types, NULL Values, Primary Keys, and Indexes. The second half of the chapter focused on how to move data into or out of tables from external data sources. Of particular importance is the ability to link to external tables, especially those residing in ODBC databases. With the ability to link to external data, Access allows you to use its full range of data analysis features without having to worry about maintaining data yourself.

In a sense, the business of designing Access tables is only a preliminary step that must be taken before data analysis can occur. In our next chapter, we'll move on to the all-important topic of *Select queries*. This type of query allows you to retrieve data from Access tables. The process of data analysis begins with the assumption that data is available and ready for perusal. With the Select query, we begin our journey into data analysis in earnest.

Chapter 4

Select Queries

In the previous chapter, we explained how to create tables in an Access database and how to link to tables in external databases. This is an essential first step in any data analysis situation. Before you can analyze data, you need to set up your data and data sources so you have something to work with.

We'll now turn to the Access queries and, more specifically, to *Select queries*. A Select query is a virtual view of data in one or more tables. For example, Select query X can present a specific view of data in tables A and B. But in addition to being based on tables, a Select query can also be based on other queries. To continue the example, this means that you can create query Y, which presents a view of data that comes from both table C and query X. Since query X is based on tables A and B, query Y really has data from tables A, B, and C.

Query Types and Views

Select queries present data drawn from tables or queries, but this is just one type of query. In total, Access allows for the creation of six query types:

- Select queries
- Make Table queries
- Append queries
- Update queries
- Delete queries
- Crosstab queries

We've already mentioned that all Access queries can be viewed in both a graphical format (known as the Design View) and as a SQL statement (the SQL View). We'll explore queries primarily in Design View, but you should be aware that queries can also be seen as a SQL statement. The term *Select query* is taken from the fact that, when viewed as a SQL statement, the statement begins with the word SELECT. This keyword indicates that we will select data to be viewed.

The six query types are shown in the Query Type section of the Ribbon under the Query Tools Design tab, as shown in Figure 4.1.

Figure 4.1
Query Types in the Ribbon.

In Figure 4.1, the Select command is highlighted, indicating that the query currently being worked on is a Select query. When you create a new query, you'll normally start by creating the query as a Select query. After the query works as desired, you can easily change the query to any other query type by simply clicking one of the commands in the Query Type section of the Ribbon and then adding a few minor modifications. You can change a query from one type to another at any time. For example, you might start out by designing a Select query, switch it to a Make Table query, and then later decide you want it to be an Append query.

Select queries are the most fundamental type of query, but let's briefly discuss the other query types to see what they do. Make Table queries are similar to Select queries, except that they create a new table to store the selected data. Append queries are similar to Make Table queries, except that they append the selected data to an existing table rather than put it in a new table. Update queries allow you to update specific fields in a table according to the specified selection criteria. Delete queries allow you to delete entire rows of data from existing tables, based on the specified selection criteria.

Make Table, Append, Update, and Delete queries are known, collectively, as *Action queries*, meaning that these queries take some action in order to modify existing data. We'll discuss these queries in detail in Chapter 11, "Action Queries."

Crosstab queries are similar to Select queries in that they merely allow you to view data. There's no updating involved. However, unlike Select queries, Crosstab queries present data in a different format with more dynamic possibilities for summarization. Crosstab queries will be covered in Chapter 12, "Crosstab Queries and Pivot Tables."

To add to the complexity of the different query types, Access also allows you to view all queries in at least three different ways:

- Design View
- SQL View
- Datasheet View

Select and Crosstab queries can also be viewed in these two additional ways:

- PivotTable View
- PivotChart View

Just as you can easily switch between the six query types, you can also easily switch between different query views. Looking at Figure 4.1 again, notice that the Results section of the Ribbon has two commands: View and Run. The View command's drop-down menu lists the following views:

- Datasheet View
- PivotTable View
- PivotChart View
- SQL View
- Design View

You will only see all five of these values if you're working with a Select or Crosstab query. If you're working with one of the four Action queries (Make Table, Append, Update, or Delete), you'll be able to select from only the Datasheet, SQL, and Design Views.

What do these views mean? The Design View is what you'll use to create and modify your queries. Access uses this view to present a graphical interface to the logic of the query. When looking at queries in this book, we'll be looking at the Design View the vast majority of the time.

The SQL View displays the SQL statement that is the basis of what's in the Design View. Behind the scenes, Access uses this SQL statement to define the data being viewed or updated. For those who are intimately familiar with SQL, this is all you really need to see to understand the query. You wouldn't necessarily need to see the query via graphical means. In fact, if you weren't using Microsoft Access, you could use this same SQL statement to select, update, or delete data from a database.

The Datasheet View is a bit more complex. For Select and Crosstab queries, the Datasheet View merely displays data. Data is displayed in the familiar spreadsheet format of rows and columns. However, for Action queries (Make Table, Append, Update, and Delete), the Datasheet View displays the data that will be affected by the action indicated by the query. For example, for Delete queries, the Datasheet View shows the data that will be deleted when the query actually runs. For Make Table queries, the Datasheet View shows the data that will be placed in the new table. For Append queries, the Datasheet View shows the data that will be appended to the specified table when the query runs.

The PivotTable and PivotChart Views allow you to view either Select or Crosstab queries as a pivot table or a pivot chart. Access pivot tables and pivot charts are very similar to what is available in Microsoft Excel. These special objects allow you to view your data in a very flexible and dynamic way. Pivot tables present data in the normal grid-like structure of a spreadsheet. Pivot charts present data in a chart format. The PivotTable and PivotChart Views are covered in detail in Chapter 12, "Crosstab Queries and Pivot Tables."

Why are the PivotTable and PivotChart Views not available for the four Action queries? The reason is that these views only make sense with regard to data that is displayed. There would be no point to displaying data in these formats for Action queries.

Let's now return to the Datasheet View to discuss one additional nuance regarding how it works. You'll notice that in addition to the View command, there's also a Run command in the Results section of the Ribbon. Here's the complication: If you're working with a Select or Crosstab query, then clicking the Run command is identical to switching to the Datasheet View. In other words, for these two query types, "running" the query means that you want to see the data that these queries select. In other words, you want to see the Datasheet View.

However, if you're working with one of the four Action queries, clicking the Run button means that you want the specified action to take place. For example, if you're working with a Delete query, you would click the Run button if you want to run the query to delete some data. This is not the same as switching to the Datasheet View. For action queries, the Datasheet View shows the data that will be affected by the action. You need to actually run the query for the action to occur.

In addition, no matter what type of query you're working with, clicking the Run button is the same as simply opening the query from the Navigation Pane. If you double-click any query in the Navigation Pane (or right-click it and then select

Open), that means that you want to open the query. *Opening* a query means that you want to *run* it.

To summarize and reinforce what all these query types and views mean, let's run through a typical example. Let's say you want to delete some data from a table. Here's one way that you can accomplish that task:

1. Create a new Select query in Design View. This sets up the selection criteria for the data you want to delete.

2. Switch the Select query to Datasheet View. This lets you see the data you'll be deleting.

3. Switch the Select query to SQL View. You might do this if you're curious to see the underlying SQL statement.

4. Switch the Select query back to Design View.

5. Switch the Select query to a Delete query. This changes the query so it can actually delete data.

6. Switch the Delete query to Datasheet View. This allows you to double check the data that will be deleted.

7. Switch the Delete query back to Design View.

8. Click the Run command. This runs the query and deletes the specified data.

Remember that as you're working on a query, you can close and save it at any time, and then return to it later. As an example, before performing the last step in the above sequence (clicking the Run command), you may have decided to simply close the query to save it for future use. If you wanted to execute the query later, you could simply open the query, which has the same effect as running it while in Design View.

Creating Queries

You have two options at your disposal when you want to create a new query. The easiest choice is to use one of the provided wizards to create the query in an automated fashion. The second option is to create the query manually. When you click on the Create tab in the Ribbon, you'll see two commands in the Queries section: Query Wizard and Query Design. These are shown in Figure 4.2.

When you click on the Query Wizard command, you're presented with a choice of four different wizards:

- Simple Query Wizard
- Crosstab Query Wizard

■ Find Duplicates Query Wizard

■ Find Unmatched Query Wizard

Figure 4.2
Query Wizard and Query Design commands.

In this section, we'll run through the Simple Query Wizard. This wizard is a quick and simple way to initiate a new query, and will provide you with an overview of the query creation process.

The other three query wizards are for specialized situations and will be covered in later chapters. The Find Unmatched Query Wizard will be discussed in Chapter 5, "Joins and Relationships." The Find Duplicates Query Wizard will be covered in Chapter 10, "Subqueries and Set Logic." The Crosstab Query Wizard will be looked at in Chapter 12, "Crosstab Queries and Pivot Tables."

All of the examples in this chapter will be based on a database with two tables named Customers and Orders. The queries will come solely from the Customers table, which contains the fields shown in Figure 4.3.

Customers	
Field Name	Data Type
CustomerID	AutoNumber
FirstName	Text
LastName	Text
City	Text
State	Text
Zip	Text

Figure 4.3
Design View of Customers table.

After the Simple Query Wizard is selected, the first window you see is shown in Figure 4.4.

This first screen in the Simple Query Wizard allows you to select one or more fields from one or more tables or queries in your database. The Tables/Queries drop-down box near the top lets you select one table or query at a time. As you select each table (or query), the Available Fields box will show all fields in that table (or query). In

Figure 4.4
Simple Query Wizard with available fields.

this example, we've selected a table named Customers. That table includes six fields: CustomerID, FirstName, LastName, City, State, and Zip.

The single-arrow icon between the Available Fields and Selected Fields lists allows you to select and move individual fields to the Selected Fields list. The double-arrow icon allows you to move all fields with one click.

Let's say we decide to put the FirstName, LastName, and State fields in our new query. After selecting those fields, the screen looks like Figure 4.5.

Figure 4.5
Simple Query Wizard with selected fields.

As seen, we've chosen to not include CustomerID, City, and Zip in our query. After clicking the Next button, we see the screen in Figure 4.6.

Figure 4.6
Simple Query Wizard title selection.

We're now nearly done with the wizard. We now need to do two things: specify a name for the query, and decide whether we want to open the query to view information or to modify the design. The wizard has automatically suggested the name "Customers Query." We'll type over this and change it to "Our Customers." We'll then select the "Modify the query design" option, which will open the query in Design View. After clicking the Finish button, we see the screen shown in Figure 4.7.

Figure 4.7
Design View of a new query.

Now that the wizard has completed its task, we find ourselves in the Design View of the query. Notice that a Design tab under Query Tools in the Ribbon has automatically opened, with a variety of new commands available for changes to query design. As can be seen by the highlighted Select command in the Query Type section, this is a Select query.

The top portion of the workspace shows all the tables (or queries) on which this query is based. In this example, only the Customers table is shown. The large grid in the center shows the three fields we've selected for the query: FirstName, Last-Name, and State.

At this point, we are free to proceed in numerous ways. We can simply save the design as is and come back to it later, or we can make any desired modifications to the design. For example, we might add additional columns or specify some selection criteria. We might want to change the query type from a Select query to some other type, such as a Delete query. We might want to change the view from Design View to some other view. For example, if we switch to Datasheet View, the query will actually run and display some data.

In the remaining sections of this chapter, we'll go through the various options in the different views. In the next section, we'll start with the Design View and make some additional modifications. We'll then examine the Datasheet View to see what the query looks like when it displays data. Finally, we'll examine the SQL View to see what the underlying SQL statements look like.

Before we embark on those details, however, let's return to the Simple Query Wizard to make one important point. In our example, we took the easiest route and selected data from only one table, the Customers table. However, the Navigation Pane shown in Figure 4.7 shows that our database contains both a Customers table and an Orders table. What would have happened if we attempted to select fields from both tables in the wizard?

As indicated by its name, the Simple Query Wizard can only handle simple queries. If we had selected fields from more than one table, we would have received a warning message saying that we've chosen fields from more than one table and that one or more tables aren't related to the others. The message would go on to state "Click OK to edit system relationships. You'll need to restart the wizard."

The *system relationships* referred to in the warning is a special feature of Access that allows you to define how tables in your database are related to each other. A key component in any database design is the relationships that exist between various tables. Access's *Relationships* manager lets you specify how tables are related to each other. This tool will be covered in the next chapter, "Joins and Relationships." The act of designing relationships is quite involved, so we'll hold off on our discussion of that issue. In the meantime, just be aware that the queries we're viewing in this chapter are somewhat simplistic, in the sense that they are based only on a single table.

The Design View

For our exploration of the Design View, we'll start with the query shown in Figure 4.7. This was the result of the query after completion of the Simple Query Wizard. Let's say that we saved and closed this query upon completion. To reinitiate work on the query, we simply select the query in the Navigation Pane, right-click, and select Design View.

Let's first examine the various portions of our work area. In the top pane, we see a rectangular box with a depiction of the Customers table. This box lists all the fields in the table. The first line in the Customers table has a single asterisk (*). The asterisk is utilized when you want to select all fields in the table. The small key icon next to CustomerID denotes that field as a primary key. As previously noted, a query can be based on more than one table. If multiple tables are involved, you'll see lines connecting the tables to indicate the relationship between the tables. Queries can be based on other queries as well as other tables. If queries are involved, they will appear the same as tables. Unlike tables, however, queries won't have a primary key.

To simplify our terminology, we'll refer to the tables and queries that can form the basis of a query as *datasets*. Thus, a dataset can be any table or query that contains data used in a query.

The large grid in the center of the workspaces is comprised of a number of elements. Each column lists a data item involved in the query. These are typically fields taken from any of the datasets (tables or queries) used in the query. Queries sometimes employ *calculated fields* in their columns. These fields are calculated from any number of fields found in the datasets. For example, one might have a column called Profit, calculated as the difference between the Revenue and Expense columns.

The grid also contains a number of predefined rows. The top row, labeled Field, lists the field name. This can be an actual column from a dataset, or a calculated column. A drop-down menu on each cell allows you to choose fields from all available fields. If there is more than one dataset in the query and if a value is not already present in the Table row, then the fields will be listed in this format:

■ DatasetName.FieldName

If the field is a calculated field, you can enter the formula for the calculation directly in the cell.

The second row, labeled Table, lists the table (or query) from which the column is taken. If a value in the Field row is already specified, then the corresponding value for the Table row is automatically populated. As with the Field row, the Table row also has a drop-down menu that allows you to choose the dataset. If the field for that column is a calculated field, there will be no value in the cell.

The third row, labeled Sort, indicates whether the query is to be sorted based on the value of that column. There are three possible sort values: Ascending, Descending, and blank. We'll discuss this particular feature later in the chapter.

The fourth row, labeled Show, specifies whether the value for that column will be displayed in the results when the query runs. Why would you have a column that isn't displayed? This might occur for columns that are used only in the selection criteria for a query. For example, you may want to exclude customers from the state of Wisconsin from appearing in your results. However, you don't want to see the State field itself. By unchecking the box in the Show row for the column with the State field, you can use that field for selection criteria but not have the field's value appear.

The fifth row, labeled Criteria, is a key row in the grid. This is what allows you to determine which rows are displayed in your results. By entering expressions in one or more columns in the grid, you can specify selection criteria ranging from simple to complex. This topic will be covered in detail in Chapter 8, "Selection Criteria."

Finally, the sixth row, labeled Or, is an extension of the Criteria row. This is sometimes needed with certain types of complex selection logic. You may be wondering why there are additional rows below the Or line. These blank rows are merely there to accommodate any additional Or conditions that may be needed.

To test our understanding of the Design View, let's now attempt to create the same query that was created previously with the Simple Query Wizard via a manual process. We'll begin by clicking the Query Design command under the Create tab. We're then presented with a screen that looks like Figure 4.8.

Essentially, we're seeing a blank query with one new feature, a Show Table box. This box allows us to select the tables or queries we want to be the basis of the new query. Note that tabs on the box let you view either tables, queries, or both. In this example, we'll select the Customers table and click the Add button and then the Close button. As the Add button is clicked, the table is immediately added to the workspace.

The only remaining task is to move desired fields from our table to the columns in the grid. There are two methods for doing that. First, you can simply double-click on any field name, which has the effect of placing that field in the next available blank column. The second method is to select a field and drag it down to the grid to the desired location.

Figure 4.8
Show Table window.

After employing either of these methods, our query appears the same as in Figure 4.7, with one difference. We have not yet named the query. At this point, it is still called Query1 and has not been saved. To give the query a name, we can utilize one of three methods. First, we can simply close the query. When the query is closed, it will ask if you want the query saved, and will prompt you for a name. The second method is to click the File tab to enter the Backstage View, and then select the Save command. This will prompt you to name the query. A final option is to click the Save icon in the Quick Access Toolbar in the upper left corner. This will also prompt you for a name.

Once a query is created, you can rename or delete it by highlighting the query in the Navigation Pane, right-clicking, and then selecting Rename or Delete.

Note that after a query has been initially created, you can go back into that query and add additional columns. To do this, double-click or drag the field as was done before. To delete a column, simply highlight the column in the grid by clicking near the top of the column in the grid, and then hit the Delete key on your keyboard. Another way to delete columns is to click anywhere in the column and then select the Delete Columns command in the Query Setup section of the Query Tools Design tab of the Ribbon.

Moving existing columns around is slightly trickier. The easiest way to move a column is to employ a cut and paste operation. Select a column, and then do a cut

(Ctrl-X, or select the Cut command on the Home tab of the Ribbon). Then insert a blank column wherever you want by selecting the Insert Columns command in the Query Tools Design tab. Then, do a paste (Ctrl-P, or the Paste command on the Ribbon).

The Datasheet View

Now that a simple query has been created, the next step is to view the data it specifies. If the query is already open in Design View, this is quite simple. It means merely switching from Design View to Datasheet View.

To do this, use the drop-down menu of the View command on the Query Tools Design tab. After selecting Datasheet View, your screen will look like Figure 4.9.

Figure 4.9
Datasheet View.

The data you see will, of course, depend on the values you happen to have in your tables.

The Datasheet View in queries is almost identical to the Datasheet View in tables. As seen in the previous chapter, the Datasheet View in tables allows you to modify or enter data. The same is true of the Datasheet View in queries. This is true for both queries based on internal tables as well as queries based on external tables for which you have update privileges. Similarly, both Table and Query Datasheet Views allow you to sort and filter data by any of the columns shown.

The only feature of the Datasheet View of tables missing in the Datasheet View of queries is the ability to add new columns. If you want to add a column to an existing table, it must be done in the table Design or Datasheet View.

The SQL View

The SQL View of a query is highly significant, but at the same time can be safely ignored. If you don't care about viewing the SQL equivalent of the queries you create, there is no need to switch to SQL View. However, if you're interested in seeing what SQL is all about, viewing your queries in the SQL View can be quite instructive.

Let's start with the query shown in Figure 4.7. If you use the View command to switch to the SQL View, you'll see a screen as shown in Figure 4.10.

Figure 4.10
SQL View.

In the SQL View, the Tabbed Documents area shows the text of a SQL statement. This SQL statement is the equivalent of the query you're working with. In terms of how data is actually retrieved from a database, the SQL statement is all that's needed. The graphical interface seen in the Design View of a query is presented solely for your convenience, to allow you to create or modify a query without having to know SQL.

At this point, we will introduce our "See the SQL" sidebars, which you'll see in this and future chapters. Since the SQL View is basically just a bunch of words, it's easier to show it as text, rather than as a screen shot.

See the SQL
_____

The SQL equivalent of Figure 4.7 is:

SELECT
Customers.FirstName,
Customers.LastName,
Customers.State
FROM Customers;

Syntax Notes:

- The SELECT keyword indicates the start of a statement that retrieves data.
- Each field that will be shown in the output follows the SELECT keyword.
- All of the fields selected are referred to as a columnlist.
- Commas separate each field in the columnlist.
- The FROM keyword is used to specify datasets used in the query. A dataset can be either a table or another query.
- Each field in the columnlist is comprised of a prefix with a dataset name (usually a table), followed by a column name. The prefix and column names are separated by a period.
- Access automatically displays the prefix in all field names, even if it isn't strictly necessary. Since this SELECT is based on only one table, the field prefixes aren't necessary. For example, the field Customers.FirstName can be changed to FirstName. Prefixes are needed only if the same field name is referenced in more than one dataset.
- A semicolon (;) is used to terminate all SQL statements.

Most of our comments and explanations concerning SQL in this book will be restricted to the "See the SQL" sidebars. Since this book's purpose is not to explain SQL, we don't want to impede the normal flow of text with explanations about SQL, outside of the sidebars. However, since this is our first mention of SQL, we'll take this opportunity to provide a bit more background material to assist in your understanding of what SQL is all about.

Let's start with a few explanations of how SQL statements appear. SQL is a language in which a single statement, although complex, contains a specific command that dictates how data will be retrieved, modified, inserted, or deleted from a database. Within this statement are various keywords that organize the statement into various clauses. By convention, all keywords are shown in all capital letters. In the statement shown in the above sidebar, the words SELECT and FROM are keywords.

SQL statements can be written on any number of lines. Spaces and lines don't matter. Thus, the original SQL statement shown in Figure 4.10 was written on two lines. The same statement, as it appears in the preceding sidebar, was written in five lines. This was done for clarity so that each item in the *columnlist* appears on a separate line.

In actuality, Access does a relatively poor job of displaying SQL statements in its SQL View. Most SQL editors, including Microsoft's own editor in SQL Server, will automatically format a SQL statement, with keywords in caps and color coded, so the statement is easy to read and comprehend. Access does not do this for you.

In addition to expanding the original SQL statement shown in the SQL View into multiple lines, we will also make three additional modifications to the SQL statements in our "See the SQL" sidebars. First, we will sometimes add additional spaces before or after words for improved readability. Second, beginning in Chapter 8, you'll see that SQL statements can utilize parentheses to clarify the logic in selection criteria. Unfortunately, Access tends to generate numerous extra parentheses in the selection criteria portion of SQL statements. This makes it difficult to distinguish between parentheses that are truly necessary and those that aren't. For the sake of clarity, we eliminate unnecessary parentheses. Finally, Access sometimes automatically inserts brackets around table or field names when building an expression. Brackets are necessary only when the table or field name contains spaces. As with parentheses, we eliminate unnecessary brackets.

To sum up, we will apply four types of modifications to SQL statements shown in our "See the SQL" sidebars:

- Reformat the SQL statement into extra lines
- Insert extra spaces for improved readability
- Eliminate unnecessary parentheses
- Eliminate unnecessary brackets

As we present queries in this book, we'll sometimes show the equivalent SQL statements in the "See the SQL" sidebars. As new elements of SQL appear in each statement, we'll include notes that explain the new features. However, let's take a moment now to preview the types of SQL statements you'll see later in the book.

The SELECT statement is the most commonly used statement in SQL. It's used to select, or retrieve, data from a database. SELECT statements can grow to be quite complex, but in generic terms, the basic SELECT can be illustrated with the following format:

```
SELECT columnlist
FROM tablelist
WHERE condition
GROUP BY columnlist
HAVING condition
ORDER BY columnlist
```

Each line in the above statement is a clause that begins with a keyword. Most SQL statements will not include all of these clauses. However, all clauses, when present, must be listed in the order shown above.

Let's now run through the clauses, one by one, to provide a general description of what they accomplish. The SELECT clause initiates the statement, and is used to list the columns (or columnlist) that will be displayed in the query. An example of a columnlist might be:

Customers.Name, Orders.OrderDate

The FROM clause initiates a listing of tables from which the query is drawn. If there is only one table involved, it is simply listed after the FROM keyword. If the query is drawn from more than one table, additional JOIN keywords will be seen, listing additional tables and specifying how they're related to each other. There are actually several variations of JOIN, which will be discussed in Chapter 5, "Joins and Relationships."

The WHERE clause is used to indicate selection criteria. It is rare to have a query without some kind of selection criteria. This allows you to specify the precise data you'd like to see. The *condition* of a WHERE clause can be quite complex. An example might be:

WHERE (Customers.State = 'IL'
AND Customers.Age > 50)
OR (Customers.State = 'WI'
AND Customers.Age > 45)

The GROUP BY clause is used to aggregate data into groups. For example, this can be utilized to group customer data by state, so various statistics on your customers can be summarized by each state. Grouping customers by state allows you to include statistics such as total or average sales by state.

The HAVING clause is similar to the WHERE clause, except that the condition expressed applies not to individual rows but to the aggregated groups specified by the GROUP BY clause. Thus, the HAVING clause is generally found only when there is also a GROUP BY. Let's say, for example, that you are using a GROUP BY clause to summarize your customers by state. The HAVING clause can be used to indicate that you only want to see states where the total sales for all customers in that state exceed a thousand dollars.

Finally, the ORDER BY clause is used to sort the output by the values in any column or expression.

In addition to the SELECT statement, other SQL statements correspond to the other types of Access queries. For example, Delete queries are satisfied via a SQL statement that begins with the keyword DELETE.

The SQL statements you'll see in the "See the SQL" sidebars in this book are not the entirety of the SQL language. Generally speaking, SQL statements can be divided into three main categories:

- DML: Data Manipulation Language
- DDL: Data Definition Language
- DCL: Data Control Language

The SELECT and all other SQL statements found in this book are part of DML. These statements allow you to manipulate data for data retrieval or modification. Besides the SELECT statement, DML includes UPDATE, DELETE, and INSERT statements to modify data in a database. DDL statements allow you to create or modify the database itself. DDL statements also allow for the creation and modification of tables and indexes. DCL statements are primarily about maintaining proper security controls for the database. This includes keywords such as GRANT and REVOKE for security issues, and COMMIT and ROLLBACK for transaction processing.

Selecting All Fields

One useful variant of the Our Customers query discussed previously is one in which you select all fields in a given table. As a matter of expediency, this often saves quite a bit of time and energy. To do this, simply double-click the asterisk (*) that appears at the end of the field list in the table. This will put a single column in the design grid, as shown in Figure 4.11.

Figure 4.11
Design View of a query selecting all fields.

See the SQL

The SQL equivalent of Figure 4.11 is:

SELECT
Customers.*
FROM Customers;

Syntax Notes:

- The use of an asterisk in the field name means "all fields."
- The preceding statement could be simplified to: SELECT * FROM Customers;

When changed to Datasheet View, all fields are displayed, as seen in Figure 4.12.

CustomerID	FirstName	LastName	City	State	Zip
1	Josephine	Smith	Los Angeles	CA	20221
2	Clark	Benham	Des Moines	IA	33333
3	Patrice	Winger	New York	NY	20202
4	Indira	Ghati	Philadelphia	PA	40444
5	Adam	Smith	Albany	NY	33333

Figure 4.12
Datasheet View of a query selecting all fields.

When the asterisk is used to select all fields, the fields are listed in the same order in which they appear in the table's Design View.

Sorting Data

So far, we've only seen how to select fields from a single table and view that data without any selection criteria. The query we've seen is about as simple as it can be. Now we'll introduce one commonly used enhancement—the ability to sort data to put it in a meaningful order.

The ability to sort data can serve many purposes in data analysis. For example:

- Sorting customers by name allows one to quickly locate a specific customer in a list.
- Sorting sales data in descending order by profit allows one to view the most profitable customers at the top of the list.
- Sorting customers by state and then by name allows one to organize data by states, and then locate customers within each state.

Let's begin by adding a sort to the query seen in Figure 4.7. To sort by the customer's last name, we simply click the cell in the Sort row under the LastName column, and then select the value Ascending. The grid in Design View now appears as in Figure 4.13.

Field:	FirstName	LastName	State
Table:	Customers	Customers	Customers
Sort:		Ascending	
Show:	✓	✓	✓
Criteria:			
or:			

Figure 4.13
Design View of a query with a sort.

See the SQL

The SQL equivalent of Figure 4.13 is:

SELECT
Customers.FirstName,
Customers.LastName,
Customers.State
FROM Customers
ORDER BY Customers.LastName;

Syntax Notes:

■ The ORDER BY keyword is used to indicate a sort.

■ The ORDER BY clause must follow all other clauses.

The Datasheet View of the query appears as in Figure 4.14.

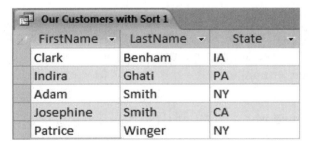

FirstName ▼	LastName ▼	State ▼
Clark	Benham	IA
Indira	Ghati	PA
Adam	Smith	NY
Josephine	Smith	CA
Patrice	Winger	NY

Our Customers with Sort 1

Figure 4.14
Datasheet View of a query with a sort.

In addition to sorting in ascending order, data can also be sorted in a descending alphabetic sequence. Whereas an ascending sort would order data from A to Z, a descending sort would place Z before A. To sort the same data in descending order by customer last name, the Design View would appear as in Figure 4.15.

Field:	FirstName	LastName	State
Table:	Customers	Customers	Customers
Sort:		Descending	
Show:	☑	☑	☑
Criteria:			
or:			

Figure 4.15
Datasheet View of a query with a descending sort.

See the SQL

The SQL equivalent of Figure 4.15 is:

```
SELECT
Customers.FirstName,
Customers.LastName,
Customers.State
FROM Customers
ORDER BY Customers.LastName DESC;
```

Syntax Notes:

■ The DESC keyword following a column listed in the ORDER BY clause indicates a sort in descending order.

■ The default for sorts is ascending, so if the DESC keyword isn't present, the sort is assumed to be in ascending order.

In addition to sorting by a single field, sorts can also be specified for multiple fields. When working with names, one would normally want to sort by last name and then by first name to ensure that the entire name is shown in alphabetical order. In this situation, the LastName column would be called the *primary sort* field and the First-Name column the *secondary sort*. To specify both a primary and secondary sort, Access requires that the primary sort be to the left of the secondary sort in the grid. Thus, the columns would need to be rearranged as shown in Figure 4.16.

Field:	LastName	FirstName	State
Table:	Customers	Customers	Customers
Sort:	Ascending	Ascending	
Show:	☑	☑	☑
Criteria:			
or:			

Figure 4.16
Design View of a query sorting on two columns.

Let's say we wanted to also sort the customers by state, and then by name. We would then need to place the State field as the first column, as shown in Figures 4.17 and 4.18.

Field:	State	LastName	FirstName
Table:	Customers	Customers	Customers
Sort:	Ascending	Ascending	Ascending
Show:	✓	✓	✓
Criteria:			
or:			

Figure 4.17
Design View of a query sorting on three columns.

Our Customers with Sort 4		
State ▾	LastName ▾	FirstName ▾
CA	Smith	Josephine
IA	Benham	Clark
NY	Smith	Adam
NY	Winger	Patrice
PA	Ghati	Indira

Figure 4.18
Datasheet View of a query sorting on three columns.

Notice that both customers in the state of New York (NY) are now together, since the primary sort field is State.

To add one final complication to our sort scenario, let's say that we want to sort only by name, but we want the first name to appear to the left of the last name in the output. As things stand, we have the LastName field to the left of FirstName. This ensures that we sort by last name, then by first name. However, if we place the last name field to the right of the first name field, it will sort by first name, then last name, which is not what we want.

The solution is to make use of the Show line in the design grid. We need to list the FirstName column twice—once to specify the sort order, and once for the actual display of the column. The column used for the sort has its Show box unchecked, as shown in Figure 4.19.

See the SQL

The SQL equivalent of Figure 4.19 is:

```
SELECT
Customers.FirstName,
Customers.LastName,
```

Customers.State
FROM Customers
ORDER BY
Customers.LastName,
Customers.FirstName;

Syntax Notes:

- The FirstName and LastName fields are listed in a different order in the SELECT columnlist and in the ORDER BY columnlist.

- In this example, the SQL View is in many ways more intuitive and understandable than the Design View. Access requires two columns in the Design View when the sort order doesn't correspond to the order in which the fields are listed.

Field:	FirstName	LastName	State	FirstName
Table:	Customers	Customers	Customers	Customers
Sort:		Ascending		Ascending
Show:	✓	✓	✓	☐
Criteria:				
or:				

Figure 4.19
Design View of a query with a sort, using the Show line.

The Datasheet View of this query is shown in Figure 4.20.

Our Customers with Sort 5		
FirstName ▾	LastName ▾	State ▾
Clark	Benham	IA
Indira	Ghati	PA
Adam	Smith	NY
Josephine	Smith	CA
Patrice	Winger	NY

Figure 4.20
Datasheet View of a query with a sort, using the Show line.

Notice that the output correctly displays Adam Smith before Josephine Smith.

When data is sorted, it is generally a good idea to display those columns involved in the sort on the far left, in the order in which the data has been sorted. This helps users intuitively grasp the sort order, since reports are generally read from top to bottom, and left to right. For example, if one is sorting by state, and then zip code, it would be best to display the state as the first field, and then the zip. The only exception to this rule might be with fields such as names, where people intuitively understand that a first name might appear to the left of the last name, even if the sort is by last name, and then first name.

Looking Ahead

We began this chapter by delineating the various Access query types and views. We noted that there are six different query types: Select, Make Table, Append, Update, Delete, and Crosstab. There are also three primary ways to view a query: Design View, SQL View, and Datasheet View. Select and Crosstab queries can also be viewed in PivotTable and PivotChart Views.

We then moved on to show how to create basic Select queries, using both the wizard and a manual process. After creating queries in Design View, we illustrated how to view the same query in Datasheet and SQL Views. "See the SQL" sidebars were introduced as a means of offering more insight into the language of SQL for interested readers.

After showing how to add fields to a query, we discussed sorts in Select queries and covered some of the nuances involved in sorting, such as ascending and descending sorts, and sorts for which the sort order doesn't correspond to the order in which fields are listed.

The queries in this chapter are still very basic, in the sense that they are drawn from data in single tables and don't involve any selection criteria. In the next chapter, we'll embrace more realistic examples of queries as we move on to the topic of joins and relationships. The ability to specify relationships between tables and join them in a single query is essential in most data analysis situations. Seldom will all your data reside in a single table.

Chapter 5

Joins and Relationships

Back in Chapter 2, we talked about the great advances of relational databases over their predecessors. The significant achievement of relational databases was their ability to allow data to be organized into any number of tables, which are related but at the same time independent of each other. Unlike in earlier databases, the relationships between tables in relational databases are not explicitly defined by a series of pointers. Instead, relationships are inferred by columns that tables have in common. These relationships are usually formalized by the definition of primary and foreign keys, but this isn't always necessary.

From the business perspective, the virtue of relational databases lies in the fact that someone can analyze business entities and then design an appropriate database that models reality with maximum flexibility.

Let's look at a common example. Most organizations have a business entity known as the customer. As such, it is typical for a database to contain a Customers table to hold this information. Such a table would normally contain a primary key to uniquely identify each customer and any number of columns with attributes describing the customer, such as name, phone, address, city, state, and birthdate.

The main idea is that all information about the customer is stored in a single table and only in that table. This simplifies the task of data updates. When a customer changes his phone number, only one table needs to be updated. However, the downside to this setup is that whenever someone needs to know anything about a customer, that person needs to access the Customer table to retrieve the information.

This brings us to the concept of a *join*. Let's say that someone is analyzing purchased products. Along with information about the products, it is often necessary to provide information about the customers who purchased each product. For example, an analyst may desire to obtain customer zip codes for a geographic analysis. The zip code is stored only in the Customers table. Product information is stored in a Products table. To get information from both customers and products, the tables must be joined together in such a way that the information matches correctly.

In essence, the promise of relational databases is fulfilled by the ability to join tables together in any desired manner.

Joining Multiple Tables

To begin our exploration of the join process, let's discuss a common situation in which a database contains information about customers and orders. Information about each of these entities is stored in tables named Customers and Orders. The Customers table might have a design such as shown in Figure 5.1, and a few rows of data as in Figure 5.2.

Customers	
Field Name	Data Type
CustomerID	AutoNumber
FirstName	Text
LastName	Text

Figure 5.1
Design View of a Customers table.

Customers		
CustomerID ▾	FirstName ▾	LastName ▾
1	William	Smith
2	Natalie	Lopez
3	Brenda	Harper
4	Adam	Petrie

Figure 5.2
Datasheet View of a Customers table.

An Orders table might have a design and data as seen in Figures 5.3 and 5.4.

Figure 5.3
Design View of an Orders table.

Figure 5.4
Datasheet View of an Orders table.

Of course, in a real life situation, tables such as these would contain many more fields and rows of data. For illustrative purposes, however, this data is sufficient to show how tables can be joined together.

First, notice that each table has a primary key, CustomerID and OrderID. The Orders table has a field named CustomerID that contains a value that points to a row in the Customers table. For example, the order with an OrderID of 4 has a value of 3 in the CustomerID field. This indicates that this order was for Brenda Harper. Also notice that there is no order for the customer with a CustomerID of 4. This is because Adam Petrie has been set up as a customer but has not yet placed an order. The Orders table only contains general information about the order, such as the date and channel. It doesn't contain details about the items ordered. This information will be seen later in a separate table.

We're now ready to create a query that selects data from both of these tables simultaneously. In our previous chapter, we saw how to create a Select query using either the Query Wizard or Query Design commands in the Queries section of the Ribbon under the Create tab. We'll utilize the Query Design command to create our queries manually, since it offers more control than the wizard.

After selecting the Query Design command, we'll select both the Customers and Orders tables in the familiar Show Table window. We then see these tables in the Design View, as in Figure 5.5.

Figure 5.5
Design View of a query.

Notice the line drawn connecting the two tables. The line connects the CustomerID of the Customers table to the CustomerID of the Orders table. This is, in fact, the field that will be used to join the two tables together. The values in this field are common values and mean the same thing in both tables. In other words, there is a *relationship* between the two tables, as indicated by the line.

How did Access figure out that these tables are related by this field? It took an educated guess, based on the fact that the field has the same name in both tables, and that CustomerID is a primary key in the Customers table. If either of these conditions weren't true, Access would have simply displayed both tables on the pane with no line drawn between them.

In situations where Access doesn't draw a line, you can draw the line yourself. This is done by clicking and dragging the mouse from one field to another.

Since Access was smart enough to join these two tables automatically for us, we're now free to select a few fields for our Design View grid. Let's choose four fields:

- CustomerID from the Customers table
- LastName from the Customers table
- OrderID from the Orders table
- OrderDate from the Orders table

After making these selections, we'll save the query as CustomerOrders. The query now appears as in Figure 5.6.

Figure 5.6
Design View of a query.

See the SQL

The SQL equivalent of Figure 5.6 is:

```
SELECT
Customers.CustomerID,
Customers.LastName,
Orders.OrderID,
Orders.OrderDate
FROM Customers
INNER JOIN Orders
ON Customers.CustomerID = Orders.CustomerID;
```

Syntax Notes:

- Each item in the columnlist has a table name and a field name, separated by a period. Since this SELECT has fields from multiple tables, it's important to include the table name.
- The INNER JOIN keyword is used to indicate additional tables.
- The ON keyword is associated with the INNER JOIN and is used to start an expression that states how the two tables being joined are related.
- This is an inner join. We'll explain the difference between inner joins and outer joins later in the chapter.
- For inner joins, the order in which the tables are listed is immaterial.

Notice that the CustomerOrders query now appears in the Navigation Pane under the Queries heading. The query has been opened in Design View. That means that we see the tables involved in the upper pane and the selected fields in the grid. We now want to see what happens when we execute the query. To do this, we can simply change the view to the Datasheet View. The results are shown in Figure 5.7.

Figure 5.7
Datasheet View of a query.

Let's now take a few moments to go over this data. The Customers and Orders tables each had four rows. Looking at the OrderID column, you can tell that we have data from all four rows from the Orders table. However, looking at the CustomerID column, you might notice that we have only three customers shown. Why is that? The answer is that the customer with a CustomerID of 4 doesn't exist in the Orders table. Since we're joining the two tables together on the CustomerID field, we have no rows in the Orders table that match the CustomerID of 4 in the Customers table.

This brings us to an important observation: This join only brought back data for which there is a match between both tables being joined. In SQL terminology, this join is known as an *inner join*. Later in the chapter, we'll talk about an alternative method of joining tables that will allow the customer information for the CustomerID of 4 to be shown, even if there are no orders for that customer. This is known as an *outer join*.

Here's a second important observation: Notice that the customer data for Natalie Lopez is repeated twice in the above results. She existed only once in the Customers table, so why is her customer data shown twice? The answer is that all possible matches are shown. Since Natalie has two rows in the Orders table, both of these rows match with her row in the Customers table, therefore bringing back her customer information twice.

Joins are not restricted to only two tables. To illustrate, let's add a third table named ItemsOrdered. This table contains the details on the ordered items. The design of this table is shown in Figure 5.8. Figure 5.9 shows some data.

Figure 5.8
Design View of ItemsOrdered table.

ItemsOrdered				
ItemID ▾	OrderID ▾	ProductID ▾	QuantityOrdered ▾	PricePerItem ▾
1	1	1	5	12.55
2	1	2	2	4.25
3	2	1	1	12.55
4	3	3	7	10.62
5	4	4	2	8.99

Figure 5.9
Datasheet View of ItemsOrdered table.

Just as the CustomerID in the Orders table pointed to a related customer, the OrderID in the ItemsOrdered table points to the related order. In other words, the OrderID tells which order each particular item was part of. Note also that we have a ProductID field with numeric values. This field is meant to point to a Products table, which would contain information about the product ordered. We won't bring in a Products table in this example, but it illustrates the notion that tables can contain pointers to more than one table.

Let's now create a query that pulls information from all three tables: Customers, Orders, and ItemsOrdered. We'll start by taking the existing query named CustomerOrders and do a copy/paste to create a new query called OrderDetails. If we go into the Design View of the new query, we can add the new table. This can be done either by clicking the Show Table command in the Query Setup section of the Ribbon under the Query Tools Design tab, or else right-clicking in the tables area and selecting Show Table. After doing this, our screen looks like Figure 5.10.

Figure 5.10
Design View of a query in progress.

After selecting the ItemsOrdered table from the Show Table window, the new table is added to the query. Finally, we'll select three fields from the new table: ItemID, QuantityOrdered, and PricePerItem. Our screen now looks like Figure 5.11.

Figure 5.11
Design View of a query with three tables.

See the SQL

The SQL equivalent of Figure 5.11 is:

```
SELECT
Customers.CustomerID,
Customers.LastName,
Orders.OrderID,
Orders.OrderDate,
ItemsOrdered.ItemID,
ItemsOrdered.QuantityOrdered,
ItemsOrdered.PricePerItem
FROM (Customers
INNER JOIN Orders
ON Customers.CustomerID = Orders.CustomerID)
INNER JOIN ItemsOrdered
ON Orders.OrderID = ItemsOrdered.OrderID;
```

Syntax Notes:

- This SELECT contains two INNER JOIN keywords, since there are three tables to be joined.
- Each INNER JOIN has a corresponding ON keyword to indicate the relationship.

■ Access automatically inserted a set of parentheses around the first two tables being joined. This was actually unnecessary. Access often inserts extra parentheses, even when not needed. In future examples, we won't show the unnecessary parentheses.

Notice that Access has automatically joined the new ItemsOrdered table to the Orders table by drawing a line connecting the OrderID fields of both tables. As before, Access was able to determine how these tables are related to each other. When we change this query to Datasheet View, we now see all seven fields that are part of the query, as seen in Figure 5.12.

OrderDetails						
CustomerID ▾	LastName ▾	OrderID ▾	OrderDate ▾	ItemID ▾	QuantityOrdered ▾	PricePerItem ▾
1	Smith	1	6/13/2011	1	5	12.55
1	Smith	1	6/13/2011	2	2	4.25
2	Lopez	2	6/13/2011	3	1	12.55
2	Lopez	3	6/14/2011	4	7	10.62
3	Harper	4	6/14/2011	5	2	8.99

Figure 5.12
Datasheet View of a query with three tables.

Queries as Virtual Tables

Up until now, all of our queries have been based on data residing in tables. One of the powerful features of Access is that it allows you to create queries that reference other queries. Once a query has been created and saved, it acts as if it were a *virtual table*. In other words, one can select data from a query as if it were an actual table. The key difference between a table and query is that a table actually contains data. A query does not contain any data. However, a query can be referenced as if it were a table with data.

In SQL terms, an Access query is like a view in SQL. In most server-based SQL databases, one can create a special object called a view. A SQL view is merely a SELECT statement that has been stored in the database. It doesn't contain any data. This is analogous to Access queries, which are basically just SQL statements. They contain no data.

Let's start with a simple example. Remembering the CustomerOrders query seen in Figure 5.6, we can create a new query that simply returns all data from the CustomerOrders query. Initiating a new query with the Query Design command, we start by selecting the CustomerOrders query under the Queries tab in the Show Table window (Figure 5.13).

Figure 5.13
Queries in the Show Table window.

The CustomerOrders query appears in Design View as if it were a table. We can then double-click the asterisk in the field list of the CustomerOrders to select all fields in the table. The resulting Design View looks like Figure 5.14.

Figure 5.14
Design View of a query selecting all fields.

When we run this query, it returns the same results seen previously in Figure 5.7. In reality, there would be no point in writing a completely trivial query like this. But now let's turn to a more practical example. Let's say we wanted to start with the CustomerOrders query and add the ItemsOrdered table to that query. We could, as was done in the prior section, start completely over and write a new query that references all three tables. This is how we developed the OrderDetails query shown in Figure 5.11.

Another way of accomplishing the same task, however, is to start with the existing CustomerOrders query and simply add the ItemsOrdered table to that query. The result of that process is shown in Figure 5.15.

A few words of explanation: In the upper panel, we see the CustomerOrders query and the ItemsOrdered table. There's no indication that one is a table and the other a query, but that's perfectly fine. Since a query is basically just a virtual table, it really makes no difference. In fact, for this reason, all tables and queries in an Access database must have unique names. You can't have a query and table with the same name. The important point to note, though, is how the two datasets are connected. In creating this query, we needed to manually draw a line between the OrderID of the CustomerOrders query and the OrderID of the ItemsOrdered table. Just as in the original

Figure 5.15
Design View of a query based on a query and a table.

OrderDetails query, this is how these datasets are related. When this query is executed, it returns the same data seen previously in Figure 5.12.

See the SQL

The SQL equivalent of Figure 5.15 is:

SELECT
CustomerOrders.CustomerID,
CustomerOrders.LastName,
CustomerOrders.OrderID,
CustomerOrders.OrderDate,
ItemsOrdered.ItemID,
ItemsOrdered.QuantityOrdered,
ItemsOrdered.PricePerItem
FROM CustomerOrders
INNER JOIN ItemsOrdered
ON CustomerOrders.OrderID = ItemsOrdered.OrderID;

Syntax Notes:

- When a query is referenced in a SELECT, it's specified as if it were a table.

Table and Column Aliases

We need to take a slight diversion at this point to talk about *aliases*. Access provides two types of aliases: table aliases and column aliases.

When utilizing tables (or queries) in queries, there are sometimes reasons why you may want to temporarily change the name by which you refer to the table. An alternate name given to a table is called an *alias*.

Table aliases are typically utilized with tables with long or cryptic names. Let's take an example of a table named OrdFurn. This table holds orders from a Furniture division. To make the table name a little clearer, we'd like to assign an alias of Furniture-Orders to the table.

Table aliases are assigned in queries, not in the table design itself. In initiating a query against the OrdFurn table, we can modify the alias by right-clicking on the table and selecting Properties. This can also be accomplished by clicking the Property Sheet command in the Show/Hide section of the Ribbon, under the Table Design tab. The Property Sheet window initially appears on the right side of the screen, as in Figure 5.16.

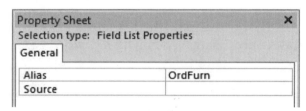

Figure 5.16
Property Sheet.

After changing the value of the Alias property from OrdFurn to FurnitureOrders, and selecting the first two fields in the table, the Design View appears as in Figure 5.17.

Figure 5.17
Design View of a query with a table alias.

Notice that the table name now appears as FurnitureOrders rather than OrdFurn in the query. The name of the underlying table, however, has not changed.

See the SQL

The SQL equivalent of Figure 5.17 is:

```
SELECT
FurnitureOrders.OrderID,
FurnitureOrders.CustomerID
FROM OrdFurn AS FurnitureOrders;
```

Syntax Notes:

- The AS keyword is used immediately after the dataset name to indicate an alias.
- Once an alias is assigned to a table, all fields in that table must reference the table alias name.

In addition to situations where you want to alter a table name to make it more understandable, there are times when a table alias is actually required—which will come into play when we discuss self joins later in this chapter, and also with subqueries in Chapter 10.

In addition to table aliases, there are also *column aliases.* Just as table aliases allow you to alter the name of a table, column aliases allow you to alter the name of a column in a query. Using the prior query as an example, let's say that you want to display different names for the columns. As the query stands, the Datasheet View of the query is shown in Figure 5.18.

Figure 5.18
Datasheet View of a query without column aliases.

Let's say you would like to change the name of the OrderID column to Furniture-OrderID when the query is run. In the Design View of the query, the column alias is added before the real column name, followed by a colon. The column alias is supplied as shown in Figure 5.19. Figure 5.20 shows the result when the query is run.

Because this query now has a column alias, the column named OrderID now appears as FurnitureOrderID.

Field:	FurnitureOrderID: OrderID	CustomerID
Table:	FurnitureOrders	FurnitureOrders
Sort:		
Show:	☑	☑
Criteria:		
or:		

Figure 5.19
Design View of a query with a column alias.

FurnitureOrdersQuery2	
FurnitureOrderID ▾	CustomerID ▾
1	1
2	2
3	1

Figure 5.20
Datasheet View of a query with a column alias.

See the SQL

The SQL equivalent of Figure 5.19 is:

SELECT
FurnitureOrders.OrderID AS FurnitureOrderID,
FurnitureOrders.CustomerID
FROM OrdFurn AS FurnitureOrders;

Syntax Notes:

■ The AS keyword is used immediately after a column name to indicate a column alias.

■ This query has both a column and a table alias. Both are indicated with the AS keyword.

Join Properties

The queries we've seen up until now have all been queries with an *inner join*. We'll now turn to queries with *outer joins*. In the query seen in Figure 5.6, we observed that not all customers appeared in the results when we ran the query. That was because the inner join in the query only displays results if there's a match between the Customers and Orders tables. Since we had one customer with no orders, we didn't see that customer in the results.

Outer joins allow us to rectify this problem. With an outer join, all customers can be seen, even if they never placed an order. The specification as to whether a join between two tables as inner or outer is made in a Joins Properties window. This window can be viewed by double-clicking the line that connects the two tables being joined.

Let's return to the CustomerOrders query of Figure 5.6, and rename it Customer Orders2. When we go into the Design View for the query and double-click the line connecting the two tables, a Join Properties window pops up, as seen in Figure 5.21.

Figure 5.21
The Join Properties window.

The Join Properties window lists the two tables, referring to them as Left Table and Right Table. The terms left and right don't necessarily relate to the physical placement of the tables; it has more to do with the order in which the tables were added to the query. As such, left and right have no particular meaning. It's just a way of referring to the two tables. Additionally, it may be that one of tables is actually a query. That, too, doesn't matter. They're still referred to as tables.

For both tables, the Join Properties window lists the table name and the field (also referred to as a column) involved in the join. Below the table and column names are three options. The first option is always "Only include rows where the joined fields from both tables are equal." This is an inner join.

The second and third options are for outer joins. The second option always includes all records from the left table and only those records from the right table where the joined fields are equal. The third option is the reverse: all records from the right table and only those records from the left table where the joined fields are equal.

In our example, we want all records from the Customers table and only those records from the Orders table that match. Therefore, we'll select the second option. After making this selection, our query design looks like Figure 5.22.

Figure 5.22
Design View of a query with an outer join.

The line connecting the two tables has now turned into an arrow, with the Customers table pointing to the Orders table. Whenever you see an arrow in a join, you know that it's an outer join. The direction of the arrow indicates which table is *primary* and which is *secondary*. In essence, you always see all records in the primary table. You see records in the secondary table if they match those in the primary table. If there is no matching record in the secondary table, you see NULL values for any fields from that table. We'll talk about how NULL values relate to outer joins shortly. The main point is that, in contrast to inner joins, outer joins have one primary and one secondary table. In inner joins, both tables are primary. When this query is executed, we see the results shown in Figure 5.23.

CustomerID ▾	LastName ▾	OrderID ▾	OrderDate ▾
1	Smith	1	6/13/2011
2	Lopez	2	6/13/2011
2	Lopez	3	6/14/2011
3	Harper	4	6/14/2011
4	Petrie		

Figure 5.23
Datasheet View of a query with an outer join.

Comparing these results to Figure 5.7, we see that there is now an extra row for the customer with a last name of Petrie. This customer had no orders. Even though there is no matching row in the Orders table for this customer, we now see his customer information.

Notice that the two fields from the Orders table appear as spaces for Petrie. These spaces in OrderID and OrderDate are actually NULL values. If you recall, we mentioned earlier that Access, unlike many other databases, does not display the word NULL when there are no values. Later, in Chapter 7, we'll learn a way to display a specific value in a field if it contains no data.

See the SQL

The SQL equivalent of Figure 5.22 is:

```
SELECT
Customers.CustomerID,
Customers.LastName,
Orders.OrderID,
Orders.OrderDate
FROM Customers
LEFT JOIN Orders
ON Customers.CustomerID = Orders.CustomerID;
```

Syntax Notes:

- This outer join uses the LEFT JOIN keyword.
- In left joins, the table on the left is always primary. The table on the right is secondary. That means that all records from the left table are returned. Records from the right table are returned if they match.
- The order in which fields are listed in the expression following the ON keyword is immaterial.
- Outer joins can also use the RIGHT JOIN keyword.
- The right join is the opposite of a left join. In a right join, the table on the right is primary. The table on the left is secondary. For example, the FROM and LEFT JOIN lines above could have been stated as the following, with the same meaning:

```
FROM Orders
RIGHT JOIN Customers
ON Customers.CustomerID = Orders.CustomerID;
```

You may be wondering why it was important to utilize an outer join in the prior example. After all, if a customer never placed an order, why would we want to see that person? That may be true, but let's now turn to another example that better illustrates the absolute need for outer joins.

Let's say that we want to join these three tables in a database: Customers, Orders, and Credits. The new table, Credits, is meant to contain information about any credit issued to a customer, typically for a returned order. Thus, the credit is related directly to the customer in a manner similar to the order. Let's further say that of the four customers shown in Figure 5.2, only one of them, Brenda Harper, has ever been issued a credit. Our credits table might look like Figure 5.24.

Credits			
CreditID ▾	CustomerID ▾	CreditDate ▾	CreditAmount ▾
1	3	6/21/2011	8.99

Figure 5.24
Datasheet View of a Credits table.

If we attempt to connect all three tables via inner joins, the table layout portion of the Design View would look like Figure 5.25.

Figure 5.25
Design View of a query with an inner join of three tables.

Notice that both the Orders and Credits are joined to the Customers table, each by the CustomerID field. If we run this query, we get back only one row of data, as shown in Figure 5.26.

CustomerOrdersCredits					
CustomerID ▾	LastName ▾	OrderID ▾	OrderDate ▾	CreditID ▾	CreditDate ▾
3	Harper	4	6/14/2011	1	6/21/2011

Figure 5.26
Datasheet View of a query with an inner join of three tables.

We get back only one row because we are utilizing inner joins, which require a complete match between two tables for any data to be shown. Since there is only one customer with a credit, we only see data for that one customer. To correct the problem, we can alter the query to utilize outer joins, as shown in Figure 5.27.

Notice that the two joins have arrows pointing in different directions. If you were to look at the Join Properties for the two joins, you'd see that the join between the Customers and Orders tables uses option 3, which is a right join in SQL terminology. The join between the Customers and Credits tables uses option 2, which is a left join in SQL terminology. The resulting Datasheet View appears as in Figure 5.28.

Figure 5.27
Design View of a query with outer joins of three tables.

CustomerID ▾	LastName ▾	OrderID ▾	OrderDate ▾	CreditID ▾	CreditDate ▾
1	Smith	1	6/13/2011		
2	Lopez	2	6/13/2011		
2	Lopez	3	6/14/2011		
3	Harper	4	6/14/2011	1	6/21/2011
4	Petrie				

Figure 5.28
Datasheet View of a query with outer joins of three tables.

The query now returns data for all customers, even if they haven't placed an order or received a credit. The cells with blank values represent NULL values. This means that the data doesn't exist for that customer.

See the SQL

The SQL equivalent of Figure 5.27 is:

```
SELECT
Customers.CustomerID,
Customers.LastName,
Orders.OrderID,
Orders.OrderDate,
Credits.CreditID,
Credits.CreditDate
FROM (Orders
RIGHT JOIN Customers
ON Orders.CustomerID = Customers.CustomerID)
LEFT JOIN Credits
ON Customers.CustomerID = Credits.CustomerID;
```

Syntax Notes:

- This query has a right join between the Orders and Customers tables. In right joins, the primary table is always is to the right of the RIGHT JOIN keyword.

- This query has a left join between the Customers and Credits tables. In left joins, the primary table is always to the left of the LEFT JOIN keyword.

With this example, the power of outer joins should now be clear. At this point, we can also reiterate the corresponding power of inner joins. While the outer join allows you to view data even when there's not a match in a second table, the inner join requires a match. As such, inner joins can be used to enforce selection criteria for your data. Let's say, for example, that you have an Orders table with complete information on all orders, and a CustomersForSurvey table that contains a single field with the CustomerIDs of customers participating in a survey. To get all information on all orders associated with any of these customers, you can simply join the two tables on CustomerID using an inner join. The inner join enforces the fact that you will see only orders from customers who are in both tables.

Finding Unmatched Records

Returning to outer joins, our example in Figure 5.22 showed how to obtain a list of all customers, including those without matching orders. We now want to address how we would produce a list of those specific customers who *do not* have matching orders. In this case, there is only one customer who meets that criterion. How would we find that specific customer? The answer is to realize that when doing an outer join, the secondary table we're attempting to match will contain NULL values. Figure 5.29 illustrates the solution.

Figure 5.29
Design View of a query for unmatched records.

To accomplish this task, we need to specify the value IS NULL in the Criteria line of the design grid under a column belonging to the Orders table. Since the Orders table doesn't have a matching row for this customer, all values for fields from the Orders table will have NULL values. In other words, the data doesn't exist. Specifying IS NULL as the criteria allows Access to select rows *without* data in the Orders table.

We haven't made any use of the Criteria line in our prior examples. The general topic of selection criteria will be covered in detail in Chapter 8. This is just a preliminary introduction to the topic.

It may strike you that this procedure of specifying IS NULL as a criteria is somewhat complex, and it is. Fortunately, Access provides a special query wizard that creates this type of query. You start by selecting the Query Wizard command in the Queries section of the Ribbon under the Create tab. After doing so, you select the Find Unmatched Query Wizard, and then answer a series of questions:

- The first screen asks which table contains the records desired in the query results. In our example, this is the Customers table.

- The next screen asks which table contains the related records. In our example, this is the Orders table.

- The next screen asks you to identify the common field in both tables. This is needed to build the join. In our example, this is the CustomerID field.

- The next screen asks which fields you want to see in the query results. In our example, this would be all three fields from the Customers table.

- The final screen asks for a name for the query.

The wizard then generates the query. The result is identical to the query we created manually in Figure 5.29.

Self Joins

The inner and outer joins seen in this chapter have dealt with various ways of combining data from multiple tables. We've also seen how queries can be used as virtual tables, allowing a query to be used as dataset in another query.

We'll now address another scenario in which tables can be used in a virtual way. The *self join* technique allows you to use the same table twice in a single query. The concept of table aliases seen earlier in this chapter allows us to redefine a table so it can be used twice in the same query, so it can be joined with itself.

The most common use of the self join is with tables that are self-referencing in nature. These tables have a column that refers to another column in the same table.

A common example of this type of relationship is a table with information about employees.

In this next example, each row in a Personnel table has a column that points to another row in the same table, representing the employee's manager. In some ways, this is similar to the concept of foreign keys. The main difference is that, whereas foreign keys point to columns in other tables, we now have columns that point to rows in the same table. Let's look at the data in the Personnel table shown in Figure 5.30.

Personnel		
EmployeeID ▾	EmployeeName ▾	ManagerID ▾
1	Susan Ford	
2	Harold Jenkins	1
3	Jacqueline Baker	1
4	Richard Fielding	1
5	Carol Bland	2
6	Janet Midling	2
7	Andrew Brown	3
8	Anne Nichol	4
9	Bradley Cash	4
10	David Sweet	5

Figure 5.30
Datasheet View of a Personnel table.

The ManagerID column shows the manager to whom each employee reports. The ID number in this column corresponds to the numbers in the EmployeeID column. For example, Harold Jenkins has a ManagerID of 1. This indicates that Harold's manager is Susan Ford, who has an EmployeeID of 1.

Similarly, it can be seen that the three people who report to Susan Ford are Harold Jenkins, Jacqueline Baker, and Richard Fielding. Notice that Susan Ford has no value in the ManagerID column. This means that she is the head of the company. She has no manager.

Now, let's say that we want to list all employees and show the name of the manager to whom each employee reports. To accomplish this, we'll create a self join of the Employees table to itself. A table alias must always be used with self joins so there's a way of distinguishing each instance of the table. The first instance of the table will be given a table alias of Employees, and the second instance will be given a table alias of Managers.

Creating this query in Access involves a few steps. We start by initiating a new query with the Query Design command, and then add the Personnel table to the query twice. Our table area of the Design View looks like Figure 5.31.

Figure 5.31
Design View of a query with a self join.

We then highlight each table and specify appropriate table aliases. We'll call the table on the left Employees and the other table Managers. We'll also manually create a relationship between the two tables by drawing a line between the ManagerID of the Employees table and the EmployeeID of the Managers table. The Design View now looks like Figure 5.32.

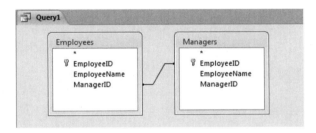

Figure 5.32
Design View of a query with a self join.

Let's pause to discuss why the relationship line was drawn as it was. Even though we have two tables in our query, they are really both derived from the same Personnel table. In SQL terminology, the term *view* is sometimes employed to refer to a table with an alias. Thus, the table with an alias of Employees can be called the Employees view.

The Employees view is used to emphasize the employees in the Personnel table. The Managers view emphasizes the managers. To understand and indicate the relationship, we must realize that the ManagerID of any employee is the same as the EmployeeID of a manager.

After the relationship has been specified, we can build the rest of the query as normal. The Design View is shown in Figure 5.33.

Field:	EmployeeName: EmployeeName	ManagerName: EmployeeName
Table:	Employees	Managers
Sort:		
Show:	✓	✓
Criteria:		
or:		

Figure 5.33
Design View of a query with a self join.

Notice that we needed to employ column aliases in this query. The EmployeeName from the Employees view is meant to be the name of the employee. We therefore gave the column an alias of EmployeeName. Similarly, the EmployeeName from the Managers view is the name of a manager. We gave this column an alias of Manager-Name. When this query is run, the results are as shown in Figure 5.34.

AllEmployees

EmployeeName	ManagerName
Harold Jenkins	Susan Ford
Jacqueline Baker	Susan Ford
Richard Fielding	Susan Ford
Carol Bland	Harold Jenkins
Janet Midling	Harold Jenkins
Andrew Brown	Jacqueline Baker
Anne Nichol	Richard Fielding
Bradley Cash	Richard Fielding
David Sweet	Carol Bland

Figure 5.34
Design View of a query with a self join.

There's actually one slight problem. Notice that Susan Ford isn't shown. This is because we utilized an inner join in the query. Since the head of the company, Susan Ford, has no manager, there is no match to the Managers view of the table. If we want Susan to be included, we merely need to change the query to utilize an outer join. Figures 5.35 and 5.36 show the new outer join and results.

Notice that the outer join specifies the Employees view as the primary table and Managers as secondary. Essentially, we want to see all employees, even if they don't have a manager. Susan Ford now appears as an employee. Since she has no manager, the ManagerName column for her row is blank, indicating a NULL value.

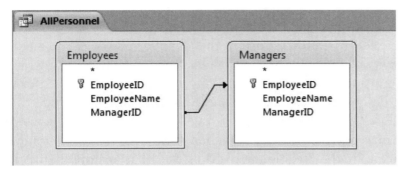

Figure 5.35
Design View of a query with a self join, using an outer join.

EmployeeName	ManagerName
Susan Ford	
Harold Jenkins	Susan Ford
Jacqueline Baker	Susan Ford
Richard Fielding	Susan Ford
Carol Bland	Harold Jenkins
Janet Midling	Harold Jenkins
Andrew Brown	Jacqueline Baker
Anne Nichol	Richard Fielding
Bradley Cash	Richard Fielding
David Sweet	Carol Bland

Figure 5.36
Datasheet View of a query with a self join, using an outer join.

See the SQL

The SQL equivalent of Figure 5.35 is:

```
SELECT
Employees.EmployeeName AS EmployeeName,
Managers.EmployeeName AS ManagerName
FROM Personnel AS Managers
RIGHT JOIN Personnel AS Employees
ON Managers.EmployeeID = Employees.ManagerID;
```

Syntax Notes:

- The Personnel table appears twice in this query. Table aliases are used to distinguish between the two views of the table.
- The table aliases in this query are indicated by the AS keyword.
- This query also utilizes column aliases, which are indicated by the AS keyword.

Relationship Tools

The Join Properties window seen numerous times in this chapter allows you to specify the relationship between two tables for the particular query you're working on. Access also provides a separate tool that lets you specify relationships between any or all tables in your entire database. This is called the Relationship Tool. Once the relationship between two tables has been specified in the Relationship Tool, you no longer need to specify it in new queries you create. When you select tables for a new query that are already known to the Relationship Tool, the relationships between those tables are automatically generated in your queries.

To illustrate the Relationship Tool, we'll start with a fresh database and include only these three tables seen previously in this chapter: Customers, Orders, and Items-Ordered. We then click on the Relationships command under the Database Tools tab on the Ribbon. We then see the familiar Add Table window, which shows all three tables. After selecting all three tables, our screen looks like Figure 5.37.

Figure 5.37
Relationship Tool.

We now simply need to draw lines between the tables to indicate the relationships. After rearranging the order of the tables on the grid and drawing the lines, our screen looks like Figure 5.38.

Notice that we made all our relationships outer joins. Orders are joined to Customers, but there need not be an order for every customer. Similarly, there need not be an item ordered for every order. Also note that the Relationship object is not visible in the Navigation Pane on the left. It can be brought up only via the Database Tools tab on the Ribbon.

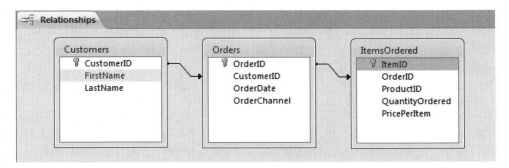

Figure 5.38
Relationships specified.

The Relationships Tool provides a few options beyond the Join Properties window seen previously in Figure 5.21. When selecting any of the relationship lines in the Relationship Tool, we see the Edit Relationships window shown in Figure 5.39.

Figure 5.39
Edit Relationships window.

The Join Type button in the Edit Relationships window allows you to select the appropriate inner or outer join. What's new is the option to Enforce Referential Integrity. This option allows you to select two additional options, a Cascade Update and a Cascade Delete. When updates or deletes are applied to rows in one table, these options can cause updates or deletes to occur automatically in related tables.

Once relationships are set up in Relationship Tools, those relationships will be created when you use the Query Design command to create a new query. This will be true even if the related fields don't have identical names.

A second advantage of setting up things in Relationship Tools is that it allows you to select multiple tables when you use the Simple Query Wizard to initiate a new query. When the wizard creates a new query involving multiple tables, it requires those tables to already be related to each other. The Relationship Tools allow those relationships to be known to the wizard.

With all these advantages, the Relationship Tools is a tremendously useful feature of Access and one that should generally be utilized. Once the relationships have been properly set up in an Access database, a user can create queries at will and be assured that the relationships are correct.

Looking Ahead

This chapter covered the important topic of how to establish relationships between tables. This is accomplished via Join Properties in a query, or in the Relationship Tools for the entire database. The ability to join and create relationships between tables allows a database to be more than just a bunch of data in individual tables. It becomes a coherent whole.

An important aspect of joins for the data analyst is the ability to distinguish between inner and outer joins. Whereas the inner join requires matches between records in two tables, the outer join allows for a one-way match, where data is present in one table but not necessarily in the other.

We also covered a number of important topics related to the process of joining tables. For example, we saw that queries can themselves be used as a type of virtual table. This allows a query to be used as input to other queries. We saw how the Find Unmatched Records Query Wizard uses an outer join and NULL values to find unmatched records. Finally, we explored the special case of self joins, which allows the same table to be referred to twice in a single query, in order to handle recursive relationships.

Our knowledge of joins and relationships gained in this chapter was largely about the mechanics of how they're accomplished. We now turn to the considerations involved in designing an entire database. In our next chapter, we'll step aside from Access for a while and examine proper database design. Although data is not always presented to the data analyst in an optimal fashion, it's useful to be aware of basic relational database design principles. This will give us the ability to think about the structure of our data in the broadest possible context.

Chapter 6

Relational Database Design

In our second chapter, we introduced the notion that relational databases are a collection of data stored in any number of tables. The tables are assumed to be related to each other in some fashion. In the prior two chapters, we showed how database designers can create primary keys and the equivalent of foreign keys with the Relationship Tool.

However, even with our knowledge of primary keys and relationships, we still have not yet addressed the basic issue of how to design a database in the first place. The main questions to address are:

- How should data be organized into a set of related tables?
- What data elements should be placed in each table?

Once tables and their data elements are defined, a database administrator can go about the business of creating foreign keys, indexes, appropriate Data Types, and so on.

There will never be a single correct answer to these two questions. Besides the fact that every organization or business is unique, it is also true that there is no definitive solution for any given business. Much depends on how flexible a business wants its data design to be. Another factor is the existence of current data. Very few organizations have the luxury of designing their databases in a vacuum, apart from what already exists.

Despite these provisos, certain database design principles have evolved over time to guide us in our quest for an optimal design structure. The most influential architect of relational database design is E.F. Codd, who published his groundbreaking article, "A Relational Model of Data for Large Shared Data Banks" in 1970. This article laid the foundation for what we now call the *relational model* and the concept of *normalization*.

Goals of Normalization

The term *normalization* refers to a specific process that allows designers to turn unstructured data into a properly designed set of tables and data elements.

The easiest way to understand normalization is to illustrate what it isn't. To do this, we'll start with the presentation of a poorly designed table with a number of obvious problems. Figure 6.1 shows a table, named Grades, that attempts to present information about all of the grades that students have received for the tests they've taken. Each row represents a grade for a particular student.

Test	Student	Date	Total Points	Grade	Test Format	Teacher	Assistant
Pronoun Quiz	Amy	3/2/2011	10	8	Multiple Choice	Smith	Collins
Pronoun Quiz	John	3/2/2011	10	6	Multiple Choice	Jones	Brown
Solids Quiz	Beth	3/3/2011	20	17	Multiple Choice	Kaplan	NULL
China Test	Karen	2/4/2011	50	45	Essay	Harris	Taylor
China Test	Alex	3/4/2011	50	38	Essay	Harris	Taylor
Grammar Test	Karen	3/5/2011	100	88	Multiple Choice, Essay	Smith	Collins

Figure 6.1
Grades table.

Let's first list the information that each column in this table is meant to provide. The columns are:

- **Test:** A description of the test or quiz given
- **Student:** The student who took the test
- **Date:** The date on which the test was taken
- **TotalPoints:** The total number of possible points for the test
- **Grade:** The number of points that the student received
- **TestFormat:** The format of the test—essay, multiple choice, or both
- **Teacher:** The teacher who gave the test
- **Assistant:** The person who assisted the teacher in this class

We'll assume that the primary key for this table is a composite key consisting of the Test and Student columns. Each row in the table is meant to express a grade for a specific test and student.

Let's now discuss two apparent difficulties with this table. First, certain data is unnecessarily duplicated. For example, you can see that the Pronoun Quiz, which was given on 3/2/2011, had a total of 10 points. The problem, however, is that this information needs to be repeated on every row for that quiz. It would be better if we could simply record the total points for that particular quiz only once.

A second problem is that data is repeated within certain single cells. We have rows for which the TestFormat is both Multiple Choice and Essay. This was done because the test had both types of questions. But this makes the data difficult to utilize. If we wanted to retrieve all tests with essay questions, how could we do that?

To be more general, the problem with this table is that it attempts to put all information into a single table. It would be much better to break down the information into separate entities, such as students, grades, and teachers, representing each entity as a separate table. The power of SQL can then be used to join tables together to retrieve any needed information.

With this discussion in mind, let's now formalize what the process of normalization hopes to accomplish. There are two main goals:

- **Eliminate redundant data**
  The preceding example clearly illustrates the issue of redundant data. But why is this important? What exactly is the problem with listing the same data on multiple rows? Besides the obvious duplication of effort, one answer is that redundancy reduces flexibility. When data is repeated, that means that any change to particular values affects multiple rows rather than just one.

- **Eliminate insert, delete, and update anomalies**
  The problem of redundant data also relates to this second goal, which is to eliminate insert, delete, and update anomalies. Let's say, for example, that one particular teacher gets married and changes her name. You would like the data to reflect the new name. Because the data is stored redundantly, you would need to update many rows of data, rather than just one.

  There are also insert and delete anomalies. If, for example, a new teacher is hired, you would like to record that somewhere in your database. However, since that teacher hasn't yet given any tests, there is nowhere to put this information, since you don't have a table specific to the entity of teachers.

Similarly, a delete anomaly would occur if you wanted to delete a row, but by doing so that would eliminate some related piece of information. Or, take another example: If you had a database of books and wanted to delete a row for a book by Henry James, and that was the only book for Mr. James, then that row deletion would not only eliminate the book but also the fact that Henry James is an author for other books that might be acquired in the future.

How to Normalize Data

We've been throwing around the term *normalization* for a while. It's now time to be more specific about what it means.

The term itself originates with E.F. Codd, and it refers to a series of recommended steps taken to remove redundancy and update anomalies from a database design. The steps involved in the normalization process are commonly referred to as first normal form, second normal form, third normal form, and so on. Although certain individuals have described steps up to sixth normal form, the usual practice is to go only through the first, second, and third normal form. When data is in third normal form, it is generally said to be sufficiently normalized.

We won't describe the entire set of rules and procedures for converting data into first, second, and third normal form. There are texts that will lead you through the process in great detail, first showing you how to transform data into first normal form, then into second form, and then finally into third normal form.

Instead, we'll summarize the rules for getting your data into third normal form. In practice, an experienced database administrator can jump from unstructured data to third normal form without having to follow every intermediate procedure. We will do the same.

The three main rules for normalizing data are as follows:

■ **Eliminate repeating data**

This rule means that no multivalued attributes are allowed. In the previous example, we would not allow a value such as "Multiple Choice, Essay" to exist in a single data cell. The existence of multiple values in a single cell creates obvious difficulties in retrieving data by any given specified value.

A corollary to this rule is that repeated columns are not allowed. In our example, the database might have been designed so that, rather than a single column named TestFormat, we had two separate columns named TestFormat1 and TestFormat2. With this alternative approach, we might have placed the value Multiple Choice in the Test Format1 column and Essay in the TestFormat2 column. This would not be permitted. We don't want to have repeated data, whether it is multiple values in a single column or multiple columns to handle similar data.

- **Eliminate partial dependencies**
  This rule refers primarily to situations where the primary key for a table is a composite primary key, meaning a key composed of multiple columns. The rule states that no column in the table can be related to only part of the primary key.

  Let's illustrate with an example. As mentioned, the primary key in the original Grades table is a composite key consisting of the Student and Test columns. The problem occurs with a column such as TotalPoints. The TotalPoints column is really an attribute of the test and has nothing to do with students. This rule mandates that all non-key columns in a table refer to the entire key, and not just a part of the key. In essence, partial dependencies indicate that the data in the table relates to more than one entity.

- **Eliminate transitive dependencies**
  This rule refers to situations where a column in the table refers not to the primary key, but to another non-key column in the same table. In this example, the Assistant column is really an attribute of the Teacher column. The fact that Assistant relates to the teacher and not to anything in the primary key (test or student) indicates that the information doesn't belong in this table.

So we've seen the problems and have talked about the rules for fixing the data. How are proper database design changes actually determined? This is where experience comes in. And there is normally not a single solution.

That said, we now present one solution to the problem. In this new design, several tables have been created from the one original table, and all data is now in normalized form. Figure 6.2 shows the new tables, along with the indicated relationships.

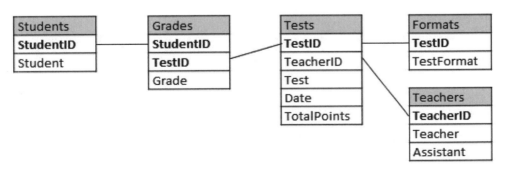

Figure 6.2
Normalized design.

The previously seen Grades table has now been expanded into a database with related tables. The primary keys in each table are shown in bold. A number of ID columns with auto-incrementing values have been added to the tables, allowing relationships between the tables to be defined. All the other columns are the same as shown before.

The main point to notice is that every entity discussed in this example has been broken out into separate tables. The Students table has information about each student. The only attribute in this table is the student name. The Grades table has information about each grade. It has a composite primary key of StudentID and TestID because each grade is tied to a student and to a specific test given.

The Tests table has information about each test given, such as the date, TeacherID, the test description, and the total points for the test.

The Formats table has information about the test formats. Multiple rows are added to this table for each test, to show whether the test is multiple choice, essay, or both.

The Teachers table has information about each teacher, including the teacher's assistant, if there is one.

Figures 6.3 through 6.7 show the data contained in these new tables, corresponding to the data in the original Grades table.

StudentID	Student
1	Amy
2	Jon
3	Beth
4	Karen
5	Alex

Figure 6.3
Students table.

TeacherID	Teacher	Assistant
1	Smith	Collins
2	Jones	Brown
3	Kaplan	NULL
4	Harris	Taylor

Figure 6.4
Teachers table.

Your first impression might be that we have unnecessarily complicated the situation, rather than improved it. For example, the Grades table is now a mass of numbers, the meaning of which is not completely obvious on quick inspection.

TestID	TeacherID	Test	Date	TotalPoints
1	1	Pronoun Quiz	3/2/2011	10
2	2	Pronoun Quiz	3/2/2011	10
3	3	Solids Quiz	3/3/2011	20
4	4	China Test	3/4/2011	50
5	1	Grammar Test	3/5/2011	100

Figure 6.5
Tests table.

TestID	TestFormat
1	Multiple Choice
2	Multiple Choice
3	Multiple Choice
4	Essay
5	Multiple Choice
5	Essay

Figure 6.6
Formats table.

StudentID	TestID	Grade
1	1	8
2	2	6
3	3	17
4	4	45
5	4	38
4	5	88

Figure 6.7
Grades table.

This is true. However, remembering the ability of Access to join tables in queries, you can also see that there is now much greater flexibility in this new design. Not only are we free to join only those tables needed for any particular analysis, but we can now add new columns to these tables much more readily, without affecting anything else.

Our information has become more modularized. For example, if we should decide that we want to capture additional information about each student, such as address and phone, we can simply add new columns to the Students table. Additionally, when we want to modify a student's address or phone later, it affects only one row in the table.

The Art of Database Design

Ultimately, designing a database is much more than simply going through the normalization procedures. Database design is really more of an art than a science, and it requires asking and thinking about relevant business issues.

In our grades example, we presented one possible database design as an illustration of how to normalize data. In truth, there are many possibilities for designing this database. Much depends on the realities of how the data will be accessed and modified. Numerous questions can be asked to ascertain that a design is as flexible and meaningful as it needs to be. Typical questions for this example might include:

- **Are there other tables that need to be added to the database?**
  One obvious choice would be a Subjects table, so you could easily select tests by subject, such as English or Math. If you did this, would you relate the subject to the test or to the teacher who gave the test?

- **Is it possible for a grade to count in more than one subject?**
  Maybe the English and Social Studies teachers are doing a combined lesson and want certain tests to count for both subjects. How would you account for that?

- **Do any teachers have their own special grading rules?**
  For example, a teacher might have a policy of dropping the lowest quiz score in a particular time period. Or, there may be a rule for test re-takes, which allows multiple grades for the same test to be averaged together.

- **Are there special analysis requirements for the data?**
  If there is more than one teacher for the same subject, do you want to be able to compare the average grades for the students of each teacher, to make sure that one teacher isn't unfairly inflating grades?

The list of possible questions is endless. But the point is that data doesn't exist in a vacuum. There is a necessary interaction between data design and requirements in the real world. Databases must be designed to allow for needed flexibility. However, there is also a danger that databases can be overly designed to a point where the data becomes unintelligible. A zealous database administrator may decide to create 20 tables to allow for every possible situation. That, too, is inadvisable. Database design is something of a balancing act in the search for a design that is sufficiently flexible but also intuitive and understandable by users of the system.

Alternatives to Normalization

We have emphasized that normalization is the overriding principle that should be followed in designing a database. In certain situations, however, there are viable alternatives that might make more sense. There are sometimes advantages to purposefully disregarding the principles of normalization when creating a database structure. This effort is referred to as *denormalization*.

For example, in the realm of data warehouse systems, many practitioners advocate utilizing a *dimensional model* for databases rather than normalization. In a dimensional model, a certain amount of redundancy is allowed and encouraged. The emphasis is on creating a data structure that more intuitively reflects business realities, and also one that allows for quick processing of data by special analytical software. As we move on to the topic of Business Intelligence later in this book, we will examine the dimensional model alternative in greater detail.

At this point, though, we'll give a brief preview of what dimensional models entail. The main idea is to create a central fact table, which is related to any number of dimension tables. The fact table contains all the quantitative numbers that are additive in nature. In our prior example, the Grade column is such a number, since we can add up grades to obtain a meaningful total grade. The dimension tables contain information on all the entities that are related to the central facts, such as time, teachers, and students.

Figure 6.8 shows what a database with a dimensional model might look like for our grades example.

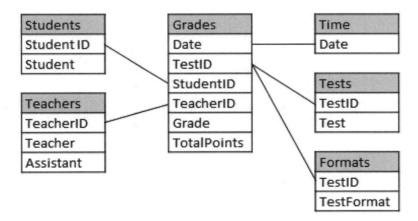

Figure 6.8
A dimensional model.

In this design, the Grades table is the central fact table. The other tables are all dimension tables.

The first four columns in the Grades table (Date, TestID, StudentID, and TeacherID) exist only to relate the table to each of the dimensions. The other two columns

(Grade and TotalPoints) have additive numeric quantities. Notice that TotalPoints is now in the Grades table. In our normalized design, it was an attribute of the Tests table. By putting both the Grade and TotalPoints in the Grades table, we can easily sum up grades and compute average grades (Grade divided by the TotalPoints) for any set of data.

Dimensional models are often ideal for certain types of analytical software that can take advantage of this structure. For example, note that the design of Figure 6.8 utilizes Time as a separate table. This is typical of dimensional models. Since much of data analysis has to do with viewing and comparing data over time, it's often useful to treat time as a separate dimension.

Looking Ahead

This chapter covered the principles of database design. We went over the basics of the normalization process, showing how a database with a single table can be converted into a more flexible structure with multiple tables, related by additional key columns. We also emphasized that database design is not merely a technical exercise. Attention must be paid to organizational realities and to considerations as to how the data will be utilized.

Finally, we briefly described the dimensional model alternative to conventional normalized designs. This construct will be covered in detail in Chapter 14, "Dimensional Modeling." At this point, just be aware that the normalized design is not the only conducive structure for data analysis.

In our next chapter, "Expressions and Functions," we return to our task of learning about Access Select queries. Now that we know about joins and relationships, we need to learn more about how to develop complex calculations on individual fields. This will be addressed by looking at various ways to create expressions in Access, and in the use of functions.

Chapter 7

Expressions and Functions

Before we get to the all-important topic of selection criteria in our next chapter, we have one preliminary topic that needs to be addressed. Up until now, we've selected only individual fields in our queries. However, when selecting data, you are not restricted to the fields that happen to be in your tables. *Expressions* and *functions* allow for a large number of additional possibilities. Expressions are the broader of the two concepts and will be covered first.

Essentially, an expression can consist of up to four different elements:

- Constants
- Identifiers
- Operators
- Functions

Constants are specific values, sometimes called *literal values*. The term *identifiers* typically refers to fields in the tables included in your queries. When a field name is included in an expression, it invokes the value of that field. Operators come in several different flavors, including arithmetic operators, such as plus (+) and minus (–), and comparison operators such as greater than (>) and equal to (=). Finally, Access contains a large number of built-in functions, which allow you to apply a large number of sophisticated calculations and formulas to your raw data.

With expressions, you do such things as:

- Perform the calculation Profit = Revenue – Expenses

- Combine a FirstName and LastName into a single value
- Use a built-in function to return the number of days between any two dates

The power of functions in Access is similar to that found in Excel. With over 160 available functions in Access, you have the ability to perform complex calculations and data manipulation on your data with little effort.

The expressions focused upon in this chapter can be specified on either the Field or Criteria rows on the query Design View grid. In other words, expressions can be used to specify the value of a field displayed when the query is run, or they can be used in selection criteria to help determine which rows are returned when a query is run. In this chapter, we'll limit our examples to expressions that appear on the Field row in the query design grid. We'll see examples of expressions on the Criteria row in the next chapter, "Selection Criteria."

Constants and Identifiers

The simplest type of expression consists of a single *constant* value, sometimes referred to as a *literal*. This specific value has nothing to do with data in a table. Examples of constants include the text value "Dog" or the number 3.

To give a simple example, Figure 7.1 shows the Design View of a query based on a single table named Donations. In this query, we added a column named "Donation Goal" with a value of 100 for all rows selected in the query.

Figure 7.1
Design View of a query with a constant.

Notice that we specified a column alias of "Donation Goal." When columns are based on something other than a single field in a table, a column alias is required so Access knows what to display as a header for that column. If no column alias is specified, Access provides a generic value such as Expr1, which isn't terribly meaningful. When run, the query appears as in Figure 7.2.

Figure 7.2
Datasheet View of a query with a constant.

In this example of a constant value, we displayed a numeric value. If we wanted to display a text value, that value would have needed to be placed within single or double quotation marks.

See the SQL

The SQL equivalent of Figure 7.1 is:

```
SELECT
Donations.PledgeDate,
Donations.PledgeAmount,
100 AS [Donation Goal]
FROM Donations;
```

Syntax Notes:

- When a constant is used in a query, it appears as a specific value.
- Access automatically placed brackets around the column alias Donation Goal. Brackets are needed around a field or column alias name if there are spaces within the field or name.

The term *identifier* refers to table column names. We've already been using identifiers as we've been creating tables. For example, let's revisit a query last seen in Figure 5.11 of Chapter 5. We adjusted the query to change all inner joins to outer joins, and we eliminated a few columns. The Design View is shown in Figure 7.3.

Figure 7.3
Design View of a query with outer joins.

We built this query by double-clicking each desired field in the two tables. This places the field in the Design Grid. For example, after clicking the LastName column, that column appears on the grid.

There's actually an alternative way of selecting fields. Let's say that we wanted to add the FirstName field to our query. We can right-click on the desired cell in the grid and select the value Build in the contextual menu. This brings up an important new window titled Expression Builder, as shown in Figure 7.4.

This Expression Builder will be key to building expressions and functions in this chapter. The top pane has the current value of the expression being built. Right now, it is blank. The bottom section is composed of three panes: Expression Elements, Expression Categories, and Expression Values. As seen, the OrderDetails element in the left pane is currently highlighted. This refers to the query currently being edited. The center pane, Expression Categories, shows the fields in this query.

To get to the FirstName field that we want to add, we need to select the plus sign (+) next to the value "Chapter 7.accdb" in the left pane. "Chapter 7.accdb" is the name of this particular database. After clicking the plus sign, we then see the objects in the database, such as Tables and Queries. We can then select the plus sign next to the Tables object to view all tables. We then select the Customers table and double-click the FirstName field to add it to the query. The Expression Builder now appears as in Figure 7.5.

The expression appears in the top pane. Unlike the identifiers previously seen, this expression is fully qualified. That means that the identifier has both the table name and the field name. Both are enclosed in square brackets, with an exclamation point (!)

Figure 7.4
Expression Builder.

Figure 7.5
Adding an Expression Value in the Expression Builder.

between them. Access sometimes uses an exclamation point (!) and sometimes uses a period (.) between the table and field names. Strictly speaking, brackets are needed only if the table or field name contains a space, but Access provides them automatically. After clicking the OK button, the expression moves to the cell in the grid where we initiated the Expression Builder, as shown in Figure 7.6.

Field:	LastName	QuantityOrdered	PricePerItem	Expr1: [Customers]![Fi
Table:	Customers	ItemsOrdered	ItemsOrdered	
Sort:				
Show:	☑	☑	☑	☑
Criteria:				
or:				

Figure 7.6
Design View of a query with an expression.

Notice two things: Since we didn't supply a column alias, Access supplied the value Expr1 as an alias. Also, note that due to the length of this expression, we can't quite see all of it. To view the entire expression, we have three choices: We can 1) manually expand the length of the column on the grid by dragging it wider, 2) go back into the Expression Builder, or 3) open up the Zoom window for that cell. The Zoom window is just like the Expression Builder except that it only shows the value of the expression. You can make modifications, but without the benefit of the various controls in the Expression Builder. The Zoom window is opened by right-clicking on the cell and selecting Zoom in the contextual menu. It's shown in Figure 7.7.

Figure 7.7
Zoom window.

As may be surmised, the Zoom window can be quite convenient for making quick modifications to expressions in your queries.

Arithmetic Operators

Moving on from constants and identifiers to operators, it should first be noted that Access categorizes operators into four groups:

- Arithmetic
- String
- Comparison
- Logical

We'll discuss Arithmetic and String operators in this chapter. Comparison and Logical operators will be saved for the next chapter, "Selection Criteria."

There are seven available arithmetic operators:

- A plus sign (+) indicates addition.
- A dash (–) indicates subtraction.
- An asterisk (*) indicates multiplication.
- A right or left slanting slash (/ or \) indicates division.
- A caret (^) indicates exponentiation.
- The value Mod indicates the modulus operation.

The plus, dash, asterisk, and slashes are used for the basic arithmetic operations of addition, subtraction, multiplication, and division. The caret is for exponents. For example, 4 ^ 2 means 4 squared, or 16. Mod is used to calculate the remainder after division has taken place. For example 33 Mod 5 equals 3, because after dividing 33 by 5, the result is 6 with a remainder of 3.

To illustrate, let's return to the prior query and add a column named SalesAmount, calculated as the result of QuantityOrdered times PricePerItem.

To accomplish the desired calculation, we place our cursor on the next available column and open the Expression Builder. If you click on Operators, and then Arithmetic, you'll see the operators shown in Figure 7.8.

Using the multiplication operator (*) and the field names under the ItemsOrdered table, you can select the appropriate elements to build the expression shown in Figure 7.9.

After clicking the OK button, the expression is moved to the grid, as shown in Figure 7.10.

Figure 7.8
Arithmetic Operators in Expression Builder.

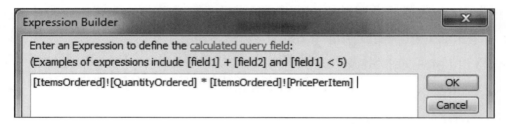

Figure 7.9
Building an expression in the Expression Builder.

Field:	LastName	QuantityOrdered	PricePerItem	FirstName: [Customer	Expr1: [ItemsOrdered]
Table:	Customers	ItemsOrdered	ItemsOrdered		
Sort:					
Show:	✓	✓	✓	✓	✓
Criteria:					
or:					

Figure 7.10
Design View of a query with an Arithmetic Operator.

See the SQL

The SQL equivalent of Figure 7.10 is:

```
SELECT
Customers.LastName,
ItemsOrdered.QuantityOrdered,
```

```
ItemsOrdered.PricePerItem,
Customers.FirstName AS FirstName,
ItemsOrdered.QuantityOrdered * ItemsOrdered.PricePerItem AS Expr1
FROM (Customers
LEFT JOIN Orders
ON Customers.CustomerID = Orders.CustomerID)
LEFT JOIN ItemsOrdered
ON Orders.OrderID = ItemsOrdered.OrderID;
```

Syntax Notes:

- Arithmetic operators, such as multiplication (*), can be inserted between identifiers to create an expression.
- To keep syntax more in line with standard SQL, we've replaced the exclamation points (!) used in Access with periods, and eliminated unnecessary brackets.

Our only remaining task is to rename the column alias from Expr1 to the desired value of SalesAmount. After doing that and running the query, we see the data shown in Figure 7.11.

OrderDetails2				
LastName ▾	QuantityOrdered ▾	PricePerItem ▾	FirstName ▾	SalesAmount ▾
Smith	5	12.55	William	62.75
Smith	2	4.25	William	8.5
Lopez	1	12.55	Natalie	12.55
Lopez	7	10.62	Natalie	74.34
Harper	2	8.99	Brenda	17.98
Petrie			Adam	

Figure 7.11
Datasheet View of a query with an Arithmetic Operator.

As seen, the expression in the SalesAmount column properly multiplied QuantityOrdered by PricePerItem.

String Operators

Just as arithmetic operators allow us to perform calculations on numeric values, string operators perform calculations on text values. There is, in fact, only one string operator: the ampersand (&) sign.

The ampersand denotes the operation known as *concatenation*. This is a fancy computer term meaning "to combine character data together." A common example of concatenation is the practice of connecting a person's first name and last name to yield a full name.

Starting a new query based on only the Customers table, let's construct a new Full-Name column from the FirstName and LastName fields of the Customers table. Figure 7.12 shows the Design View for a query that accomplishes this.

Field:	FirstName	LastName	FullName: [Customers]![FirstName] & ' ' & [Customers]![LastName]	
Table:	Customers	Customers		
Sort:				
Show:	✓	✓	✓	
Criteria:				
or:				

Figure 7.12
Design View of a query with a String Operator.

Notice that there are the three components to the expression that makes up the Full-Name column: the first name, a constant value of space, and the last name. The space is necessary so that a space is inserted between the first and last names. When run, the Datasheet View for the query appears as in Figure 7.13.

CustomerName		
FirstName ▾	LastName ▾	FullName ▾
William	Smith	William Smith
Natalie	Lopez	Natalie Lopez
Brenda	Harper	Brenda Harper
Adam	Petrie	Adam Petrie

Figure 7.13
Datasheet View of a query with a String Operator.

See the SQL

The SQL equivalent of Figure 7.12 is:

```
SELECT
Customers.FirstName,
Customers.LastName,
Customers.FirstName & ' ' & Customers.LastName AS FullName
FROM Customers;
```

Syntax Notes:

- The ampersand (&) operator is used to denote concatenation.
- Concatenated fields often require a literal space to separate values. Single quotes are used to designate the literal space.

We've now seen both Arithmetic and String operators. As mentioned, Comparison and Logical operators will be covered in the next chapter, "Selection Criteria."

Functions

Similar to the expressions that can be created with arithmetic and string operators, functions provide another way to manipulate data. The expressions we've seen have involved operators that connect multiple fields. In contrast, functions are often performed on a single column.

What is a function? A function is merely a rule for transforming one value (or values) into another value, using a specific formula. For example, the function MID can be used to determine that the first initial of the name Joan is J.

A function can be based on any number of input values. There are even functions that have no inputs, such as the DATE function, which simply returns the current date. However, all functions, regardless of the number of inputs, always return a single output value.

In general, there are two basic types of functions: scalar and aggregate. The term *scalar* comes from mathematics and refers to an operation done on a single number. In computer usage, it means that the function is performed on data in a single row. For example, the LTRIM function removes leading spaces from one specified value.

In contrast, *aggregate* functions are meant to be performed on a larger set of data. For example, the SUM function can be used to calculate the sum of all the values of a specified column.

Access categorizes functions into 14 categories:

- Arrays
- Conversion
- Database
- Date/Time
- Domain Aggregate

- Error Handling
- Financial
- General
- Inspection
- Math
- Messages
- Program Flow
- SQL Aggregate
- Text

Access offers well over 160 functions in all these categories. In this book, we will cover only a few representative examples of some of the more useful functions that are important for the data analyst.

In this chapter, we'll discuss a number of Text, Date/Time, Math, Financial, Conversion, and Inspection functions. These are all scalar functions that operate on single values. The Text, Date/Time, and Math functions are basic functions that operate, respectively, on Text, Date/Time and Numeric data. Financial functions are a special class of Math functions used for financial analysis. Conversion and Inspection functions are useful for transforming or testing the Data Types of data.

Program Flow functions will be discussed in the next chapter, "Selection Criteria." These functions can be used to apply logic to the values that appear in query columns.

The SQL Aggregate functions are the important aggregate functions mentioned previously. Since these functions apply to sets or groups of data, we will leave our discussion of them to Chapter 9, "Summarizing Data."

Text Functions

Text functions are those that enable you to manipulate text data. In common usage, text functions are sometimes called *string functions*. We'll cover five examples of text functions: LEFT, RIGHT, MID, UCASE, and TRIM.

To select functions with the Expression Builder, you simply select Functions, then Built-In Functions, and then the desired category. After selecting a function, Access places a template for the function in the main entry box in the Expression Builder. This is illustrated in Figure 7.14.

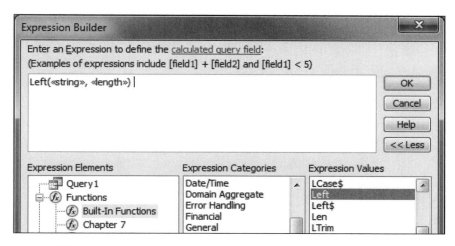

Figure 7.14
Building an Expression with a Function.

In this example, we've selected the LEFT function. The template for the function reads:

- Left («string», «length»)

This indicates that there are two parameters required as input for the function: a *string* value and a *length*. The LEFT function is used to select a specified number of characters from a string, starting on the left side. The *string* parameter is the value for which the function will be applied. The *length* parameter specifies how many characters to capture.

Notice that there are parentheses around the two parameters. This is true of all functions. Functions are specified by a name followed by any number of parameters within parentheses. If there is more than one parameter, they will be separated by commas. It's possible for a function to have no parameters, in which case the parentheses will still be present but will have nothing within them.

If you want complete information on a function, you merely need to click on the link for the function shown at the bottom of the Expression Builder. This will open an Access Help window with information on the function.

The template that appears in the Expression Builder is a placeholder for values you want to enter. In this example, we'll replace *string* with the identifier [FirstName]. This can be done by simply double-clicking on the FirstName field in the Expression Builder. We'll replace the *length* parameter with the value 1, meaning that we want the first initial of the first name. Finally, we'll replace the generic column alias with

"Initial" to indicate that this is the first initial. After doing this, the Design View of the query appears as in Figure 7.15.

Figure 7.15
Design View of a query with a LEFT function.

See the SQL

The SQL equivalent of Figure 7.15 is:

SELECT
Customers.FirstName,
Customers.LastName,
LEFT ([FirstName], 1) AS Initial
FROM Customers;

Syntax Notes:

■ Functions appear in SQL statements exactly as they appear in the Expression Builder.

When run, the data appears as in Figure 7.16.

The next three text functions we'll discuss are RIGHT, MID, and UCASE. The templates for these functions are:

■ Right («string», «length»)

■ Mid («string», «start», «length»)

■ UCase («string»)

TextFunctions1

FirstName ▾	LastName ▾	Initial ▾
William	Smith	W
Natalie	Lopez	N
Brenda	Harper	B
Adam	Petrie	A

Figure 7.16
Datasheet View of a query with a LEFT function.

The RIGHT function is used to select a specified number of characters from the right side of a string. MID is employed to select characters from the middle of a string, with a specified start position and length. The UCASE function converts a string to all capital letters.

These three functions are illustrated by the Design and Datasheet Views shown in Figures 7.17 and 7.18.

Field:	LastName	Right: Right([LastName],2)	Mid: Mid([LastName],2,3)	UCase: UCase([LastName])
Table:	Customers			
Sort:				
Show:	✓	✓	✓	✓
Criteria:				
or:				

Figure 7.17
Design View of a query with RIGHT, MID, and UCASE functions.

TextFunctions2

LastName ▾	Right ▾	Mid ▾	UCase ▾
Smith	th	mit	SMITH
Lopez	ez	ope	LOPEZ
Harper	er	arp	HARPER
Petrie	ie	etr	PETRIE

Figure 7.18
Datasheet View of a query with RIGHT, MID, and UCASE functions.

In this example, we specified a selection of the two right-most characters for the RIGHT function. We therefore see a value of "th" for Smith. For the MID function, we specified 3 characters, starting in position 2. We therefore see a value of "mit" for Smith. Finally, the UCASE function merely converts all characters in the string to uppercase.

To illustrate our final text function, TRIM, we'll need to add a new row to the Customers table for a customer with the name of Jane Doe. The unique characteristic of this row will be that it contains five spaces in the FirstName field before the name.

The TRIM function eliminates, or trims, all leading and trailing spaces around a text value. The template for the function is:

■ Trim («string»)

Figures 7.19 and 7.20 show the Design and Datasheet Views for a query with the TRIM function applied to the FirstName field.

Field:	FirstName	LastName	Trim: Trim([FirstName])
Table:	Customers	Customers	
Sort:			
Show:	✓	✓	✓
Criteria:			
or:			

Figure 7.19
Design View of a query with a TRIM function.

TextFunctions3

FirstName ▼	LastName ▼	Trim ▼
William	Smith	William
Natalie	Lopez	Natalie
Brenda	Harper	Brenda
Adam	Petrie	Adam
Jane	Doe	Jane

Figure 7.20
Datasheet View of a query with a TRIM function.

As seen, the TRIM function successfully eliminated the leading spaces before the first name of Jane.

Composite Functions

An important characteristic of functions, whether they are text, date/time, or math, is that two or more functions can be combined to create composite functions. A composite function with two functions can be said to be a function of a function.

To illustrate, let's return to the LEFT and TRIM functions. We've seen that the LEFT function selects a specified number of characters from the left side of a text value.

The TRIM function can get rid of any leading spaces. The question we'll pose is: How would one select the first initial for Jane Doe? If we just use the LEFT function to select the first character, we'll get a space. We don't really want to use the MID function to get the first initial, because we can't predict exactly how many spaces exist to the left of the name.

The solution is to use both the LEFT and TRIM functions in combination. The template for a composite function that accomplishes this is:

■ Left (Trim («string»), «length»)

This is really two functions in one. Composite functions always contain an *inner* and an *outer* function. The inner function is performed first, and then the outer function is performed on the result. If there are more than two functions involved, the calculation proceeds from the innermost function to the outermost function. In this case, the inner function is:

■ Trim («string»)

This does the trim of the string. The outer function is:

■ Left («string», «length»)

When the outer function is performed, the string value is replaced by the result of the inner function. Putting it all together with the string name, the desired length, and column alias, the function appears as:

■ Initial: Left (Trim ([FirstName]), 1)

The solution is shown in Figures 7.21 and 7.22.

Field:	FirstName	LastName	Initial: Left(Trim([FirstName]),1)
Table:	Customers	Customers	
Sort:			
Show:	✓	✓	✓
Criteria:			
or:			

Figure 7.21
Design View of a query with a composite function.

As seen in Figure 7.22, the composite function has successfully returned the first initial of every first name, even if the FirstName field includes leading spaces.

In this example, the order in which the individual functions in the composite function were specified was significant. We needed to perform the TRIM function prior

Figure 7.22
Datasheet View of a query with a composite function.

to the LEFT function for the composite. In other words, the following two expressions are not functionally equivalent:

- Left (Trim ([FirstName]), 1)
- Trim (Left ([FirstName], 1))

However, the order of functions is not always critical. For example, if you wanted to trim spaces from an expression and convert that expression to uppercase, you would create a composite function with the TRIM and UPPER functions. In that situation, it wouldn't matter which function was performed first. You could first trim the expression, and then convert to uppercase, or you could convert to uppercase first. In other words, the following two expressions are functionally equivalent:

- UCase (Trim ([FirstName]))
- Trim (UCase ([FirstName]))

In essence, functions can be combined as building blocks to create composite functions. This allows data analysts to create customized complex expressions.

Date/Time Functions

Date/Time functions allow for the manipulation of date and time values. These functions are often of critical importance, as much of data analysis is sensitive to dates and time. For example, one might want to:

- View data falling within a specific date range
- View yesterday's sales data
- Compare average sales on Mondays with average sales on Tuesdays
- Compare this month's sales with the same month last year

- Determine how many days have elapsed since a customer last placed an order
- Display dates in a format that includes the day of the week

In this chapter, we'll provide examples of ways to perform date calculations and display dates in different formats. The topic of data selection will be held off until the next chapter. To provide a taste of some of the possibilities, we'll cover these five examples of date/time functions: DATE, DATEADD, DATEDIFF, MONTH, and YEAR.

The simplest of the date/time functions is one that returns the current date. This is the DATE function. The template for this function is:

- Date ( )

In fact, one would not normally use the DATE function by itself in the Field row of a query. Users seldom want to know the current date as part of returned data. A more practical example would be one in which users are shown the number of days that have elapsed between an order date and the current date, for orders which have not yet been paid. Another use of the DATE function, which will be shown in the next chapter, involves using it to select records that fall within a period of time relative to the current date, such as orders in the last 10 days.

Access provides two other functions similar to the DATE function: TIME and NOW. The TIME function returns the current time. The NOW function returns both the date and time.

The next Date/Time functions we'll discuss are DATEADD and DATEDIFF. DATEADD is used to add a specific period of time to a date. DATEDIFF allows you to calculate the length of time that exists between two dates, measured in any unit of time. The templates for these two functions are:

- DateAdd («interval», «number», «date»)
- DateDiff («interval», «date1», «date2», «firstdayofweek», «firstweekofyear»)

In DATEADD, the amount of time to be added is specified via *interval* and *number* parameters. The *interval* parameter can accept string values such as "d" for days. If you look at the Help screen for this function, you'll find that there are many other options for the interval parameter—for example, "m" for month or "ww" for week. Additionally, the *number* parameter can be a negative number, allowing you to calculate a date before the specified date.

In DATEDIFF, the first three parameters, *interval, date1,* and *date2* are required. The last two are optional.

To illustrate, we'll use these functions against the Donations table seen earlier in this chapter. We'll use the DATEADD function to add 20 days to the PledgeDate field. DATEDIFF will be used to calculate the number of days between the PledgeDate and DateReceived.

The expressions we'll place in the query are:

- DaysAdded: DateAdd ("d", 20, [PledgeDate])
- DaysBetween: DateDiff ("d", [PledgeDate], [DateReceived])

Figure 7.23 shows the results.

DonationID	PledgeDate	DateReceived	DaysAdded	DaysBetween
1	4/11/2011	4/25/2011	5/1/2011	14
2	4/11/2011	4/26/2011	5/1/2011	15
3	4/11/2011	4/27/2011	5/1/2011	16
4	4/12/2011	4/26/2011	5/2/2011	14
5	4/12/2011	4/29/2011	5/2/2011	17

Figure 7.23
Datasheet View of a query with DATEADD and DATEDIFF functions.

As seen, the DATEADD function was used in the DaysAdded column to add 20 days to the PledgeDate. Using the DATEDIFF function, the DaysBetween column shows the number of days between PledgeDate and DateReceived. With a quick adjustment to the parameter values, the DATEADD function could just as easily have subtracted 3 months from PledgeDate, and DATEDIFF could have calculated the number of weekdays between the two dates.

See the SQL

The SQL equivalent of Figure 7.23 is:

```
SELECT
Donations.DonationID,
Donations.PledgeDate,
Donations.DateReceived,
DATEADD ("d", 20, PledgeDate) AS DaysAdded,
DATEDIFF ("d", PledgeDate, DateReceived) AS DaysBetween
FROM Donations;
```

Syntax Notes:

- The specific format of functions varies among different SQL implementations. For example, although most SQL databases have a DateDiff function, the number of parameters and allowed values for parameters will often be different.

Finally, the MONTH and YEAR functions return the month and year, respectively, of a specified date. To illustrate the usefulness of these functions, let's say you want to calculate the first day of the current month. You may want to do that, for example, if you want to select rows with a date prior to the first day of the current month. To create this expression, you'll need to create a composite function with the DATE, MONTH, and YEAR functions. The trick is to concatenate these three expressions:

- The month of the current month
- The text literal "/1/"
- The year of the current month

An expression that accomplishes this is:

- FirstDayOfMonth: Month (Date ( )) & "/1/" & Year (Date ( ))

FirstDayOfMonth is the column alias. Let's now break down how the composite function works. Let's say that the current date is 04/15/2012. DATE ( ) gives the current date. MONTH (DATE ( )) gives the month of the current date, which is 4 in this case. Similarly, YEAR (DATE ( )) gives the year of the current date, which is 2012. Putting this all together, we're concatenating 4, plus "/1/" plus 2012, which produces 4/1/2012.

Format Properties

It is sometimes desirable to display dates in a format other than the standard mm/dd/yyyy. Let's take a slight detour from functions to discuss how this is accomplished. Just as Excel allows you to modify the format of a cell, independent of the contents of that cell, Access also allows you to modify the format of a data item via its *Format property*. Formatting properties apply not only to dates, but also to numbers.

As an example, let's return to the query result shown in Figure 7.2. The date is shown in mm/dd/yyyy format, and the numbers are integers. To change the format, you simply need to right-click on a cell in the Design View of the query and select Properties. Alternatively, you can select Property Sheet in the Show/Hide section of the Ribbon under the Design tab.

In either case, you'll see a property box appear, which looks like Figure 7.24.

If you're working with a Date/Time field, you'll see four possibilities for formatting: General Date, Long Date, Medium Date, and Short Date. If you're on a numeric field, you'll see values such as General Number, Fixed, Currency, and Percent.

Figure 7.24
Property Sheet.

To illustrate the power of formatting, let's change the Format property for the date field to Long Date, and change the Format property of the two numeric values to Fixed. The result of the query now appears as in Figure 7.25.

PledgeDate	PledgeAmount	Donation Goal
Monday, April 11, 2011	25.00	100.00
Monday, April 11, 2011	50.00	100.00
Monday, April 11, 2011	60.00	100.00
Tuesday, April 12, 2011	50.00	100.00
Tuesday, April 12, 2011	75.00	100.00

Figure 7.25
Datasheet View of a query with altered formats.

As expected, the date now appears in a longer format, and the numbers have two fixed decimal places.

Math and Financial Functions

Math functions allow for the manipulation of numeric values. Financial functions are a special subset of mathematical functions that allow for standard financial calculations. Relative to Excel, Access provides far fewer math and financial functions, since these functions tend to be less important in the normal usage of Access. However, four math functions worth mentioning are ROUND, INT, SQR, and LOG. The templates for these functions are:

■ Round («number», «precision»)

■ Int («number»)

- Sqr («number»)

- Log («number»)

The ROUND function takes a specified *number* and rounds it to the desired *precision*. For example, if a precision of 2 is specified for the number 876.2386, the result will be 876.24. A precision of 3 will result in 876.239. The *precision* value can also have a value of 0. This has the effect of rounding to the nearest integer value. The *precision* parameter can't have a negative value.

The INT function converts the specified number to an integer, simply by dropping any decimal places. It doesn't do any rounding.

As might be guessed, the SQR function takes the square root, and LOG takes the log of a *number*.

Turning to financial functions, we'll first note that Access provides only 13 financial functions, compared to the more than 50 in Excel. We'll illustrate what can be done with financial functions with the PV and FV functions.

The PV function calculates the present value of a stream of future payments. The FV function is very similar, except that it calculates the future value of prior payments. These two functions are commonly used to give financial analysts the ability to consider the time value of money when comparing cash flows in different time periods. The templates for the two functions are:

- PV («rate», «num_periods», «payment», «future_value», «type»)

- FV («rate», «num_periods», «payment», «present_value», «type»)

The first three parameters of both functions, *rate, num_periods,* and *payment,* are required. The *rate* is the interest rate for the period. For example, if you will be paying 12% interest in 12 monthly payments, the *rate* for the period is 1% or .01. The *num_periods* parameter is the number of periods in the stream of payments. For example, if there are to be 3 years of monthly payments, then *num_periods* is 36. The *payment* is the payment per period. The last two parameters for each function are optional. For PV, you can specify the *future_value* as a single value. For FV, you can specify the *present_value* as single value. The *type* parameter allows you to override the default on timing, which is that the payments are assumed to occur at the end of each period.

To illustrate these functions, let's work with numbers from a Finance table, with three relevant columns: Rate, Periods, and Payment. The values in these columns will be used as input to both the PV and FV functions. Let's also add in our ability to formulate composite functions, and add the ROUND function to both PV and FV to round the result to the nearest integer value. The Query Design appears as in Figure 7.26.

Figure 7.26
Design View of a query with PV and FV functions.

The first three columns of this query show the values from the Rates, Periods, and Payment fields of the Finance table. These values are used as input to the PV and FV functions, shown in the last two columns. Since the contents of these PresentValue and FutureValue columns are too large to display on screen, we'll utilize the Zoom window to view the contents of those cells:

- PresentValue: Round (PV ([Rate] / 12, [Periods], [Payment]), 0)
- FutureValue: Round (FV ([Rate] / 12, [Periods], [Payment]), 0)

We'll examine how these functions work in a minute. But first, let's look at the results of the query, shown in Figure 7.27.

Rate	Periods	Payment	PresentValue	FutureValue
0.05	12	-100	1168	1228
0.07	24	-100	2234	2568
0.08	12	-100	1150	1245

Figure 7.27
Datasheet View of a query with PV and FV functions.

The results computed the present and future value for a stream of payments based on the given rate, periods, and payment amount. For example, the first row indicates that the present value of a future stream of twelve monthly $100 payments (assuming a dollar currency) at 5% annual interest is $1168. The future value of a prior stream of twelve monthly $100 payments at 5% annual interest is $1228.

Let's now look at the formulas in greater detail. The present value calculation is a composite function with this template:

- Round (PV («rate», «num_periods», «payment»), «precision»)

The inner function, which is computed first, is PV. It consists of three parameters, *rate*, *num_periods*, and *payment*. The value of the rate parameter has been divided by 12 to translate the yearly rate of 5% to a monthly rate. This nicely illustrates that operators (such as division) are often used in combination with functions. The outer function, ROUND, is wrapped around the PV function to round the result to the nearest integer. The result of the PV function is used as the *number* parameter in the ROUND function. To this, it adds 0 as the value for the *precision* parameter to round the result to the nearest integer.

Conversion and Inspection Functions

All of the aforementioned functions relate to specific ways to manipulate Text, Numeric, or Date/Time Data Types. But you may need to convert data from one data type to another, or convert NULL values to something meaningful. The remainder of this chapter will cover functions that can be used in these situations.

Access provides several dozen Conversion functions. Functions in this category allow you to convert expressions from one Data Type to another. We'll illustrate the process with the CDATE function, which converts text data to a true Date/Time Data Type. The template for the function is simple:

- CDate («expression»)

This function accepts just one expression parameter and converts it to a date. We'll illustrate the use of this function with the query shown in Figure 7.28.

See the SQL

The SQL equivalent of Figure 7.28 is:

```
SELECT
MiscDates.DateField,
```

CDATE (DateField) AS TrueDate
FROM MiscDates;

Syntax Notes:

■ The CDATE function is specific to Access. If you're running SQL on standard SQL databases such as Microsoft SQL Server, you'll usually use the CAST keyword to convert data types from one format to another.

Figure 7.28
Design View of a query with a CDATE function.

In this query, we are drawing data from the MiscDates table. In this table, the Date-Field field is actually a text field. This can sometimes present a problem. Even though the field contains dates, those dates can't be used with date/time functions because Access doesn't recognize them as dates. By using the CDATE function, those values can be converted to true dates. When the query in 7.28 is run, the results are as shown in Figure 7.29.

ConversionFunctions	
DateField ▾	TrueDate ▾
03/18/2011	3/18/2011
05-06-2011	5/6/2011
4/2/11	4/2/2011
07-APR-2011	4/7/2011

Figure 7.29
Datasheet View of a query with a CDATE function.

As seen, CDATE converted the dates found in the DateField field to a standard format. Notice that even though the original dates were in a variety of formats, CDATE was able to accomplish the correct conversion.

In addition to the Conversion functions, Access also provides ten Inspection functions. The one Inspection function of particular interest is ISNULL.

As mentioned previously, Access allows data in individual cells to contain NULL values. These values represent the absence of data. The problem with NULL values is that they display as spaces. This means that when one sees spaces in a query result, it may not be clear whether that value represents spaces or a NULL value.

The ISNULL function provides some assistance with this. The template of the function is:

- IsNull («expression»)

The function is simple. When a value is inserted into the *expression* parameter, the function returns a value of either 0 or –1. A value of –1 means that the expression contains a NULL value. A value of 0 means that it's not NULL.

Taking an example, the query shown in Figure 7.30 joins the Customers and Orders tables. The data contains a few customers who have never placed orders. When joining these tables with a left join, we'll encounter a few orders with NULL values, because orders don't exist for those customers. In this query, we'll specify the OrderID field in three different ways, as explained next.

Figure 7.30
Design View of a query with an ISNULL function.

When this query is run, the result is as seen in Figure 7.31.

CustomerID ▾	LastName ▾	OrderID1 ▾	OrderID2 ▾	OrderID3 ▾
1	Smith	1	0	1
2	Lopez	2	0	2
2	Lopez	3	0	3
3	Harper	4	0	4
4	Petrie		-1	No Order
5	Doe		-1	No Order

Figure 7.31
Datasheet View of a query with an ISNULL function.

Since they're not visible in Figure 7.30, the expressions for the OrderID1, OrderID2, and OrderID3 columns are:

- OrderID1: OrderID
- OrderID2: IsNull ([OrderID])
- OrderID3: IIf (IsNull ([OrderID]), "No Order", [OrderID])

The first column, with column alias OrderID1, is simply the OrderID. This displays the OrderID as is. For those rows with NULL values for this field, the cell appears with spaces.

The second column, with the column alias OrderID2, specifies the OrderID as the expression in the ISNULL function. For those rows with NULL values for the OrderID, the cell appears as either 0 or –1. A value of –1 means that the field contains a NULL value. Of course, the display of a 0 or -1 is far from ideal. This leads us to the OrderID3 column.

The third column, with the column alias OrderID3, utilizes the ISNULL function in conjunction with another function called IIF. We'll go over the IIF function formally in the next chapter in the section on Condition Logic, so this is just a preview of the function, showing another way that it can be used. The IIF function has this template:

IIf («expression», «truepart», «falsepart»)

We've created a composite function by placing the entire result of the ISNULL function in the *expression* parameter of the IIF function. We then specified the value "No Order" for the *truepart* parameter. The OrderID field is specified for the *falsepart* parameter. In other words, if the ISNULL function evaluates to true, we display the value "No Order." Otherwise, we display the value of the OrderID field.

See the SQL

The SQL equivalent of Figure 7.30 is:

```
SELECT
Customers.CustomerID,
Customers.LastName,
Orders.OrderID AS OrderID1,
ISNULL (OrderID) AS OrderID2,
IIF (ISNULL (OrderID), "No Order",OrderID) AS OrderID3
FROM Customers
LEFT JOIN Orders
ON Customers.CustomerID = Orders.CustomerID;
```

Syntax Notes:

■ If you're running SQL on Microsoft SQL Server, you'll find that the ISNULL function in that database allows for two parameters: the expression to evaluate, and the value to display if the expression is NULL. This allows NULL values to be handled without resorting to a composite function.

Looking Ahead

Expressions and functions play a critical role in the endeavor of presenting data in a useful manner. We began this chapter with the observation that expressions can consist of any combination of literals, identifiers, operators, and functions. We covered arithmetic and string operators, while leaving comparison and logical operators for the next chapter. We then discussed a variety of functions in a number of categories: Text, Date/Time, Math, Financial, Conversion, and Inspection.

A lot of this material on functions is necessarily dry, because there are simply so many available functions with widely varying capabilities. It's impossible to discuss every nuance of every available function. The thing to remember is that the syntax for functions can be easily obtained in the Access Help window when they need to be used. Access Help is context sensitive, so you merely need to click the Help button when you're viewing any particular function. This provides a quick guide to syntax and functionality.

The importance of functions cannot be overstressed. Without functions, very little can be accomplished in the way of data presentation and selection. Functions are like prepackaged formulas that serve as building blocks for many aspects of data manipulation. Additionally, the ability to create composite functions from two or more functions is a significant way to extend their power even further. Hopefully, the examples of composite functions shown in the chapter will give you an idea of some of the possibilities.

In our next chapter, "Selection Criteria," we'll finally encounter the task of selecting the data that you truly want to see. The expressions and functions that we've seen on the Field line of the Design View of queries will now be extended to the Criteria line. To the arithmetic and string operators we've already seen, we'll add comparison and logical operators. More importantly, the next chapter will cover a topic known as *Boolean Logic*. This will give you the ability to create complex logical expressions that can be used to specify the precise data that will be retrieved in a Select query.

Chapter 8

Selection Criteria

Up until this point, our queries have always brought back every possible row from the tables referenced in the query. This would rarely be the case in real-world situations. Normally, one would only be interested in retrieving data that meets certain criteria. By addressing the topic of selection criteria, this chapter will address that shortcoming.

If you're selecting customers, you would typically want to see only a subset of all your customers. If you're retrieving orders from your customers, you probably only want to see orders that meet certain conditions or that fall within a particular date range. Rarely does someone want to simply see everything. Data analysis is typically directed toward a small subset of all available data in order to analyze or view one particular aspect or situation.

Specifying Criteria

Selection criteria in Access queries begin with the Criteria line of the Design View grid. Working from the Donations table seen in the previous chapter, let's start with the simplest possible example of selection criteria. In the query shown in Figure 8.1, we're selecting all rows from the Donations table where the FirstName equals Janet.

As shown, we have entered the value "Janet" on the Criteria line of the grid under the DonorFirstName column. This accomplishes the selection of that value. Note that we did not need to type in the quotation marks. Access provides quotes automatically, since it knows it's a Text field.

Figure 8.1
Design View of a query with one selection criteria.

See the SQL

The SQL equivalent of Figure 8.1 is:

SELECT
Donations.DonationID,
Donations.DonorFirstName,
Donations.DonorLastName
FROM Donations
WHERE Donations.DonorFirstName = "Janet";

Syntax Notes:

- All selection criteria is initiated with a WHERE keyword. The WHERE clause immediately follows the FROM clause.

- An equality condition is specified with an equals sign (=). The equals sign is needed even if it doesn't appear in the Design View.

- In this example, Access automatically inserted numerous parentheses in the WHERE clause. As mentioned in Chapter 4, we remove all unnecessary parentheses in our "See the SQL" sidebars. This is done when the parentheses don't affect the logic. Access originally displayed this WHERE clause as: WHERE (((Donations.DonorFirstName) = "Janet"))

The Donations table includes the data shown in Figure 8.2.

When the query is run, it appears as in Figure 8.3.

As expected, the query selected only one row of data, for the donation from Janet Crawford.

Figure 8.2
Datasheet View of Donations table.

Figure 8.3
Datasheet View of a query with one selection criteria.

Comparison Operators

In the above example, the value "Janet" implied a condition of equality. If we had typed an equals sign (=) in front of Janet, the result would be the same.

The equals sign is referred to as a *comparison* operator in Access. Here's a list of the basic comparison operators:

Operator	Meaning
=	Equals
<>	Does not equal
>	Is greater than
<	Is less than
>=	Is greater than or equal to
<=	Is less than or equal to

Access provides three additional comparison operators: BETWEEN, IN, and LIKE. These will be discussed later in this chapter.

We've already seen an example of the equals (=) operator. Let's look at an example of one of the others. Figure 8.4 shows a query where we select donations with a pledge amount greater than or equal to $50 (assuming dollars as the currency). The result is shown in Figure 8.5.

As expected, we only see rows where the PledgeAmount is 50 or more. The $25 pledge from William McIntyre is excluded.

Field:	DonationID	DonorFirstName	DonorLastName	PledgeAmount
Table:	Donations	Donations	Donations	Donations
Sort:				
Show:	✓	✓	✓	✓
Criteria:				>=50
or:				

Figure 8.4
Design View of a query with comparison operator.

Donations Query 2

DonationID	DonorFirstName	DonorLastName	PledgeAmount
2	Janet	Crawford	50
3	Lynn	Sanchez	60
4	Cary	Newman	50
5	Andrew	Myers	75

Figure 8.5
Datasheet View of a query with comparison operator.

Comparison operators, even comparisons of inequality such as greater than (>), aren't restricted to situations involving numeric data. For example, with respect to dates, it's often desirable to select data greater than (or less than) a particular date. Inequality comparisons can also be used with text data. In our example, if we wanted to select donors with a last name that begins with the letters M to Z, we would specify criteria as shown in Figure 8.6, with a result shown in Figure 8.7.

Field:	DonationID	DonorFirstName	DonorLastName	PledgeAmount
Table:	Donations	Donations	Donations	Donations
Sort:				
Show:	✓	✓	✓	✓
Criteria:			>="M"	
or:				

Figure 8.6
Design View of a query with compare on text data.

Donations Query 3

DonationID	DonorFirstName	DonorLastName	PledgeAmount
1	William	McIntyre	25
3	Lynn	Sanchez	60
4	Cary	Newman	50
5	Andrew	Myers	75

Figure 8.7
Datasheet View of a query with compare on text data.

The result excludes the donation from Janet Crawford, as her last name begins with a letter that comes before M.

Limiting Rows

What do you do if you want to select a small subset of rows in a table, but you don't care which rows are returned? Let's say that you have a table with 100,000 rows, and you want to see just a few rows of data to see what it looks like. It wouldn't make sense to use normal selection criteria for this purpose, since you don't care which rows are returned.

The solution is to use the Top Values property of the query to limit the number of rows returned. This property can be specified in two ways. First, you can bring up the Property Sheet for the query, which will list the Top Values property. An easier method, though, is to simply make a selection on the Ribbon. In the Query Setup section of the Ribbon under the Query Tools Design tab, you'll find a command named Return. This section of the Ribbon is shown in Figure 8.8. Next to the Return command, you'll see a drop-down box that allows you to select a value, either as a number or a percent. The default value is All.

Figure 8.8
Return command on the Ribbon.

Using our Donations table as an example, we'll select a value of 3. When you select the drop-down box, you'll find values such as 5 and 25, but these can be overwritten with any number. We won't specify any other selection criteria. When the query is executed, we see the result shown in Figure 8.9.

DonationID	DonorFirstName	DonorLastName	PledgeAmount
1	William	McIntyre	25
2	Janet	Crawford	50
3	Lynn	Sanchez	60

Figure 8.9
Datasheet View of a query with Top Values value of 3.

We now see only three rows from the Donations table. Note that this is not a random sample. Access brings back the first three rows, as they're physically stored in the database.

The Top Values property can also be specified as a percent. If we rerun this query, specifying 40% rather than 3, we'll see only two rows of data (40% of the five rows in the Donations table is two).

See the SQL

The SQL equivalent of Figure 8.9 is:

```
SELECT
TOP 3
Donations.DonationID,
Donations.DonorFirstName,
Donations.DonorLastName,
Donations.PledgeAmount
FROM Donations;
```

Syntax Notes:

- The Top Values property is specified with the TOP keyword immediately after the SELECT keyword.
- If the Top Values property is specified as a percent, the SQL keyword will be TOP PERCENT. For example, a selection of 50% would be stated as TOP PERCENT 50.
- The TOP and TOP PERCENT keywords are valid in Microsoft SQL Server. Other databases may utilize a different syntax.

These examples of the Top Values property are interesting but of limited analytic value. A much more significant use of Top Values comes into play when this property is combined with a sort.

In our Donations table example, let's say we wanted to see the two largest donations ever made. This can be accomplished by specifying a Top Value of 2, combined with a descending sort. The query appears as in Figures 8.10 and 8.11, showing the Ribbon and Design View. Figure 8.12 shows the results when run.

Figure 8.10
Return command on the Ribbon with value of 2.

Field:	DonationID	DonorFirstName	DonorLastName	PledgeAmount
Table:	Donations	Donations	Donations	Donations
Sort:				Descending
Show:	✓	✓	✓	✓
Criteria:				
or:				

Figure 8.11
Design View of a query with Top Values and a sort.

Donations Query 5

DonationID ▾	DonorFirstName ▾	DonorLastName ▾	PledgeAmount ▾
5	Andrew	Myers	75
3	Lynn	Sanchez	60

Figure 8.12
Datasheet View of a query with Top Values and a sort.

Why was the sort specified in descending order? When sorted in descending order, the rows are arranged from the highest to the lowest values. We want to see only the two rows with the highest value for the PledgeAmount field. Therefore, only a descending sort makes sense. If we had sorted the data in an ascending order, we would have seen those rows with the lowest pledge amounts.

See the SQL

The SQL equivalent of Figures 8.10 and 8.11 is:

```
SELECT
TOP 2
Donations.DonationID,
Donations.DonorFirstName,
Donations.DonorLastName,
Donations.PledgeAmount
FROM Donations
ORDER BY Donations.PledgeAmount DESC;
```

Syntax Notes:

- As seen, the TOP keyword can be combined with an ORDER BY clause to return rows based on a sorted order.
- If the DESC (descending) option for the ORDER is specified, the query will return those rows with the highest values. The ASC (ascending) option will return rows with the lowest values.

There are numerous other possibilities for an effective use of the Top Values property, used in combination with a sort. For example, if we had wanted to see the top 10% of donations, we would simply specify a percentage for the Top Values property. Or if we wanted to see the top three donations from the state of California (assuming we had a State field in the table), we would specify that selection criteria for the state, while still sorting the data in descending order by PledgeAmount.

Focus on Analysis: Random Samples

Analysts are sometimes called upon to select a random sample from a dataset for further testing. The RND (random) function in Access is a mathematical function that allows this to occur. The template for the RND function is:

- RND («number»)

The RND function operates on any field in your query with a numeric value. The function returns a random value between 0 and 1. Once that number is obtained from the function, you can sort the query on that column and use the Top Values property to return any desired number of records.

One caveat is that the field specified in the RND function must be a number, and preferably a positive number. Negative and zero values can result in duplicate random numbers. The ideal field to use is one with an AutoNumber data type. If your data doesn't contain such a field, you can utilize an Append query to copy your data to a new table with an AutoNumber field. Append queries are covered in Chapter 11, "Action Queries."

As an example, let's say you have a table with a column named NumericField, containing positive numeric values. To generate the random sample, simply add a column to your query with this value on the Field line:

- RND (NumericField)

Specify either an Ascending or Descending sort on the Sort line and uncheck the box on the Show line. Then select any desired value for the Top Values property. Specifying 25% will generate a random set of 25% of your data.

Due to the nature of random samples, this query will generate a different result every time the query is run. If you want to save the random sample values, you can modify the query to a Make Table, as explained in Chapter 11, to save the data.

Pattern Matching

We'll now turn to a related situation in which the data to be retrieved is not precisely defined. In contrast to tests of pure equality with the equals (=) comparison operator, we'll examine the need to retrieve data based on inexact matches with words or phrases. For example, you may be interested in finding businesses whose name contains the word "bank."

The process of finding inexact matches within an expression is often referred to as *pattern matching*. The LIKE operator in Access is a special comparison operator that allows for such matches. In conjunction with the LIKE operator, *wildcard* characters are used to specify the nature of the match.

The most common wildcard characters are the asterisk (*) and percent sign (%). These characters both mean "any character." The asterisk is used for data found in Access tables. The percent sign is generally used for data found in linked external tables.

Let's illustrate with an example taken from a table with Movie titles, shown in Figure 8.13.

Movies	
MovieID ▾	MovieTitle ▾
1	Love Actually
2	His Girl Friday
3	Love and Death
4	Sweet and Lowdown
5	Everyone Says I Love You
6	Down with Love
7	North by Northwest

Figure 8.13
Datasheet View of Movies table.

Our first task is to find movies that contain the word "love" anywhere in the title. A query that accomplishes this is shown in Figure 8.14. The results are in Figure 8.15.

Field:	MovieID	MovieTitle
Table:	Movies	Movies
Sort:		
Show:	☑	☑
Criteria:		Like "*love*"
or:		

Figure 8.14
Design View of a query with the LIKE operator.

The expression that accomplishes the selection of movie titles with the word "love" is simple: the operator LIKE, followed by "*love*". The asterisks on either side of love indicate that any characters may precede or follow the word. This can include situations where no characters precede or follow. The criteria specified by the LIKE operator isn't case sensitive, so "love" is evaluated the same as "LOVE".

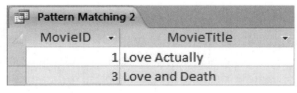

Pattern Matching 1

MovieID ▾	MovieTitle ▾
1	Love Actually
3	Love and Death
5	Everyone Says I Love You
6	Down with Love

Figure 8.15
Datasheet View of a query with the LIKE operator.

See the SQL

The SQL equivalent of Figure 8.14 is:

SELECT
Movies.MovieID,
Movies.MovieTitle
FROM Movies
WHERE Movies.MovieTitle LIKE "*love*";

Syntax Notes:

■ The asterisk (*) wildcard applies to data in Access tables. For external tables, the wildcard to use is usually the percent sign (%).

One variant of this type of pattern matching selection criteria is a search where the desired word appears only at the beginning or end of the phrase. For example, you may want to find only movies for which the word "Love" appears at the very beginning of the phrase. This is accomplished with the following selection criteria:

Like "love*"

When run, this query produces the result shown in Figure 8.16.

Pattern Matching 2

MovieID ▾	MovieTitle ▾
1	Love Actually
3	Love and Death

Figure 8.16
Datasheet View of a query with the LIKE operator.

We now see only movies that begin with the word "love". Similarly, an asterisk can be placed at the end of the search criteria to find movies that end with love. What if you wanted to find movies with "love" in the middle of the title, but not at the beginning or end? The solution is to specify the following search criteria:

"* love *"

Notice that a space has been inserted between the word "love" and the asterisk wildcards on either side. This ensures that there is at least one space on either side of the word. When run, this query produces the result shown in Figure 8.17.

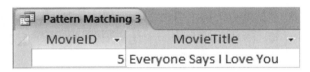

MovieID	▾	MovieTitle	▾
	5	Everyone Says I Love You	

Figure 8.17
Datasheet View of a query with the LIKE operator.

Besides the asterisk (or percent) wildcards, a few additional wildcard characters provide slightly different functionality. A question mark (?) or underscore (_) is a wildcard for exactly one character. The question mark is for data in Access; the underscore is for external tables. For example, the string T?E will match with the words THE or TIE, but not the words THEM or TABLE.

Another option for wildcards is the ability to specify a characterlist with multiple characters within brackets. When a characterlist is utilized, the match must be with exactly one character in the list. For example, the string P[EA]T will match PET or PAT, but not PIT or PLANT. You can also specify a negative characterlist, meaning that it will match with any characters *not* in the list. This type of character is denoted by an exclamation point (!) at the start of the list. For example, the string P[!EA]T will match PIT but not PET, PAT, or PLANT.

Boolean Logic

So far, the selection criteria we've seen in this chapter has involved simple situations, such as:

- DonorFirstName = "Janet"
- PledgeAmount >= 50

In the real world, data selection is often far from this straightforward. Accordingly, we'll now turn our attention to ways of specifying some more complex logical conditions in selection criteria.

The ability to devise complex logical conditions is sometimes called *Boolean logic*. This term, taken from mathematics, refers to the ability to formulate complex conditions that are evaluated as either true or false. In our prior example, for the criteria PledgeAmount >= 50, the procedure would be to evaluate each row in the result as either true or false for each row. The object is to return only data for which it is true that PledgeAmount is greater than or equal to 50. With Boolean Logic, we can combine multiple logical conditions into a single expression, which is then evaluated as either true or false.

Thus, with Boolean logic, the conditions for selection criteria can become more complex. The principle keywords used to create Boolean logic are AND, OR, and NOT. In Access terminology, these are referred to as *logical operators*. In proper combination, the AND, OR, and NOT operators, along with parentheses, can specify just about any logical expression that can be imagined.

One of the chief benefits of the Access graphical interface is its ability to let you specify complex logical expressions by separating them out into different cells on the query Design View grid. If you were to take an Access query and convert it to the underlying SQL statement, you'll find that many sets of parentheses are often needed to clarify the intent of the statement. Access, however, allows you to specify expressions through purely graphical means, without having to resort to parentheses. You can therefore create most (but not all) logical expressions in Access without parentheses.

In this section, we'll start with some simple examples of Boolean logic. In our next section, "Advanced Boolean Logic," we'll cover examples that utilize more complex expressions, and we'll explain how parentheses can be employed.

The following examples will be taken from the OrderSummary table shown in Figure 8.18.

OrderID ▾	CustomerName ▾	State ▾	City ▾	Zip ▾	QuantityPurchased ▾	PricePerItem ▾
1	Jake Jones	FL	Miami	33136	4	2.75
2	Lois Cook	CA	Los Angeles	90017	10	1.25
3	Ellen Sanchez	NY	New York	10036	5	4.35

Figure 8.18
Datasheet View of OrderSummary table.

We'll begin with selection criteria that utilizes the AND operator. Let's say we want to select rows where the quantity purchased is greater than 3, and also less than 7. The grid of the Design View of such a query appears as in Figure 8.19. The result is shown in Figure 8.20.

Field:	CustomerName	QuantityPurchased
Table:	OrderSummary	OrderSummary
Sort:		
Show:	☑	☑
Criteria:		>3 And <7
or:		

Figure 8.19
Design View of a query with an AND operator in one column.

Boolean Query 1	
CustomerName ▾	QuantityPurchased ▾
Jake Jones	4
Ellen Sanchez	5

Figure 8.20
Datasheet View of a query with an AND operator in one column.

The AND operator means that all conditions must evaluate to true for the row to be selected. In this situation, there are two implied parts to the condition:

- QuantityPurchased > 3
- QuantityPurchased < 7

Since these conditions are connected with an AND, they must both be true for the row to be selected. In this example, both conditions apply to the same column, QuantityPurchased. They can therefore both be placed in the same cell in the design grid.

The result of this query is the selection of the rows for Jake Jones and Ellen Sanchez. The row for Lois Cook was not returned. Why? Lois purchased a quantity of 10, which, in fact, does satisfy the first condition (QuantityPurchased > 3). However, the second condition (QuantityPurchased < 7) is not satisfied, and therefore is not true. When using the AND operator, all conditions specified must be true.

See the SQL

The SQL equivalent of Figure 8.19 is:

```
SELECT
OrderSummary.CustomerName,
OrderSummary.QuantityPurchased
FROM OrderSummary
```

WHERE OrderSummary.QuantityPurchased > 3
AND OrderSummary.QuantityPurchased < 7;

Syntax Notes:

■ Since both parts of the expression with the AND operator apply to the same column, Access permits you to enter the criteria in a single cell in an abbreviated manner: > 3 AND < 7. However, the SQL statement always breaks this abbreviated format into multiple expressions, separated by an AND.

■ As before, Access inserts numerous parentheses in this query when displaying it in the SQL View. In this example, none of the parentheses are necessary, so they aren't shown.

Let's look at another example of the AND operator—this time with the conditions applying to two different columns. Let's say we want to select all rows where the quantity purchased is less than 8, and the state is New York (NY). The query shown in Figure 8.21 accomplishes this task. The result is shown in Figure 8.22.

Field:	CustomerName	QuantityPurchased	State
Table:	OrderSummary	OrderSummary	OrderSummary
Sort:			
Show:	✓	✓	✓
Criteria:		<8	"NY"
or:			

Figure 8.21
Design View of a query with an AND operator in two columns.

Boolean Query 2		
CustomerName ▾	QuantityPurchased ▾	State ▾
Ellen Sanchez	5	NY

Figure 8.22
Datasheet View of a query with an AND operator in two columns.

In this situation, the two conditions are:

■ QuantityPurchased < 8

■ State = "NY"

Unlike the prior example, these two conditions apply to two different columns. They therefore needed to be separated and placed in different cells. This leads to an important observation about how the Design View grid works with AND conditions: If selection criteria is specified in multiple cells on the same line in the Design Grid, there is always an implied AND condition between those criteria.

In other words, we might have a situation with multiple columns that are part of the same AND condition. In these cases, the AND operator does not appear anywhere on the grid. The AND is implied to exist between expressions in more than one column on the same line.

Let's now turn to the OR operator. Whereas the AND operator meant that all conditions must evaluate to true for the row to be selected, the OR operator means that the row will be selected if any of the conditions is determined to be true.

The simplest example of an OR operator is one in which all conditions apply to the same column. As an example, let's say we want rows where the state equals Florida (FL) or California (CA). The query and results appear in Figures 8.23 and 8.24.

Field:	CustomerName	State
Table:	OrderSummary	OrderSummary
Sort:		
Show:	☑	☑
Criteria:		"FL" Or "CA"
or:		

Figure 8.23
Design View of query with an OR operator in one column.

Boolean Query 3	
CustomerName ▾	State ▾
Jake Jones	FL
Lois Cook	CA

Figure 8.24
Datasheet View of query with an OR operator in one column.

The OR operator means that at least one condition must evaluate to true for the row to be selected. In this situation, there are two implied parts to the condition:

- State = "FL"
- State = "CA"

Since these conditions are connected with an OR, it's sufficient that either one be true for the row to be selected. In this example, both conditions apply to the same column. They can therefore both be placed in the same cell in the design grid.

The result of this query is the selection of the rows for Jake Jones and Lois Cook. The row for Ellen Sanchez was not returned, since her state is NY.

Let's move on to a case where the OR operator applies to expressions in two different fields. In this example, we want rows where the quantity purchased is greater than 8, or the price per item is greater than 3. The query appears as in Figure 8.25 and the result is shown in Figure 8.26.

Field:	CustomerName	QuantityPurchased	PricePerItem
Table:	OrderSummary	OrderSummary	OrderSummary
Sort:			
Show:	✓	✓	✓
Criteria:		>8	
or:			>3

Figure 8.25
Design View of query with an OR operator in two columns.

CustomerName ▾	QuantityPurchased ▾	PricePerItem ▾
Lois Cook	10	1.25
Ellen Sanchez	5	4.35

▦ **Boolean Query 4**

Figure 8.26
Datasheet View of query with an OR operator in two columns.

This query is the first we've seen that makes use of the Or line of the Design View grid. Since these conditions apply to two different columns, we can't simply place them both on the same Criteria line. This is because multiple cells on the same Criteria line have an implied AND condition between them. We want to specify an OR condition. Access provides the Or line for just this purpose.

Notice, also, that Access provides a bunch of additional blank lines below the Or line on the grid. These extra lines are for additional OR conditions, if they're needed.

See the SQL

The SQL equivalent of Figure 8.25 is:

```
SELECT
OrderSummary.CustomerName,
OrderSummary.QuantityPurchased,
OrderSummary.PricePerItem
FROM OrderSummary
WHERE OrderSummary.QuantityPurchased > 8
OR OrderSummary.PricePerItem > 3;
```

Syntax Notes:

- The use of the OR operator in SQL is analogous to the AND.

Why are the rows for Lois Cook and Ellen Sanchez displayed, and not the row for Jake Jones? The row for Lois Cook is selected because it meets the requirements of the first condition (QuantityPurchased > 8). It doesn't matter that the second condition (PricePerItem > 3) isn't true for Lois, because only one condition needs to be true for an OR condition.

Likewise, the row for Ellen Sanchez is selected because the second condition (PricePerItem > 3) is true for that row. The row for Jake Jones isn't selected because it doesn't satisfy either of the two conditions.

As mentioned at the beginning of this section, the NOT operator is another basic logical operator. Within the context of the Access graphical interface, it is usually not needed. However, here's a simple example of using NOT. Let's say you want to select rows from customers who are not in Florida. One could specify this by using either of these expressions in the Criteria line under the State column:

- Not "FL"
- <> "FL"

In other words, you can use either the NOT logical operator or the not equals (<>) comparison operator to signify a simple not equal condition. You may then wonder why the NOT logical operator is needed at all. In Boolean logic, the NOT is often used to negate a complex logical expression in parentheses. This will be illustrated in the next section.

Focus on Analysis: Relative Dates

A common task in data analysis is the selection of dates that are relative to the current date. For example, you may want to view yesterday's sales data, or sales from the prior calendar month. Here are two generic formulas that accomplish that.

To select data from the prior day, one needs to construct a composite function with the DATEADD and DATE functions. The DATE function provides the current date, and the DATEADD function computes a date one day prior to that date. To select dates from the prior day, simply place the following expression on the Criteria line under the date you want to select on:

- DATEADD ("d", -1, DATE ( ))

Selecting data from the prior month requires a more complex expression. The trick is to create an expression with this general structure: >= [the first day of the prior calendar month] AND < [the first day of the current calendar month]. The expression to compute the first day of the prior or current calendar months requires a composite function with the DATEADD, DATE, MONTH, and YEAR functions.

To select data from the prior month, put this expression in the Criteria row in the column under the date you want to select on:

- >= MONTH (DATEADD ("m", -1, DATE())) & "/1/" & YEAR (DATEADD ("m", -1, DATE ( ))) AND < MONTH (DATEADD ("m", 0, DATE ( )) & "/1/" & YEAR (DATEADD ("m", 0, DATE ( )))

Advanced Boolean Logic

We now turn to some more complex examples of Boolean Logic, which involve combining AND and OR operators in a single query. Continuing with the OrderSummary table, let's say that you want all orders where the state is either California or Florida, and where the quantity purchased is greater than 8. The Design and Datasheet Views for such a query are shown in Figures 8.27 and 8.28.

Field:	CustomerName	QuantityPurchased	State
Table:	OrderSummary	OrderSummary	OrderSummary
Sort:			
Show:	✓	✓	✓
Criteria:		>8	"CA" Or "FL"
or:			

Figure 8.27
Design View of a query with OR and AND conditions.

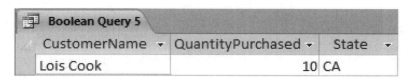

CustomerName ▾	QuantityPurchased ▾	State ▾
Lois Cook	10	CA

Figure 8.28
Datasheet View of a query with OR and AND conditions.

It was critical to place the selection of California OR Florida in a single cell. It would have been incorrect to design the query as shown in Figure 8.29.

The problem with the query of Figure 8.29 is that CA and FL were placed on separate lines in the grid. Each Criteria line in the grid represents an entire condition that is evaluated on its own. If there is more than one Criteria line in the query, there is an implied OR between the lines. In Figure 8.29, the query is evaluated as meaning to select all orders in California with a quantity purchased greater than 8, or all orders from Florida. This was not the original intent. If the query of Figure 8.29 is run, it will bring back not only Lois Cook, but also Jake Jones of Florida.

Field:	CustomerName	QuantityPurchased	State
Table:	OrderSummary	OrderSummary	OrderSummary
Sort:			
Show:	✓	✓	✓
Criteria:		>8	"CA"
or:			"FL"

Figure 8.29
Design View of an incorrect query with OR and AND conditions.

As mentioned, one of the benefits of Access is its graphical interface that allows you to specify complex selection expressions without knowing any SQL syntax. However, the downside is that it becomes increasingly easy to inadvertently design a query in error when the criteria start to get complex.

As an alternative, we want to introduce another way that this query can be expressed, in which all aspects of selection logic are placed in a single cell. This allows you to specify everything in one place and not have to worry about how Access will evaluate it. The downside to this approach, however, is that you need to know a bit more about how SQL logic works.

Figure 8.30 shows the same query as Figure 8.27, expressed in this new way. The key cell in this query is the top cell in the last column. Since the entire content of the cell isn't visible, we utilize the Zoom window to display the entire content, as shown in Figure 8.31.

Field:	CustomerName	QuantityPurchased	State	Expr1: [QuantityPurch
Table:	OrderSummary	OrderSummary	OrderSummary	
Sort:				
Show:	✓	✓	✓	✓
Criteria:				True
or:				

Figure 8.30
Datasheet View of a query with a single logical expression.

First, note that the Show box for the fourth column is unchecked. That means that this column is only being used for data selection, and won't appear in the query results. The expression on the Field line, shown in Figure 8.31, shows the expression to be evaluated. The selection criteria is simply a value of True. This means that if the expression is True for any given row of data, then that row will be selected. Since the expression represents a Boolean value of True or False, that expression can be selected simply based on it being true or false.

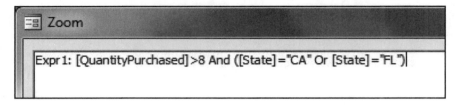

Figure 8.31
Zoom window of a cell in a query with a single logical expression.

Also note that brackets have been placed around each field name. This was automatically done by Access. As noted before, brackets are necessary only if a field name contains spaces, but Access adds them in, nevertheless.

The key addition to this query is the set of parentheses around the selection of California OR Florida. Parentheses are used in SQL expressions to eliminate ambiguity. There are actually three parts to this logical expression:

■ QuantityPurchased > 8

■ And State = "CA"

■ Or State = "FL"

The parentheses are needed in order to specify what is evaluated first. Is it (QuantityPurchased > 8 And State = "CA"), or is it (State = "CA" Or State = "FL")? If parentheses are not present, SQL will use a rule of evaluating any AND conditions prior to OR conditions. In this case, it would first evaluate (QuantityPurchased > 8 And State = "CA"), which is contrary to the intent of the query.

To sum up, by using this technique of placing an entire logical expression in a single cell, you have more direct control over how logic is evaluated. The downside, however, is that the expression must be entirely accurate and have correct syntax. For example, you must type in the needed quote marks around text fields.

Finally, note that in this case it was not necessary to type the brackets around the field names. Access automatically does this for you. Access also added the Expr1 column alias seen before the expression.

See the SQL

The SQL equivalent of Figure 8.30 is:

```
SELECT
OrderSummary.CustomerName,
OrderSummary.QuantityPurchased,
OrderSummary.State
FROM OrderSummary
WHERE (QuantityPurchased > 8
AND (State = "CA"
OR State = "FL")) = True;
```

Syntax Notes:

- When a single expression is stated in Access, with a corresponding selection of either True or False, that entire expression appears in the SQL statement as is.
- As normal, Access adds numerous sets of unnecessary parentheses. The example above shows the needed sets of parentheses.
- When testing for equality with True, a set of parentheses must be placed around the entire expression being compared with True.
- The above WHERE clause can be restated without the test for True, as in:

```
WHERE QuantityPurchased > 8
AND (State= "CA"
OR State = "FL")
```

In the prior example, we were able to design the query in two ways—one that makes use of the Design View grid to separate the various conditions into separate cells, and one that places the entire logical expression in a single cell. We now turn to a query for which it is essential to use the single logical expression approach.

In this next example, we want to view orders that are either 1) from the state of California, or 2) from the state and Florida and from either the city of Miami or zip code 33136. Zip code 33136 happens to be one particular zip code in the city of Orlando.

If we attempt to lay out this logic using the grid, we can get as far as the Design View shown in Figure 8.32, but will then encounter a problem.

The dilemma is that we now need to add to the second criteria line that, in addition to the order being from Florida, the order must also be from either Miami or zip 33136. However, since the city and zip are two different columns, we can't place this OR condition (City = Miami Or Zip = 33136) in a single column. One solution is to place this logical expression in a new column, as shown in Figure 8.33. Figure 8.34 shows the result when this query is run.

Field:	CustomerName	State	City	Zip	
Table:	OrderSummary	OrderSummary	OrderSummary	OrderSummary	
Sort:					
Show:	☑	☑	☑	☑	
Criteria:		"CA"			
or:		"FL"			

Figure 8.32
Design View of a query in progress.

Field:	CustomerName	State	City	Zip	([City]="Miami" Or [Zip]="33136")
Table:	OrderSummary	OrderSummary	OrderSummary	OrderSummary	
Sort:					
Show:	☑	☑	☑	☑	☐
Criteria:		"CA"			
or:		"FL"			True

Figure 8.33
Design View of a query with a single logical expression.

Boolean Query 9			
CustomerName ▾	State ▾	City ▾	Zip ▾
Jake Jones	FL	Miami	33136
Lois Cook	CA	Los Angeles	90017

Figure 8.34
Datasheet View of a query with a single logical expression.

As seen, we have placed a single logical expression in a new column to handle the Miami OR 33136 problem. The evaluation of TRUE for this expression is on the second criteria line, so it's associated with the selection of the state of Florida.

Another approach for the same query would be to place all the logic in a single logical expression, using all needed parentheses. That solution is shown in Figures 8.35 and 8.36.

Field:	CustomerName	State	City	Zip	[State]="CA" Or ([State
Table:	OrderSummary	OrderSummary	OrderSummary	OrderSummary	
Sort:					
Show:	☑	☑	☑	☑	☐
Criteria:					True
or:					

Figure 8.35
Design View of a query with all logic in a single logical expression.

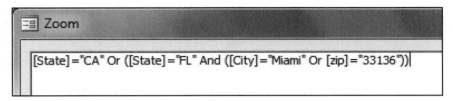

Figure 8.36
Zoom window of a cell in a query with a single logical expression.

There is one new feature of this logical expression that we haven't seen before. The parentheses in this expression are nested, in the sense that one set of parentheses is inside another set. The inner set of parentheses is:

- (City = "Miami" Or Zip = "33136")

Whenever there are nested parentheses, the inner set is evaluated first. The outer set of parentheses is:

- (State = "FL" And `[results of inner set of parentheses])

To evaluate this outer set, we take the results of the inner set of parentheses and add it in to the outer set. Remember that all Boolean expressions are evaluated as either true or false. The parentheses specify the order in which the evaluation is done.

Note the relative simplicity of this query. Once you get used to the idea of using parentheses, it's often helpful to specify all of your selection logic in one place rather than rely on the graphical interface to separate it.

See the SQL

The SQL equivalent of Figure 8.35 is:

```
SELECT
OrderSummary.CustomerName,
OrderSummary.State,
OrderSummary.City,
OrderSummary.Zip
FROM OrderSummary
WHERE (State = "CA"
OR (State = "FL"
AND (City = "Miami"
OR Zip = "33136"))) = TRUE;
```

Syntax Notes:

- As normal, Access adds numerous sets of unnecessary parentheses. This example shows the needed sets of parentheses.
- The WHERE clause can be restated without the test for TRUE, as:

WHERE State = "CA"
OR (State = "FL"
AND (City = "Miami"
OR Zip = "33136"))

Before leaving the topic of Boolean logic, let's briefly revisit the NOT operator. As illustrated by the following example, the NOT operator is generally not needed in Access. Let's say that you want to retrieve orders that are not from Florida or California. Your first thought might be to enter the following expression under the State column:

- Not ("FL" Or "CA")

This is a valid expression in standard SQL. However, Access will automatically take the criteria under the State column and put it in a separate column as a logical expression, as shown in Figures 8.37 and 8.38.

Field:	CustomerName	State	([OrderSummary].[Stat
Table:	OrderSummary	OrderSummary	
Sort:			
Show:	☑	☑	☐
Criteria:			False
or:			

Figure 8.37
Design View of a query with a NOT operator.

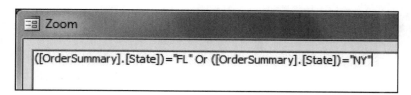

Figure 8.38
Zoom window of a cell in a query with a NOT operator.

Note that Access tests the new logical expression for FALSE. This is the equivalent of using the NOT operator. Complex expressions you enter with a NOT operator will be converted in such a manner.

To add one more twist to this example, this query can be expressed in a completely different way, without using the NOT operator or testing for FALSE. This solution is shown in Figures 8.39 and 8.40.

Field:	CustomerName	State
Table:	OrderSummary	OrderSummary
Sort:		
Show:	☑	☑
Criteria:		<> "FL" And <> "CA"
or:		

Figure 8.39
Design View of a query with two not-equal comparison operators.

CustomerName ▾	State ▾
Ellen Sanchez	NY

Boolean Query 12

Figure 8.40
Datasheet View of a query with two not-equal comparison operators.

This gives the same result as the prior query. In other words, these two queries are logically equivalent:

- Not ("FL" Or "CA")
- <> "FL" And <> "CA"

You may need to think a bit to realize why these two expressions are equivalent. At any rate, this provides yet another reason why the NOT operator is generally unnecessary in Access.

BETWEEN and IN

Access provides two special comparison operators, BETWEEN and IN, that allow you to simplify expressions that would ordinarily require the OR or AND operators.

The BETWEEN operator allows you to abbreviate an AND expression with greater than or equal to (>=) and less than or equal to (<=) operators into one simple expression. As an example, let's say you want to select all rows from the OrderSummary table with a quantity purchased between 5 and 9. Without the BETWEEN operator, the selection criteria to place under the QuantityPurchased column would be:

- >= 5 And <= 9

This equivalent expression utilizes the BETWEEN operator:

■ Between 5 And 9

The BETWEEN operator always requires a corresponding AND placed between the two numbers. The Design and Datasheet Views of this query are shown in Figure 8.41 and 8.42.

Figure 8.41
Design View of a query with a BETWEEN operator.

Query with Between	
CustomerName ▾	QuantityPurchased ▾
Ellen Sanchez	5

Figure 8.42
Datasheet View of a query with a BETWEEN operator.

Note the relative simplicity of the BETWEEN operator. Also notice that the BETWEEN keyword is equivalent only to the greater than or equal to (>=) and less than or equal to (<=) operators. It can't be used to express something simply greater than (>) or less than (<) a range of numbers. In this example, the row for Ellen Sanchez is selected since the quantity is equal to 5, and therefore is between 5 and 9.

See the SQL

The SQL equivalent of Figure 8.41 is:

```
SELECT
OrderSummary.CustomerName,
OrderSummary.QuantityPurchased
FROM OrderSummary
WHERE OrderSummary.QuantityPurchased BETWEEN 5 AND 9;
```

Syntax Notes:

■ The BETWEEN and IN operators appear in SQL exactly as they do in Access.

Just as the BETWEEN operator represents a special case of the AND operator, the IN operator allows for a special case of the OR operator. Let's say you want to see rows where the state is Florida or California. Without the IN operator, the selection criteria to place under the State column would be:

■ "FL" Or "CA"

An equivalent expression with the IN operator is:

■ In ("FL", "CA")

The IN operator places the desired values in a set of parentheses, separated by commas. The Design View of such a query is shown in Figure 8.43.

Field:	CustomerName	State
Table:	OrderSummary	OrderSummary
Sort:		
Show:	✓	✓
Criteria:		In ("FL","CA")
or:		

Figure 8.43
Design View of a query with an IN operator.

The usefulness of the IN operator may not be obvious in this example where only two states are listed. However, the IN can just as easily be used in situations where you want to list dozens of specific values. This greatly reduces the amount of typing required for such a statement. Another handy use for the IN operator arises in situations where you want to use data from Excel in an Access query. If you want to obtain multiple values from adjacent cells in a spreadsheet for your query, Excel allows you to copy those values with a comma delimiter. This result can then be pasted inside the parentheses following the IN operator.

One final note about the IN operator: There is a second way to use IN, which is substantially different from the syntax just discussed. In the second format of the IN operator, an entire query is specified within the parentheses, allowing the columnlist in that second query to be made available to the main query. This is called a *subquery*, which will be covered in detail in Chapter 10, "Subqueries and Set Logic."

Testing for NULL Values

It was stated previously that the Boolean logic in SQL evaluates complex expressions as either true or false. This assertion was not completely accurate. When evaluating the selection criteria, there are actually three possibilities: true, false, and unknown.

The possibility of unknown derives from the fact that columns in SQL databases are sometimes allowed to have a NULL value. As mentioned in Chapter 3, NULL values are those for which there is an absence of data.

We've already seen the ISNULL function in Chapter 7, which allows us to test an expression for NULL values and then display an appropriate value if the expression contains NULLs.

In addition to the ISNULL function, Access provides a special constant called NULL that allows you to test the presence or absence of NULL values in selection criteria. If you look at the available constants in the Expression Builder, you'll see the four values shown in Figure 8.44.

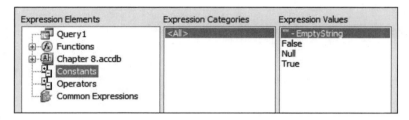

Figure 8.44
Constants in the Expression Builder.

We've already seen the TRUE and FALSE constants utilized in some of the advanced Boolean queries. The set of double quotes is used for fields with no data. The NULL constant is used to test for NULL values. To emphasize the point, a test for NULL values is different from using the double quotes to test for no data. When a field exists but has no data in it, it can successfully test for no data. The test for NULLs applies when there is literally no row of data present.

To illustrate, let's look at a query with a left join between the previously seen Customers and Orders tables. We want to see all Customers who have never placed an order. The query that accomplishes this is shown in Figures 8.45 and 8.46.

As seen, Adam Petrie and Jane Doe have never placed an order. There are no rows in the Orders table that match their rows in the Customers table. The IS NULL criteria specified that we only want to see rows where there is a NULL value in the OrderID column. In reality, we could have specified the IS NULL criteria for any column in the Orders table. The main point is that the row doesn't exist.

There are other situations when a table allows a specific column to contain NULL values, where the test for NULL applies only to that column and not to all columns in the row.

Figure 8.45
Design View of a query that tests for NULL values.

Figure 8.46
Datasheet View of a query that tests for NULL values.

Note that we could also reverse the logic and test a column to find only rows where that column does not contain NULLs. In that case, you simply specify IS NOT NULL rather than IS NULL.

Conditional Logic

So far, the logic we have seen in this chapter has been applied strictly to rows. When the logic of the selection criteria is evaluated, the result is either the display or non-display of a row of data. We now want to discuss a way in which logic can be applied to the columns specified in a query. Essentially, we're going to look at a technique where logic is associated with the value of a single column in a query. This is sometimes referred to as *conditional logic*. It's called conditional because the value that will be displayed for the indicated column is based on a logical expression.

Access provides two special Program Flow functions to handle conditional logic: IIF and SWITCH. We'll begin with an illustration of the IIF function, which is the simpler of the two. IIF stands for "Immediate If." This term is used to distinguish the function from the IF keyword found in VBA, SQL, and Access Macros.

The template for the IIF function is:

■ IIf («expression», «truepart», «falsepart»)

Let's say that we have a Clients table with a list of client names. Included in the table is a column that indicates their sex, as either M (male) or F (female). We want to see a list of our clients, but we want to spell out the sex as either Male or Female rather than M and F. Figures 8.47 and 8.48 show the Design and Datasheet Views of a query that accomplishes this goal.

Figure 8.47
Design View of a query with an IIF function.

ClientName	Sex1	Sex2
Bob Carter	M	Male
Louise Parker	F	Female
Ronald Kraft	M	Male
Melanie Downe	F	Female

Figure 8.48
Datasheet View of a query with an IIF function.

This query displays two columns with the sex of the client. The column named Sex1 shows the original data in the table. The column named Sex2 translates that value to either Male or Female. The IIF function works nicely with this task because Sex has only two values: M or F. The first parameter of the function is the *expression*, which in this case is given the value:

- Clients.Sex = "M"

The *truepart* parameter has the value Male and the *falsepart* parameter has the value Female. If the expression doesn't have a value of M, the function returns the *falsepart* or Female.

The IIF function works with these two-valued expressions, but most categorizing in the real world involves more than two values. This is where the SWITCH function comes in. The template for the SWITCH function is:

- Switch («expr-|0», «value-|0»)

The template for this function includes a vertical bar, which indicates that each parameter can be repeated any number of times. To illustrate, let's look at a Foods table containing information about various foods. Some sample data is shown in Figure 8.49.

Foods		
FoodID	CategoryCode	Description
1	F	Apple
2	S	Mustard
3	V	Carrot
4	B	Tea

Figure 8.49
Datasheet View of a Foods table.

In this set of data, the CategoryCode column is a code for the type of food, where F means fruit, S means spice, V means vegetable, and B means beverage. The goal of the next query will be to translate this code to a meaningful name. We'll want to see a name only for the fruits and vegetables. We want all other categories to be called "Other." The assumption in this exercise is that there is not already a table that performs this translation. If there were such a table, it could merely be added to the query with a join by the CategoryCode column, and then supply the description from that table.

In the absence of such a table, we'll rely on the SWITCH function to perform the translation. Figure 8.50 shows the query that accomplishes this. Figure 8.51 shows the Zoom window with the SWITCH function and Figure 8.52 shows the result.

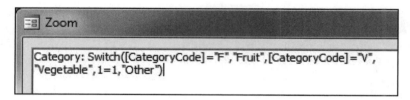

Field:	CategoryCode	Category: Switch([Cat	Description
Table:	Foods		Foods
Sort:			
Show:	☑	☑	☑
Criteria:			
or:			

Figure 8.50
Design View of a query with a SWITCH function.

▦ Zoom

Category: Switch([CategoryCode]="F","Fruit",[CategoryCode]="V", "Vegetable",1=1,"Other")|

Figure 8.51
Zoom window of a cell in a query with a SWITCH function.

▦ Conditional Logic 2

CategoryCode ▾	Category ▾	Description ▾
F	Fruit	Apple
S	Other	Mustard
V	Vegetable	Carrot
B	Other	Tea

Figure 8.52
Datasheet View of query with a SWITCH function.

See the SQL

The SQL equivalent of Figure 8.50 is:

```
SELECT
Foods.CategoryCode,
SWITCH (CategoryCode = "F", "Fruit", CategoryCode = "V", "Vegetable", 1=1, "Other") AS
Category,
Foods.Description
FROM Foods;
```

Syntax Notes:

■ The SWITCH function is not a part of standard SQL. In its place, SQL offers something called the CASE expression. The CASE expression uses a series of WHEN-THEN clauses to specify the expressions and values, an ELSE to specify the default, and an END to end the expression. The equivalent of the above, utilizing a CASE expression, is:

```
SELECT
Foods.CategoryCode,
```

```
CASE
WHEN CategoryCode = "F" THEN "Fruit"
WHEN CategoryCode = "V" THEN "Vegetable"
ELSE "Other"
END AS Category,
Foods.Description
FROM Foods;
```

As seen, the SWITCH function consists of six different parameters. The first four parameters give the expression and resulting value for fruit and vegetable.

The value of the fifth parameter is: 1=1. This expression illustrates a little trick that can be used to specify a default value for the SWITCH function. Since it's always true that 1 equals 1, this expression always evaluates to true. The SWITCH function works by evaluating the various expressions until one is found that is true. So in this example, if the tests for F and V aren't found to be true, the 1=1 expression will kick in and supply a value of "Other" to be returned from the function.

We've illustrated conditional logic with examples using the IIF and SWITCH functions on the Field line of the query design grid. In fact, however, these functions are also quite useful in the Criteria or Sort lines of the design grid. For example, one can specify conditional logic in selection criteria to select records with criteria that are only evaluated when the query is run. Rather than hard-coding specific selection criteria, it can be determined in a dynamic fashion, dependent on how an IIF or SWITCH function is evaluated.

As an example of using conditional logic on the Criteria line, let's say you have a query that selects items where the description equals Glove. You'd like to change the criteria so that the type of item selected depends on some attribute of the customer. For items from customer type X, you want to select Gloves, but for items from customer type Y, you want to select Socks. This can be accomplished by placing an expression with a SWITCH function on the Criteria line of the query.

Focus on Analysis: Division by Zero

The fundamental laws of arithmetic dictate that division by zero is not permitted. Not only is it not permitted, but it's also said to be an impossibility. Accordingly, Access displays this unpleasant message when division by zero is attempted: #Div/0!

As a result, special care must be taken to ensure that division by zero never occurs. The IIF function easily takes care of the problem. To generalize the situation, let's say that we are creating an expression in this format:

- Numerator / Denominator

To make certain that division by zero doesn't occur, simply substitute the following:

- IIF (Denominator = 0, 0, Numerator / Denominator)

This expression substitutes the value 0 when division by zero is attempted.

Parameters

All the previous queries had selection criteria that needed to be specified in advance. In most cases, this is something very specific, such as OrderDate = "12/15/2011". Conditional logic added the ability to formulate an expression in your criteria that is evaluated at runtime. However, the ability to add *parameters* to queries adds complete flexibility to selection logic.

Parameters can be substituted for any expression in the selection criteria, allowing the user to specify that expression's value when the query runs. Here's an example, taken from the Donations table seen at the beginning of this chapter. The Design View is shown in Figure 8.53.

Field:	DonationID	DonorLastName	PledgeDate
Table:	Donations	Donations	Donations
Sort:			
Show:	☑	☑	☑
Criteria:			[Please enter a Pledge Date]
or:			

Figure 8.53
Design View of a query with a parameter.

Notice that the Criteria under the PledgeDate column contain a few words within square brackets. The brackets indicate that this is a parameter, with a value to be determined when the query is run. These brackets should not be confused with the brackets that often appear around table and field names.

When the query is opened in Datasheet View, the user first sees the Enter Parameter Value window as shown in Figure 8.54.

The text in the window corresponds to the value specified in the selection criteria. After entering a date in the text box and clicking OK, the query runs with the date supplied and immediately displays the Datasheet View. For example, if the date 4/12/2011 is entered, the resulting Datasheet View is as seen in Figure 8.55.

Figure 8.54
Enter Parameter Value window.

Donations Query 6		
DonationID	DonorLastName	PledgeDate
4	Newman	4/12/2011
5	Myers	4/12/2011

Figure 8.55
Datasheet View of a query with a parameter.

Adding parameters allows you to generalize your queries. Rather than have separate queries for each situation, you can create a single query and allow the user to specify the needed values at runtime.

Also, queries can contain multiple parameters, either in different columns or within the same column. If there are multiple parameters, the user supplies the various values one at a time.

Finally, Access provides a way to maintain all the parameters in a query in a special Query Parameters window. This window has the added benefit of allowing you to specify a Data Type for each parameter, ensuring that the value is entered in an appropriate format. To illustrate both the Query Parameters window and the ability to use multiple parameters in a query, let's expand on the last example, to enter a date range for the date selection. We'll start by opening the Query Parameters window by clicking the Parameters icon in the Ribbon, found in the Show/Hide section in the Design tab under Query Tools. This is shown in Figure 8.56.

Figure 8.56
The Parameters command.

Once the command is clicked, Access displays the Query Parameters window. We'll then enter the two parameters we want to use, as shown in Figure 8.57.

Figure 8.57
Query Parameters window.

We then simply enter an expression on the Criteria line under the PledgeDate column, as shown in Figure 8.58.

Field:	DonationID	DonorLastName	PledgeDate
Table:	Donations	Donations	Donations
Sort:			
Show:	☑	☑	☑
Criteria:			Between [Start date] And [End date]
or:			

Figure 8.58
Design View of a query with two parameters.

When the query is run, the user will be prompted to enter two different dates, which are then combined as a date range to select appropriate rows. The results with date range 4/11/2011 to 4/12/2011 are shown in Figure 8.59.

Donations Query 7

DonationID	DonorLastName	PledgeDate
1	McIntyre	4/11/2011
2	Crawford	4/11/2011
3	Sanchez	4/11/2011
4	Newman	4/12/2011
5	Myers	4/12/2011

Figure 8.59
Datasheet View of a query with two parameters.

Looking Ahead

This chapter covered the important topic of how to create expressions of selection logic. We started with basic comparison operators such as equals (=) and greater than (>). We then introduced the Top Values property of a query as a useful way of limiting the number of rows returned to a finite number. Pattern Matching was discussed as a method to match text data when the exact value of a field isn't known.

We then turned to the main topic of this chapter, Boolean logic. Using AND and OR operators to create complex expressions of logic is key to the ability to retrieve the specific sets of desired data. As logical expressions become more complex, however, the idiosyncrasies of the Access Design View grid become apparent. One needs to be aware of both the logic that is desired and the means by which that logic can be specified in the grid.

After covering the essentials of Boolean logic, we looked at a number of related topics, such as the BETWEEN and IN operators, and NULL values. As an adjunct to Boolean logic, conditional logic provides the ability to apply logic to the value or selection of a single column. As such, conditional logic is an important tool in the data analyst's arsenal, and one that is often overlooked. Finally, we discussed the ability of parameters to generalize a query by allowing a user to provide the necessary values at the time the query is run.

In our next chapter, we move on to the subject of summarization. In this all-important topic, we'll look at ways to combine data into groups and utilize special aggregate functions to summarize the values in those groups. The ability to summarize data is a critical component of data analysis, as it allows you to transform your raw data into a more concise and meaningful display of values. We'll also extend the current topic of selection criteria to be able to specify criteria on an entire group of data. For example, rather than select customers who have purchased more than $100 on a specified date, we may want to see only states where the total purchases from all customers in that state exceeded $10,000 on a specified date.

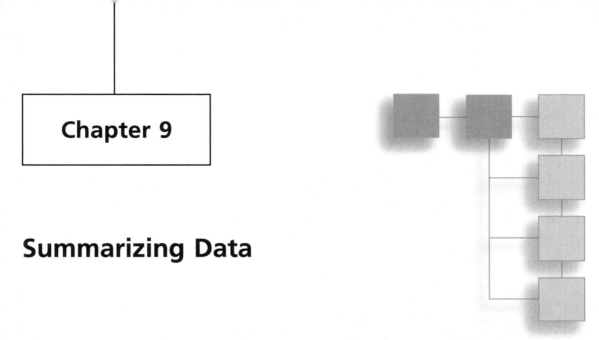

Chapter 9

Summarizing Data

Up until now, we've been looking at data as it already exists in a database. Sure, we've used some functions to move things around, and we've created some additional calculations, but the rows we've retrieved have always corresponded to rows in the underlying database. We'll now turn to various methods of summarizing our data. In many ways, this is the essence of the data analysis process. The ability to summarize data in a meaningful way is key to deriving useful insights from a sea of numbers and words.

Although it's possible to provide a summary of all of your data at once, it's often useful to break data into groups and then summarize each group separately, combining all groups into a useful whole. The computer term usually associated with this type of endeavor is *aggregation*, which means "to combine into groups." Aggregating and summarizing data is a fundamental way to move beyond a mere display of data to something approaching useful information.

Distinct Values

Before turning to true aggregation, let's discuss a more elementary way to summarize data. When selecting specific columns from any number of tables, one often wants to see only the distinct values for those columns. For example, we may wish to see a list of customers who have met some specific criteria regarding orders they have placed. In doing so, we only want to see each customer one time. We don't want to see the customer name repeated for every order they may have placed.

Access provides a property called *Unique Values* that allows you to eliminate duplicate values for the columns shown in your query. When creating a new query, the default value for this property is No, which means that that the property setting is ignored. When this property is set to a value of Yes, a feature is added to the query that ensures that there will be no duplicate rows in the output.

Note that the ability to specify distinct values via the Unique Values property isn't quite the same as finding or eliminating duplicate data that already exists. In Chapter 10, "Subqueries and Set Logic," we'll look at specific ways to identify and delete duplicate records. At this point, we only want to produce output that *avoids* the display of duplicate values.

To illustrate, we'll work with the SongTitles table shown in Figure 9.1.

SongID	Artist	Album	Title
1	The Beatles	Abbey Road	Because
2	The Beatles	Abbey Road	Carry That Weight
3	The Beatles	Revolver	Good Day Sunshine
4	The Rolling Stones	Let It Bleed	Gimme Shelter
5	The Rolling Stones	Flowers	Ruby Tuesday
6	Paul McCartney	Ram	Too Many People

Figure 9.1
Datasheet View of SongTitles table.

Let's say you want to see a list of artists in the table. This can be accomplished by starting a new query and changing the Unique Values property for the query to Yes. This is shown in Figure 9.2.

Property Sheet ✕
Selection type: Query Properties

General	
Description	
Default View	Datasheet
Output All Fields	No
Top Values	All
Unique Values	Yes
Unique Records	No

Figure 9.2
Property Sheet.

After this property is set, the design of the query is straightforward, as shown in Figures 9.3 and 9.4.

Figure 9.3
Design View of a query with Unique Values property.

Figure 9.4
Datasheet View of a query with Unique Values property.

Remember that the Unique Values property works only on those fields shown in the display. Since the only field shown is Artist, the query simply returns a list of unique artists. To see distinct combinations of both artists and albums, you'd merely change the query to add the Album column, as shown in Figures 9.5 and 9.6.

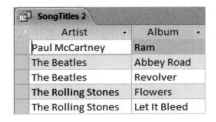

Figure 9.5
Design View of a query with two columns and Unique Values property.

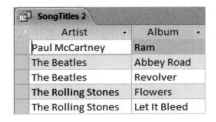

Figure 9.6
Datasheet View of a query with two columns and Unique Values property.

Notice that Abbey Road is listed only once, even though there are two songs from that album in the table. This is because the Unique Values property causes only distinct values from the listed columns to be shown.

See the SQL

The SQL equivalent of Figure 9.5 is:

```
SELECT
DISTINCT
SongTitles.Artist,
SongTitles.Album
FROM SongTitles;
```

Syntax Notes:

■ The keyword DISTINCT is used to implement the Unique Values property. The word DISTINCT appears once before all columns in the columnlist.

Finally, you may have noticed that Figure 9.2 showed another property similar to Unique Values called Unique Records. Since the Unique Records property serves a fairly obscure purpose, we won't cover it in this text. In brief, it allows you to select unique records, ignoring the specific selected fields, but it has an effect only when pulling data from more than one table.

Aggregate Functions

The functions discussed in Chapter 7 were all *scalar functions*. These functions were all performed on values in a single row. In contrast, *aggregate functions* are used with groups of data. The aggregate functions available in Access are: COUNT, SUM, AVG, MIN, MAX, STDEV, STDEVP, VAR, and VARP.

SUM and AVG provide a sum and average of a group of numbers. MIN and MAX give the minimum and maximum values of a group. There are two variants of the COUNT function, the most common of which simply gives a count of the number of rows returned. STDEV and VAR give the standard deviation and variance of a group of numbers representing a sample of data. STDEVP and VARP are minor variants that give the same statistics for an entire population.

All of the aggregate functions have a single parameter, which can be any expression. For example, the template for the SUM function is:

■ Sum («expression»)

Our aggregate function examples will be taken from the following two tables with information about students, Fees and Grades. The data in these tables is shown in Figures 9.7 and 9.8.

FeeID	Student	FeeType	Fee
1	Kevin	Gym	30
2	Kevin	Lunch	10
3	Kevin	Trip	8
4	Michelle	Gym	30
5	Becky	Lunch	10

Figure 9.7
Datasheet View of Fees table.

GradeID	Student	GradeType	Grade
1	Colleen	Quiz	92
2	Colleen	Quiz	95
3	Colleen	Homework	84
4	Lois	Quiz	62
5	Lois	Quiz	81
6	Lois	Homework	
7	Ronald	Quiz	58
8	Ronald	Quiz	74
9	Ronald	Homework	88

Figure 9.8
Datasheet View of Grades table.

Starting with the SUM function, let's say that you want to see the total amount of gym fees paid by all students. This can be accomplished with the query shown in Figures 9.9 and 9.10.

Field:	Total Fees: Sum([Fee])	FeeType
Table:		Fees
Sort:		
Show:	☑	☐
Criteria:		"Gym"
or:		

Figure 9.9
Design View of a query with SUM function.

Figure 9.10
Datasheet View of a query with SUM function.

The first column in the Design View shows the amount being summed. The SUM function is specified on an expression consisting solely of the Fee column of the Fees table. A column alias of Total Fees has been applied to the column. The second column in the query has the selection criteria. The criteria will select only records where the FeeType column equals "Gym".

It's important to note that the second column with the selection criteria does not have the Show line checked. This indicates that the value of the FeeType column is not shown in the query. In fact, the query would be invalid if we had checked the Show box in the second column. The reason for this has to do with the nature of aggregation. Once aggregation is introduced into a query, you can't mix aggregated with non-aggregated values in the display. In our example, it wouldn't make sense to attempt to list the values of the FeeType column for individual rows, since the rest of the query shows an aggregated value with a single row.

See the SQL

The SQL equivalent of Figure 9.9 is:

```
SELECT
SUM (Fee) AS [Total Fees]
FROM Fees
WHERE Fees.FeeType = "Gym";
```

Syntax Notes:

- This query has a single aggregated value in the columnlist. The aggregation function SUM appears in the query as it does in Access.

- In this example, there are required brackets around the column alias, since it contains a space.

The AVG, MIN, and MAX functions are similar to SUM. Figures 9.11 and 9.12 show a query using all three of these functions, in separate columns, to compute the average, minimum, and maximum quiz grades from the Grades table.

Field:	Average Grade: Avg([grade])	Lowest Grade: Min([grade])	Highest Grade: Max([grade])	GradeType
Table:				Grades
Sort:				
Show:	☑	☑	☑	☐
Criteria:				"Quiz"

Figure 9.11
Design View of a query with AVG, MIN, and MAX functions.

Grades 1		
Average Grade ▾	Lowest Grade ▾	Highest Grade ▾
77	58	95

Figure 9.12
Datasheet View of a query with AVG, MIN, and MAX functions.

The output shows the average, minimum, and maximum grades of all quizzes in the Grades table. These numbers have been computed separately, based on each function. Note that, once again, the column with the selection criteria must remain as not shown. The three columns with aggregate values are compatible with each other, since they each return one row.

The COUNT function is slightly more complex, in that it can be used in two different ways. The most common usage of the COUNT function is to return a count of all selected rows, regardless of the values in any particular column. As an example, the query in Figures 9.13 and 9.14 returns a count of all rows from the Grades table with homework grades.

Field:	Row Count: Count(*)	GradeType
Table:		Grades
Sort:		
Show:	☑	☐
Criteria:		"Homework"
or:		

Figure 9.13
Design View of a query with a COUNT function.

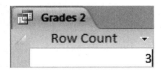

Grades 2	
Row Count ▾	
3	

Figure 9.14
Datasheet View of a query with a COUNT function.

The result indicates that there are three rows in the Grades table with homework grades. Notice that an asterisk (*) was used as the value of the expression for the COUNT function. Back in Chapter 3, we noted that the asterisk means "all fields." In this situation, the asterisk provides a shorthand method of specifying that we want to count rows pertaining to all fields in the table. We aren't interested in the count of any specific field.

This leads us to the second format of the COUNT function, which is applied to a specific field. The query shown in Figures 9.15 and 9.16 replaces the function COUNT (*) with COUNT (Grades). The intent of the query is to provide a count of the number of rows where there is a value in the Grades table, subject to the selection criteria.

Field:	Row Count: Count([Grade])	GradeType
Table:		Grades
Sort:		
Show:	☑	☐
Criteria:		"Homework"
or:		

Figure 9.15
Design View of a query with a COUNT function against a column.

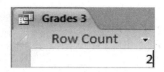

Figure 9.16
Datasheet View of a query with a COUNT function against a column.

This time, the result is 2 rather than 3. The reason for the difference? Notice that one of the rows in the Grades table, with GradeID = 6, has no value in the Grades column. Although it can't be discerned from Figure 9.8, this row of data has a NULL value in the Grades column. Since there is no data in this column for this row, the COUNT function did not include that row as it computed the count. Thus, for the specified selection criteria, there are only two rows with data in the Grades table.

One final comment about the COUNT function: In standard SQL, it's possible to combine the Unique Values property discussed earlier in this chapter with the COUNT function in such a way as to provide a count of distinct values in a table or query. For example, let's say you have a table with four rows, two of which have the same value in one particular column. In SQL, one can create a COUNT DISTINCT expression to count the distinct values of that column. This would return a value of 3. However, this syntax isn't valid in Access. The only way to provide a count of distinct values in Access is to utilize a subquery. This will be demonstrated in the next chapter.

Grouping Data

The preceding examples of aggregation are interesting, but are of somewhat limited value. The real power of the aggregation functions becomes evident once we introduce the concept of grouping data.

Using the Totals command, found in the Show/Hide section of the Query Tools Design tab in the Ribbon, one can cause a new line to appear in the Query Design grid: the Total line. The Totals command is represented with the Greek letter Sigma (Σ), as shown in Figure 9.17.

Figure 9.17
Totals command.

The Total line on the Design view grid allows you to organize your data into groups. The cell on the Total line allows you to select a value from a drop-down list, indicating how you would like to handle aggregation for that column of the grid. The values in the drop-down list are:

- Group By
- Sum
- Avg
- Min
- Max
- Count
- StDev
- Var
- First
- Last
- Expression
- Where

Selecting GROUP BY means that you want to create groups based on the expression on the Field line in that column. The next seven values, from SUM to VAR, represent functions. These indicate that you want to aggregate based on that function type. For example, a selection of SUM means that you want to apply the SUM function to the expression on the Field line of that column.

The next two items, FIRST and LAST, are two aggregation functions we haven't seen before. These functions are similar to MIN and MAX in the sense that they cause one particular value to be selected for display. However, whereas MIN and MAX select the lowest or highest value, FIRST and LAST select the value of whatever record happens to be encountered first (or last) as the grouping is created. It's basically an arbitrary value.

Selecting EXPRESSION means that you wish to apply some other selection criteria to the group specified by the GROUP BY column. This will be discussed later in the chapter in the "Selection Criteria on Aggregates" section.

Finally, selecting WHERE means that this column is for selection criteria on the underlying rows and has nothing to do with the group. As usual, the criteria itself is entered on the Criteria line.

We'll start with a simple example taken from the Grades table. Let's say that we want to analyze grades based on the grade type. In other words, we want to separate the data into two groups, quizzes and homework, and then see the average grade for each group. Figures 9.18 and 9.19 show such a query.

Field:	GradeType	Average: Grade
Table:	Grades	Grades
Total:	Group By	Avg
Sort:		
Show:	☑	☑
Criteria:		
or:		

Figure 9.18
Design View of a query with a GROUP BY and AVG.

Grades 4	
GradeType ▾	Average ▾
Homework	86
Quiz	77

Figure 9.19
Datasheet View of a query with a GROUP BY and AVG.

See the SQL

The SQL equivalent of Figure 9.18 is:

SELECT
Grades.GradeType,
AVG (Grades.Grade) AS Average
FROM Grades
GROUP BY Grades.GradeType;

Syntax Notes:

- The GROUP BY clause indicates columns or expressions by which the grouping is applied.
- The selection of AVG in the Total line results in the AVG function being utilized.

Note the simplicity of the Design View. The first column specifies the column that creates the groups. The GROUP BY keyword on the Total line accomplishes this. The second column contains the AVG value on the Total line. This indicates that the AVG function will be applied to the Grade column to produce an average for each group. When grouping is in place, it isn't necessary to type the function name on the Field line. Instead, the Total line indicates which function will be used.

Also note that we added a sort to this query—sorting the results by the GROUP BY expression in the first column. When grouping data, it's generally a good idea to place the GROUP BY column to the far left and sort on that column, so the grouping is obvious to anyone viewing the results.

Finally, notice that even though there is one row in the underlying Grades table with a NULL value for the Homework type, the average grade was computed as 86, a relatively high value. In other words, Access is smart enough to ignore rows with NULL values when computing an average. If you had wanted the NULL value to be counted as a 0, then the ISNULL and IIF functions could have been used to convert the NULL to a 0, as previously explained in Chapter 7. A new Design View with this modification is shown in Figures 9.20.

When run, this query will now display an average grade for Homework of 57.33. In order for this query to work, we needed to change the value of the Total line in the second column from AVG to EXPRESSION. This is because we are no longer specifying a simple value for which we can apply the AVG function. We've specified a complex expression using both the AVG and IIF functions.

Field:	GradeType	Average: Avg(IIf(IsNull([Grade]),0,[Grade]))
Table:	Grades	
Total:	Group By	Expression
Sort:		
Show:	✓	✓
Criteria:		
or:		

Figure 9.20
Design View of a query with a GROUP BY and an expression.

The concept of groups can be extended so the groups are based on more than one column. Let's say, for example, that we want to group on both the grade type and students. A query that accomplishes this is shown in Figures 9.21 and 9.22.

Field:	GradeType	Student	Average: Grade
Table:	Grades	Grades	Grades
Total:	Group By	Group By	Avg
Sort:	Ascending	Ascending	
Show:	✓	✓	✓
Criteria:			
or:			

Figure 9.21
Design View of a query with two GROUP BY columns.

Grades 6		
GradeType ▾	Student ▾	Average ▾
Homework	Colleen	84
Homework	Lois	
Homework	Ronald	88
Quiz	Colleen	93.5
Quiz	Lois	71.5
Quiz	Ronald	66

Figure 9.22
Datasheet View of a query with two GROUP BY columns.

The result shows a breakdown not only of grade types, but also of students. The average grades are computed on each group. Note that the homework row for Lois is blank. This represents a NULL value.

This query is sorted by the values in the first two columns. The order of those columns is significant for the sort. However, if there were no sort in the query, the order of the first two columns would *not* be significant.

Let's continue our examination of the GROUP BY operation with a slightly more complex query. In this example, we want to look only at grades for one student, Colleen. We want to group her grades by grade type, but this time we want to include not only an average, but also a count of the number of grades received. Additionally, we would like to see Colleen's name in the output. Figures 9.23 and 9.24 show the solution.

Field:	Student: Student	GradeType	Average: Grade	Grade Count: Grade	Student
Table:	Grades	Grades	Grades	Grades	Grades
Total:	First	Group By	Avg	Count	Where
Sort:		Ascending			
Show:	☑	☑	☑	☑	☐
Criteria:					"Colleen"
or:					

Figure 9.23
Design View of a query with GROUP BY, function, and criteria columns.

Grades 7			
Student ▾	GradeType ▾	Average ▾	Grade Count ▾
Colleen	Homework	84	1
Colleen	Quiz	93.5	2

Figure 9.24
Datasheet View of a query with GROUP BY, function, and criteria columns.

See the SQL

The SQL equivalent of Figure 9.23 is:

```
SELECT
FIRST (Grades.Student) AS Student,
Grades.GradeType,
AVG (Grades.Grade) AS Average,
COUNT (Grades.Grade) AS [Grade Count]
FROM Grades
WHERE Grades.Student = "Colleen"
GROUP BY Grades.GradeType
ORDER BY Grades.GradeType;
```

Syntax Notes:

- When a query contains both a WHERE and a GROUP BY, the WHERE clause always precedes GROUP BY.
- When a query contains both a GROUP BY and an ORDER BY, the GROUP BY clause always precedes ORDER BY.

A number of design elements bear noting. The second column specifies the GROUP BY for this query. Grouping is done only by GradeType. The fifth column contains the selection criteria. The WHERE value on the Totals line indicates that this is normal selection criteria, not associated with any groups. Any rows that don't contain a value of "Colleen" in the Student field will be ignored. The three remaining columns represent aggregate functions. The third column uses the AVG function to give the average grade for each group. The fourth column uses the COUNT function to give a count of the number of rows in each group.

The new feature of this query is the first column, which uses the FIRST function to display the student name. If you recall, once aggregates are introduced into a query, you can't mix aggregated and non-aggregated values. To display the student name in this query, we can't merely include the Student field without it being associated with an aggregate function. This is where the FIRST function comes in. This function means that, within each group, the first row encountered will be used to display the Student field. Since we're selecting only records with the name "Colleen," it doesn't really matter which row is selected. They will all contain the value "Colleen". We could have used the LAST function for this same purpose.

Let's conclude our discussion of the GROUP BY with an example that utilizes a function that creates partitions of data in specified ranges. The PARTITION function is a special function in the Database category with this general format:

- Partition («number», «start», «stop», «interval»)

As an example, the following values in the PARTITION function create ranges that begin with 1 and end with 100, in intervals of 5, from a field named Grade:

- Partition (Grade, 1, 100, 5)

Applying this concept to our table of grades, the query shown in Figure 9.25 produces a count of the number of grades that fall within each of these intervals. The output is shown in Figure 9.26.

Field:	Range: Partition([Grade],1,100,5)		Count: Grade	Grade
Table:			Grades	Grades
Total:	Group By		Count	Where
Sort:				
Show:		☑	☑	☐
Criteria:				Is Not Null
or:				

Figure 9.25
Design View of a query with a PARTITION function.

Grades 8	
Range ▾	Count ▾
56: 60	1
61: 65	1
71: 75	1
81: 85	2
86: 90	1
91: 95	2

Figure 9.26
Datasheet View of a query with a PARTITION function.

Notice that a GROUP BY was applied to the column with the PARTITION function. This allowed grouping to be created for the ranges specified by the function. The column with the COUNT provides a count of the number of rows in each partition. The WHERE expression eliminates the row with NULL values in the Grade field. As seen, the combination of the PARTITION with a GROUP BY effectively creates a frequency distribution for this set of grades.

Focus on Analysis: The Mode

The three principal ways to measure central tendency in a data set are through the mean, mode, and median. Access already provides a function (AVG) that easily computes the mean, or average. The mode of a data set is the value that occurs most frequently. Excel provides a function to compute the mode, but Access does not.

To compute the mode of a field in Access, the first step is to find the frequency with which each value occurs. This is accomplished by setting up a query with two components: a GROUP BY column and a COUNT column. For example, if you want to get frequencies for field AAA, place field AAA in two different columns. In one column, do a GROUP BY on the Total line. This creates the grouping for that field. In the second column, do a COUNT on the Total line, and sort that column in descending order. That creates the frequencies for each group. Since the second column is sorted in descending order, you'll see the groups with the highest frequencies listed first.

If you want to take the next step and compute the mode for field AAA, simply look at the first row of the results. The value with the highest frequency is the mode. Alternatively, you can indicate a Top Values property of 1 for the query, which means that it will return only one row, which will be the row with the highest frequency.

Selection Criteria on Aggregates

We need to include one more topic in our discussion of summarizing data. Once groups are created, selection criteria become a bit more complex. When applying any kind of selection criteria to a query with groups, one must ask whether the selection criteria applies to the individual rows or to the entire group.

To illustrate the concept of selection criteria against a group, let's say you want to see a list of students who have an average quiz grade of 70 or higher. You'd like to see each student name and their average. In this situation, it would not be correct to simply exclude those rows with a quiz grade less than 70. You need to compute the average for each student, and then either include or exclude that student based on their average grade for quizzes. Figures 9.27 and 9.28 show the solution.

Field:	Student	Average: Grade	GradeType
Table:	Grades	Grades	Grades
Total:	Group By	Avg	Where
Sort:	Ascending		
Show:	☑	☑	☐
Criteria:		>=70	"Quiz"
or:			

Figure 9.27
Design View of a query with an AVG criteria against a group.

Student	Average
Colleen	93.5
Lois	71.5

Figure 9.28
Datasheet View of a query with an AVG criteria against a group.

There are two sets of selection criteria in this query. First, there is selection against individual rows, specifying that we only want to see rows where the GradeType equals "Quiz". This is accomplished with a WHERE on the Total line. Second, there is selection on the Student group specifying that the average grade for each group must be at least 70. This is accomplished by adding criteria to the second column with AVG on the Total line.

See the SQL

The SQL equivalent of Figure 9.27 is:

```
SELECT
Grades.Student,
AVG (Grades.Grade) AS Average
FROM Grades
WHERE Grades.GradeType = "Quiz"
GROUP BY Grades.Student
HAVING AVG (Grades.Grade) >= 70
ORDER BY Grades.Student;
```

Syntax Notes:

- The HAVING clause is used for selection criteria associated with a GROUP BY group.
- When a query contains both a HAVING and a GROUP BY clause, the HAVING clause is always placed immediately after the GROUP BY clause.

Let's take a slightly more complex example. In this case, we only want to see students who have at least two quizzes with a grade of 60 or higher. The solution is shown in Figures 9.29 and 9.30.

Field:	Student	Count: Count(*)	GradeType	Grade
Table:	Grades		Grades	Grades
Total:	Group By	Expression	Where	Where
Sort:	Ascending			
Show:	✓	✓	☐	☐
Criteria:		>=2	"Quiz"	>=60
or:				

Figure 9.29
Design View of a query with a COUNT criteria against a group.

Figure 9.30
Datasheet View of a query with a COUNT criteria against a group.

The first column in the Design View indicates that we are grouping the data by Student. The third and fourth columns have the selection criteria for individual rows. The GradeType must equal "quiz" and the Grade must be greater than or equal to 60. The tricky part of this query is the second column. This column indicates that we only want to see results if there are at least two rows for the student. The COUNT function is somewhat different from all the other aggregate functions in the sense that a count is not applied to the actual values of any field. We simply want a count of rows. To accomplish this, we used the EXPRESSION value on the Totals line, in combination with an expression on the field line of COUNT (*) and selection criteria that the count must be greater than or equal to 2.

See the SQL

The SQL equivalent of Figure 9.29 is:

```
SELECT
Grades.Student,
COUNT(*) AS Count
FROM Grades
WHERE Grades.GradeType = "Quiz"
AND Grades.Grade >= 60
GROUP BY Grades.Student
HAVING COUNT(*) >= 2
ORDER BY Grades.Student;
```

Syntax Notes:

■ The selection criteria against the group in this example use the COUNT function.

We could have accomplished the same thing by using the Design View shown in Figure 9.31.

Field:	Student	Count: Student	GradeType	Grade
Table:	Grades	Grades	Grades	Grades
Total:	Group By	Count	Where	Where
Sort:	Ascending			
Show:	✓	✓	☐	☐
Criteria:		>=2	"Quiz"	>=60
or:				

Figure 9.31
Design View of a query with a COUNT criteria against a group.

The difference in this alternate version is in how the second column was specified. In Figure 9.31, we used the COUNT value on the Total line rather than EXPRESSION, indicating that we want to use the COUNT function. The difficulty with this is in deciding which field to count. We chose the Student field because that field has data in every row. As a result, we consider this alternative version of the query to be a less straightforward solution.

Looking Ahead

In this chapter, we covered several forms of aggregation, beginning with the simplest —that of selecting distinct values. We then introduced the class of functions known as aggregate functions. Unlike the scalar functions covered in Chapter 7, aggregate functions operate on more than one row of data. The real power of aggregate functions becomes apparent when they are used in conjunction with groups, which allow for the aggregation of data by group. Grouping is implemented in Access via the Total line of the Design View grid. Finally, we covered selection criteria against groups of data, which allows you to select data based on a characteristic of the entire group.

Our next chapter, "Subqueries and Set Logic," moves into an area involving more complex queries. Subqueries are essentially a query within a query. This is analogous to composite functions, which are a function within a function. Just as composite functions allow for more flexible expressions, subqueries allow for more complex expressions of logic, and provide certain capabilities not available in standard queries. For example, subqueries allow you to identify duplicate records within a table. Set logic involves using SQL code to combine two independent queries in a logical fashion. Like subqueries, set logic allows multiple queries to be combined together to retrieve data that could not be retrieved with a single query.

Chapter 10

Subqueries and Set Logic

In Chapter 7, we talked about composite functions. These functions contained other functions. Similarly, it is possible for Access queries to contain other queries. Queries contained within other queries are called *subqueries*.

The topic of subqueries is somewhat complex, primarily because there are many different ways in which they can be used. Subqueries can be placed in many different parts of a query, each with different nuances and requirements. Also, as a query contained within another query, subqueries can be related to and dependent on the main query, or they can be completely independent of the main query. Again, this distinction results in different usage requirements. Finally, subqueries can be used not only in Select queries, but also in other query types, such as Delete and Append. In this chapter, however, we'll restrict our discussion of subqueries to Select queries.

No matter how subqueries are used, they add a great deal of flexibility to the retrieval process. In many cases, subqueries provide functionality that can be accomplished by other means. In such instances, personal preferences will come into play, as you decide whether you want to utilize a subquery solution. However, as will be seen, there are certain situations where subqueries are essential for the task.

The second main concern of this chapter, set logic, is in some ways a natural extension of the topic of subqueries. Whereas subqueries are a query within a query, set logic involves having two independent queries logically tied together. The typical use of set logic is to connect two queries via the UNION operator. This means that the results of query A and query B are combined into a single query to yield the results of both individual queries together.

Another connection between subqueries and set logic is the fact that both techniques require, in most cases, some awareness of SQL. As mentioned in Chapter 3, the SQL View of queries shows the SQL statement underlying the query. This SQL View can generally be ignored. However, in the case of most subqueries and set logic situations, the SQL involved in the query will be more apparent and significant.

With that, let's begin our discussion with an outline of the basic types of subqueries.

Using Queries as a Data Source

A subquery is a query contained within another query. It isn't saved as a separate query, but exists only within another query. In terms of the SQL statements that underlie all queries, a subquery is a SELECT statement inserted inside another SELECT statement. In SQL, the subquery is generally enclosed in parentheses and given its own alias, so the results can be distinguished from those of the main query.

Apart from how Access handles subqueries, there are three types of subqueries in SQL databases:

- A subquery can represent a data source.
- A subquery can represent a specific column.
- A subquery can be part of an expression in selection criteria.

Let's begin with subqueries that represent a data source. In doing so, we need to point out that the second and third types of subqueries are easily handled by the Access Design View grid. When a subquery represents a specific column, it appears in the Field line of the grid. When a query is part of the selection criteria, it appears in the Criteria line of the grid.

However, the graphical interface of Access can't easily handle subqueries that represent data sources. This is because the Design View grid doesn't have an element that represents an entire data source. Within the context of Access, data sources are either tables or queries.

This means that in Access, subqueries that represent data sources are much more easily represented as an independent query. That independent query is then referenced in a second query, and is typically joined together with other tables or queries. These independent queries are saved on their own, and then referenced as a data source in other queries.

It must be said, however, that it is possible to create subqueries that represent data sources in Access. The main problem, though, is that these subqueries can't be represented in the Access Design View. If you want to work with subqueries as data sources, you need to work entirely in SQL View. The "Focus on Analysis" sidebar in this section includes an example of a subquery used as a data source that is handled entirely via the SQL View.

To illustrate the process of creating a separate query as a data source, let's say we have the Customers and Orders tables shown in Figures 10.1 and 10.2.

Customers	
CustomerID ▾	CustomerName ▾
1	Gloria Carter
2	Penelope Wilson
3	Sam Johnson

Figure 10.1
Datasheet View of Customers table.

Orders			
OrderID ▾	CustomerID ▾	OrderAmount ▾	OrderType ▾
1	1	22	Cash
2	2	11	Credit
3	2	5	Credit
4	2	8	Cash
5	3	9	Credit
6	3	10	Credit
7	2	4	Cash

Figure 10.2
Datasheet View of Orders table.

We would like to see a list of customers, along with a total sum of the cash orders they have placed. We want to see all customers, even if they have never placed a cash order. Our strategy in this situation is to break the problem into two separate queries. The first query will be a list of customers and the total amount of cash orders they've placed. This is shown in Figures 10.3 and 10.4.

The only table used in this query is the Orders table. By grouping the Orders table by CustomerID, this query returns the total order amount for cash orders. This query is saved with the name CashOrders.

The next query, shown in Figures 10.5 and 10.6, takes the results of the CashOrders query and uses it to display the total amount of cash orders for every customer.

This second query takes the results of the first query, the CashOrders query, and combines it with the Customers table to produce the final results. As shown, Sam Johnson has a blank in the CashOrders column, indicating that he has never placed a cash order. Of course, we could have taken an extra step and used the ISNULL and IIF functions to display a zero rather than the blank, or NULL, value.

Figure 10.3
Design View of a query to be used as a data source.

Figure 10.4
Datasheet View of a query to be used as a data source.

Figure 10.5
Design View of a query using another query as a data source.

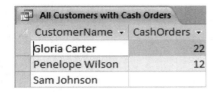

Figure 10.6
Datasheet View of a query using another query as a data source.

Note the relative simplicity of the solution. With the use of some complex functions and selection logic, it would have been possible to produce these results with only one query. This is shown in Figure 10.7. However, by breaking the problem into two separate queries, we modularized and simplified the final solution.

Figure 10.7
Design View of an alternate query.

Focus on Analysis: The Median

In Chapter 9, we learned how to compute an average and a mode. The median provides a third way to measure central tendency in a set of data. If a set of numbers is sorted from low to high, then the median is the number exactly in the middle. If there is an even number of values in the set, the median is an average of the middle two numbers. It's quite easy to pick out the median in a set of numbers. All you have to do is sort the numbers, and then find the row (or rows) in the middle. As it turns out, however, it's quite complex to come up with a formula for computing the median. There are many approaches. The best we can do is to supply one example of a formula, which you can plug into your data as desired. The following assumes that you want to compute the median of a field named ValueField in a table named MyTable. Enter the following SQL statement into the SQL View of a query:

```
SELECT (A.Value1 + B.Value2) / 2 AS Median
FROM
(SELECT TOP 1 ValueField AS Value1 FROM MyTable
WHERE ValueField IN (SELECT TOP 50 PERCENT ValueField from MyTable AS Temp)
ORDER BY ValueField DESC) AS A,
(SELECT TOP 1 ValueField AS Value2 FROM MyTable
WHERE ValueField IN (SELECT TOP 50 PERCENT ValueField from MyTable AS Temp
ORDER BY ValueField DESC) ORDER BY ValueField) AS B;
```

The basic structure of the above statement is:

SELECT (A.Value1 + B.Value2) / 2 AS Median
FROM (*a subquery with the lowest number in the upper 50% of the table*) AS A,
(*a subquery with the highest number in the lowest 50% of the table*) AS B

This query takes the average of the lowest number in the upper 50% of the data, and the highest number in the lower 50%. Notice that there are two separate data sources (A and B) after the FROM keyword. However, these data sources are not joined together. They simply exist as two independent data sources, which each supply part of the median calculation.

In Chapter 9, we mentioned that Access doesn't provide the COUNT DISTINCT expression that is part of standard SQL. This syntax allows one to produce a count of distinct values in a column. However, this type of logic can be applied in Access by using a separate query as a data source. To illustrate the solution, let's say we have a table with four rows with information about Animals, as shown in Figure 10.8.

| Animals | | |
AnimalID ▾	AnimalType ▾	Price ▾
1 Dog		50
2 Dog		30
3 Cat		10
4 Bird		15

Figure 10.8
Datasheet View of a table with duplicate values.

We would like to produce a statistic that counts the number of unique animals. It isn't possible to accomplish this with a single query, but it can be done with the use of a second query used as a separate data source. We first need to create a query, such as shown in Figure 10.9.

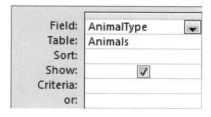

Figure 10.9
Design View of a query with Unique Values.

We're giving this query the name UniqueAnimals. This query has the Animals table as its source, and has the Unique Values property set to Yes. When this query is run, it produces three rows of data with these values: Bird, Cat, and Dog.

The second step is to create a query that uses UniqueAnimals as its data source. This query is shown in Figures 10.10 and 10.11.

Field:	Count of Unique Animals: AnimalType
Table:	UniqueAnimals
Total:	Count
Sort:	
Show:	☑
Criteria:	
or:	

Figure 10.10
Design View of a query using another query as a data source.

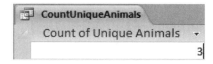

Figure 10.11
Datasheet View of a query using another query as a data source.

This second query is now able to utilize the Count function to count rows. Since there are only three rows in the UniqueAnimals query, this produces the desired effect. With the use of a second query used as a data source, we have been able to produce a count of the number of distinct values of the AnimalType column in the Animals table.

See the SQL

The SQL equivalent of Figure 10.9 is:

```
SELECT
DISTINCT Animals.AnimalType
FROM Animals;
```

The SQL equivalent of Figure 10.10 is:

```
SELECT
COUNT (UniqueAnimals.AnimalType) AS [Count of Unique Animals]
FROM UniqueAnimals;
```

Syntax Notes:

■ Access requires two queries to do a count of distinct values in a column. In standard SQL, these two queries can be combined into a single query with this syntax:

```
SELECT
COUNT (DISTINCT Animals.AnimalType)
FROM Animals;
```

Finding Duplicate Records

The previous example wasn't really a subquery, since it involved two separate queries. We now turn to true subqueries, in which one query is wholly contained within the other. The easiest way to begin is with the query wizard that Access provides for finding duplicate records. As will be seen, this wizard produces a query with a complex subquery structure. The data in this example is taken from a table with sports teams, shown in Figure 10.12.

TeamID	Team	Type
1	Chicago Cubs	Baseball
2	Chicago White Sox	Baseball
3	New York Yankees	Baseball
4	Los Angeles Dodgers	Baseball
5	Atlanta Braves	Baseball
6	Chicago Cubs	Baseball

Figure 10.12
Datasheet View of Teams table.

The object of this next query is to find duplicate records in this list. A single column will determine whether the record is a duplicate: the Team field. To initiate the wizard, we click the Query Wizard command on the Ribbon, select the "Find Duplicates" Query Wizard, and then run through the following steps:

■ When asked "Which table or query do you want to search for duplicate values?" select the Teams table.

■ When asked "Which fields might contain duplicate information?" select the Team field.

- When asked "Do you want the query to show fields in addition to those with duplicate values?" select the TeamID and Type fields.

- Specify a name for the query as Duplicate Teams.

The new query now appears as in Figures 10.13 and 10.14.

Field:	Team			TeamID	Type
Table:	Teams			Teams	Teams
Sort:	Ascending				
Show:		☑		☑	☑
Criteria:	In (SELECT [Team] FROM [Teams] As Tmp GROUP BY [Team] HAVING Count(*)>1)				
or:					

Figure 10.13
Design View of a Find Duplicates query.

Duplicate Teams		
Team ▼	TeamID ▼	Type ▼
Chicago Cubs	6	Baseball
Chicago Cubs	1	Baseball

Figure 10.14
Datasheet View of a Find Duplicates query.

The Find Duplicates Query Wizard produced this complex query. How can you tell that this query contains a subquery? Note the SELECT statement on the Criteria line under the Team field. In essence, the criteria for selection is a complete query.

See the SQL

The SQL equivalent of Figure 10.13 is:

```
SELECT
Teams.Team,
Teams.TeamID,
Teams.Type
FROM Teams
WHERE Teams.Team IN
(SELECT Team FROM Teams AS Tmp GROUP BY Team HAVING Count(*) > 1)
ORDER BY Teams.Team;
```

Syntax Notes:

- Subqueries used as selection criteria appear in the WHERE clause of the main query.
- Subqueries are enclosed in parentheses.

Unless you've been studiously following the "See the SQL" sidebars in this book, or already have some knowledge of SQL, you probably have no idea as to what this statement means. That's all right. To assist, we'll present a trick that will allow you to gain an understanding of what Access did in the Find Duplicates wizard. Looking at the contents of the Criteria cell, you'll see that it consists of the IN operator followed by a long expression in parentheses. We previously encountered the IN operator in Chapter 8, with reference to expressions such as:

- IN ("FL", "CA")

In the current situation, rather than list specific text values for the IN operator, we're specifying an entire SQL statement, which will return a list of text values when executed. The SQL statement following the IN operator is:

- SELECT Team FROM Teams AS Tmp GROUP BY Team HAVING COUNT(*) > 1

To see what this SELECT statement means, we can take the SQL statement itself and create a query based on that statement. This is the procedure:

- Copy the entire SELECT statement from the cell.

- Click the Query Design command in the Ribbon to start a new query.

- On the Add Table window, click the Close button without selecting any tables.

- On the View command in the Ribbon, switch the view to SQL View.

- Do a Paste, copying over any words that appear on the screen.

- On the View command in the Ribbon, switch the view to Design View.

The resulting query is shown in Figures 10.15 and 10.16.

Now that the subquery is shown in the familiar Access Design View, we can get a sense of what it is. Perhaps the only confusing aspect of the query shown in Figure 10.15 is the table with the name Tmp. If you were to go into the properties of the query, you'd see that this is an alias for the Teams table. The second column in the query, with the selection criteria on the Count(*) field, specifies selection criteria on an aggregate. The group is being selected only if there is more than one record in the group. As seen in Figure 10.16, only one group satisfies the condition. The main query uses the result of this subquery to select all matching records, thus producing a list of duplicates.

Figure 10.15
Design View of Subquery converted into a query.

Figure 10.16
Datasheet View of Subquery converted into a query.

Using Subqueries as Criteria

The Find Duplicates query wizard seen in the previous example created a query in which the selection criteria is an entire query, thus forming a subquery. The format of the expression in the selection criteria was:

- IN (SQL SELECT statement)

The resulting subquery was decidedly complex, and in fact would have been even more complex had we selected more than one field to determine whether rows are duplicates. To reinforce the idea that subqueries can be used as selection criteria for purposes other than finding duplicates, let's illustrate with a simpler example.

Returning to our Customers and Orders tables, let's say we want to retrieve a list of customers who have ever paid cash for any order they placed. This can be accomplished without subqueries, as seen in Figures 10.17 and 10.18.

Figure 10.17
Design View of a query including criteria without a subquery.

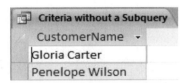

Figure 10.18
Datasheet View of a query including criteria without a subquery.

The main complexity in this query is in the use of GROUP BY. Even though we're selecting only rows from the Orders table with an OrderType of "Cash", we still need to group by customers in order to return just one row per customer.

Figure 10.19 shows a different solution to the same problem. This formulation uses a subquery as selection criteria, and has the same result.

The subquery solution is in some ways simpler and in other ways much more complex. The simplicity lies in the fact that this query requires only one table as a data source—the Customers table. The Orders table is handled in the subquery. Additionally, there is no GROUP BY needed, since the main query only selects from the Customers table. However, the complexity comes from the fact that one needs to manually enter a SQL statement in the criteria. This criteria specifies that we only want CustomerIDs in the Customers table that are also in rows in the Orders table where the OrderType is "Cash".

Figure 10.19
Design View of a query including criteria with a subquery.

The purpose of this example has been to provide a sense of the possibilities for using subqueries in selection logic. For this particular example, there would be little point in using a subquery if you're not sufficiently familiar with SQL. However, for more difficult problems, utilizing the subquery format might be necessary. If you find the need to use subqueries, but aren't comfortable with SQL, remember that Access can write the SQL for you. In the preceding example, one could have created a query with just the subquery, as shown in Figure 10.20.

Field:	CustomerID	OrderType
Table:	Orders	Orders
Sort:		
Show:	☑	☐
Criteria:		"Cash"
or:		

Figure 10.20
Design View of a subquery saved as a query.

The query in Figure 10.20 is the subquery of Figure 10.19, seen in Design View. After creating the subquery design, one can simply switch to SQL View and copy the SQL statement. That SQL statement can then be pasted into the main query.

Using Subqueries as Fields

We've talked about using subqueries as a data source and as selection criteria. The final general use of subqueries we'll talk about is as a field. In this type of subquery, the entire subquery appears on the Field line of the Design View grid. The result of the subquery is displayed as a column in the query.

In addition to classification of subqueries as data sources, criteria, or fields, there is another way to classify subqueries: as *correlated* or *uncorrelated*. The subqueries we've seen so far have been uncorrelated subqueries. The terms *correlated*. and *uncorrelated* describe whether the subquery is related to the query in which it is contained. Uncorrelated subqueries are unrelated. When a subquery is unrelated, it is completely independent of the outer query. Uncorrelated subqueries are evaluated and executed only once as part of the main query.

In contrast, correlated subqueries are specifically related to the main query. Because of this explicit relationship, correlated subqueries need to be evaluated for each row returned, and can produce different results each time the subquery is executed. Additionally, correlated subqueries can't be created or executed on their own, as was done in the example of Figure 10.20.

Our next example will illustrate both of these concepts: subqueries as a data source and correlated subqueries. In fact, subqueries used as a field are usually correlated subqueries. The best way to explain is with an example. Returning to the Customers and Orders tables, let's say we want to produce a list of the total number of orders each customer has placed. This query can be handled in the traditional manner without a subquery, as shown in Figures 10.21 and 10.22.

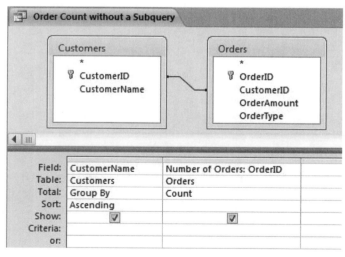

Figure 10.21
Design View of a query without a subquery.

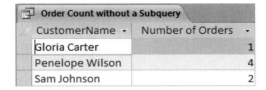

Figure 10.22
Datasheet View of a query without a subquery.

The complexity of this query lies in the fact that it requires grouping and selection criteria on an aggregated count. It also requires both the Customers and Orders tables as data sources. In contrast, the same query can be written with a subquery as a data source, as shown in Figure 10.23.

Figure 10.23
Design View of a query with a correlated subquery.

In the Design View, the subquery is on the Field line of the second column. However, Access doesn't fully display correlated subqueries in the grid. To view the contents of the cell with the correlated subquery, you need to view the Zoom window, as shown in Figure 10.24.

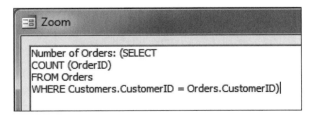

Figure 10.24
Zoom window of a correlated subquery.

Let's now look at this query in some detail. As before, the subquery is expressed entirely in SQL. The main query has only the Customers table as its dataset. The subquery retrieves data from the Orders table. Notice, however, that the WHERE clause in the subquery matches the CustomerID in the Customers table and the CustomerID in the Orders table to do the join. The unusual aspect is that the Customers table is *not* a data source in the subquery. It's only a data source in the main query. This is what makes this a *correlated* subquery. The subquery cannot be executed on its own. If run by itself, the subquery would error because the reference to the CustomerID column of the Customers table doesn't exist within the context of the subquery. The correlated subquery computes the total order count for each customer. From a processing standpoint, this is somewhat inefficient, since the subquery needs to be executed for every customer.

See the SQL

The SQL equivalent of Figure 10.24 is:

```
SELECT
Customers.CustomerName,
(SELECT COUNT (OrderID) FROM Orders
WHERE Customers.CustomerID = Orders.CustomerID) AS [Number of Orders]
FROM Customers
ORDER BY Customers.CustomerName;
```

Syntax Notes:

■ As with uncorrelated subqueries, correlated subqueries are surrounded by parentheses.

Note that since the subquery isn't valid on its own, we can't use the trick to design the subquery as a separate query, and then paste the SQL into the main query. This makes correlated subqueries substantially more difficult, since they require a basic knowledge of SQL.

Focus on Analysis: Moving Averages

In Chapter 9, we saw how to use the AVG aggregate function to compute an average. A more complex variant is the ability to create a moving average for a time series of data. For example, you might want to compute an average of only those transactions that have occurred during the past week. The tricky part is that "last week" has a different meaning for every row of data. The assumption in computing moving averages is that there is one record per date in your dataset. Each of these records has some value that you want to average over time.

To accomplish this, one needs to insert a correlated subquery into the Field line of a query. A special property of this correlated subquery is that it will access the same table that's in the main query. For this reason, a table alias needs to be used in the subquery to keep references to the two tables straight. This situation regarding aliases is similar to the self joins seen in Chapter 5.

As an example, let's say that your query has a single data source: a table named MyTable. This table has a date field named DateField and a field for which you would like to compute a moving average, named ValueField. To compute a moving average for ValueField, you need to enter the following expression on the Field line in a column in your query:

Moving Average: (SELECT AVG (Temp.ValueField) FROM MyTable AS Temp where Temp.DateField BETWEEN DATEADD ("d", -x, MyTable.DateField) AND MyTable.DateField)

In the above expression, x represents the number of days you want to go back in time when computing the moving average. The data source in the subquery is referred to as Temp. The subquery computes the average in the Temp table, based on a date range of records in the main query.

Union Queries

In Chapter 5, we introduced the idea of joining multiple tables together in a single query. Earlier in this chapter, we explained that a query could be used as a data source for another query. Later, in discussing subqueries, we showed that queries could contain other queries within them. These contained queries are referred to as subqueries. In all of these situations, the result is a single query, which may or may not reference or contain other queries. In SQL terms, the result is a query with a single SELECT statement.

We now want to turn to a technique in which multiple queries are combined to form a composite query. In SQL terms, we will create a single SQL statement that contains more than one SELECT statement. The SELECT statements exist independently, in a single query. This is not quite the same as a subquery. In a subquery, one query exists inside another query. In this new technique, the two queries exist side by side. The results of each query are combined to form a larger result.

The concept of combining queries in this manner is often referred to as *set logic*—a term taken from mathematics. Each query can be referred to as a *set* of data. In general, there are four different possibilities for combining information from multiple sets. Assuming that we have data in set A and in set B, we can combine the sets as follows:

- Data that is in set A or in set B
- Data that is in both set A and in set B
- Data that is in set A, but not in set B
- Data that is in set B, but not in set A

Access only allows for the first possibility, combining data that is in set A or in set B. Other databases, such as Microsoft SQL Server, allow for the other three possibilities, but those other scenarios are, in fact, rarely needed or used.

To accommodate this technique, Access provides a Union command in the Query Type section of the Ribbon, under the Design Query Tools tab. This is shown in Figure 10.25.

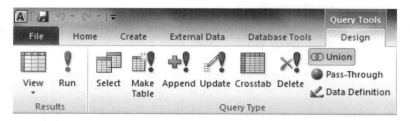

Figure 10.25
The Union command.

The Union command initiates a Union query. To illustrate, we'll say that we have data in a Purchases table, which has information on purchases that a company has made from its vendors, and a Returns table, which has data on returns made to vendors. The data in these tables is shown in Figures 10.26 and 10.27.

Purchases

PurchaseID	PurchaseDate	PurchaseAmount	VendorID
1	6/13/2011	50	1
2	6/13/2011	40	2
3	6/14/2011	25	1
4	6/15/2011	50	3
5	6/16/2011	35	2
6	6/20/2011	30	4

Figure 10.26
Datasheet View of Purchases table.

Returns

ReturnID	ReturnDate	ReturnAmount	VendorID
1	6/16/2011	25	1
2	6/17/2011	20	2
3	6/18/2011	25	1
4	6/20/2011	5	3

Figure 10.27
Datasheet View of Returns table.

Both the Purchases and Returns tables contain a field named VendorID. The VendorID points to a record in a Vendors table with information on the vendor from whom the item was purchased or returned. The interesting aspect of these tables is that, even though the data in them is related, they are essentially independent of each other. There's no common field that links the Purchases and Returns tables. A single return may be related to a single purchase or to multiple purchases. Note also that the data in this example is simplistic in the sense that we're leaving out additional fields that would normally appear, such as information on the product purchased or returned, quantity purchased, and price per item.

To illustrate the use of a Union query, we'll create a query that displays all purchases and returns between the dates of 6/13/2011 and 6/19/2011. We want to see each purchase or return on a separate line in the results.

The solution is to break down the query into two separate queries, which will later be combined via the Union command. The Design View of the two individual queries appears in Figures 10.28 and 10.29. We'll hold off on showing the Datasheet View until we've combined the queries.

Figure 10.28
Design View of a query of the Purchases table.

Notice that the second column in both queries has a literal that states the type of data in the query—either a "Purchase" or a "Return". After the data is combined, this column will let the user know what type of data they're looking at. Notice also that both queries have the same number of columns and the same exact names for each column. If the queries pull data with different field names, those columns are given identical alias names. For example, both the PurchaseAmount and ReturnAmount fields have a column alias of "Amount". This is a requirement of Union queries. In general, there are three rules for queries combined with a Union command:

- All queries combined must have the same number of columns selected.

- All columns in each query must be in the same order.

- All corresponding columns must have the same or compatible data types.

Figure 10.29
Design View of a query of the Returns table.

Now that we have two compatible queries, the next task is to combine them. The process for this is somewhat convoluted, in that it involves copying and pasting SQL code into a single query, and typing in some additional SQL code. Here's how it's done with the Purchases Query and Returns Query that we already created:

1. Open both the Purchases Query and Returns Query in Design View.

2. Switch each query to SQL View. The screen now appears as in Figure 10.30.

3. Click the Query Design command in the Ribbon to initiate a new query.

4. In the Show Table window, click the Close button without selecting any tables or queries.

5. Click the Union command in the Ribbon. This automatically puts the query in SQL View. The main part of the screen will be blank.

6. Return focus to the Purchases query and copy the SQL statement.

7. Switch focus to the new query, and do a paste in the blank screen. Delete the semicolon at the end of the statement.

8. Type the word UNION on a new line after the SQL statement. The screen now appears as in Figure 10.31.

9. Switch focus to the Returns query and copy the SQL statement.

10. Switch focus to the new query, and do a paste on the line after the UNION keyword. Delete the semicolon at the end of the statement. The screen now appears as in Figure 10.32.

11. There is one task remaining, and that is to add a sort to the query. We want to sort the results by date. Enter the following at the end of the statement: ORDER BY Date;

12. The screen now appears as in Figure 10.33. Save the query with a desired name.

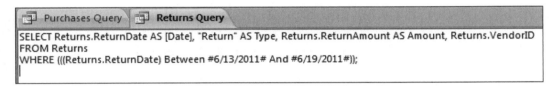

Figure 10.30
SQL View of Returns Query.

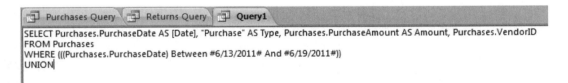

Figure 10.31
SQL View of Union query after one query copied.

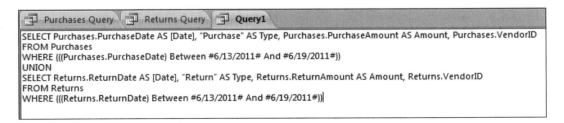

Figure 10.32
SQL View of Union query after two queries copied.

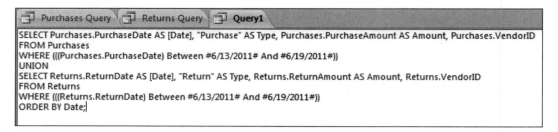

```
SELECT Purchases.PurchaseDate AS [Date], "Purchase" AS Type, Purchases.PurchaseAmount AS Amount, Purchases.VendorID
FROM Purchases
WHERE (((Purchases.PurchaseDate) Between #6/13/2011# And #6/19/2011#))
UNION
SELECT Returns.ReturnDate AS [Date], "Return" AS Type, Returns.ReturnAmount AS Amount, Returns.VendorID
FROM Returns
WHERE (((Returns.ReturnDate) Between #6/13/2011# And #6/19/2011#))
ORDER BY Date;|
```

Figure 10.33
SQL View of Union query after two queries and a sort.

We can now open the new query in Datasheet View. Notice that we cannot see Union queries in Design View. This is because Access can't represent Union queries in the Design View grid. Figure 10.34 shows the new query in Datasheet View.

Date	Type	Amount	VendorID
6/13/2011	Purchase	40	2
6/13/2011	Purchase	50	1
6/14/2011	Purchase	25	1
6/15/2011	Purchase	50	3
6/16/2011	Purchase	35	2
6/16/2011	Return	25	1
6/17/2011	Return	20	2
6/18/2011	Return	25	1

Figure 10.34
Datasheet View of a Union query.

The results of this Union query show the purchases and returns together. The second column indicates whether the amount was for a purchase or a return. Since we added a sort to the query, the data is sorted by date.

At this point, it is useful to step back and talk about why it was necessary to design this as a Union query. Why couldn't we simply join these two tables together in the usual fashion? First, in this example with limited data fields, there was simply no field that could serve as a link to join the Purchases and Returns together.

To examine alternate possibilities, let's imagine that the Returns table had a field named PurchaseID that linked the Returns record to the Purchases table. In that situation, we could create a query with an outer join to join the Purchases table to the

Returns table. However, even in this alternate scenario, there is still often a valid reason for utilizing a Union query. Unlike normal queries, Union queries have the ability to return separate rows for related data. In contrast, when tables are joined in the usual manner, the matching data appears on the same row. As such, Union queries are a useful way to present data from related tables on separate rows.

Looking Ahead

In this chapter, we've seen subqueries used in three different ways: as a data source, in selection criteria, and as a calculated column. When subqueries are used as a data source, Access doesn't have a way of displaying that query in Design View. The entire query must be created in SQL View. For that reason, it's generally best to create a separate query, which is then saved and used as a data source for another query.

We also looked at examples of both correlated and uncorrelated subqueries. We've really only touched on some of the uses of subqueries. What complicates the matter is that many subqueries can be expressed in other ways. Whether or not you choose to utilize subqueries depends on your personal taste and willingness to deal directly with SQL code.

Finally, we discussed the related topic of set logic and Union queries. With this technique, multiple queries can be combined into one query that returns the results of each query on separate rows. The creation of Union queries requires a complex procedure of copying and pasting SQL code. For this reason, these queries are not for the faint of heart. However, they are often an essential tool for pulling together related data.

In our next chapter, "Action Queries," we'll address queries that alter data. This includes queries that modify, delete, or insert data into tables. Just to give one example of the usefulness of these queries, let's say that you want to create a Union query but don't want to deal with the complexities of SQL code. Using Action queries, you can break down the process into multiple steps and achieve the same result. Essentially, the two queries that were combined together in a Union query can be executed separately to insert data into a new table. This would be followed by a Select query that pulls data from the table. This produces the same result as if it were all done via a single Union query.

Chapter 11

Action Queries

The queries discussed in Chapters 4 through 10 have all been Select queries. These are the mainstay of the data analyst, as they all involve retrieving data in the particular way that the data needs to be viewed. There are, however, occasions for the modification of data. Access provides several query types that modify data in various ways. These queries are known collectively as *Action queries*. There are four types of Action queries:

- Make Table queries
- Append queries
- Update queries
- Delete queries

In brief, Make Table queries insert rows of data into a new table. Append queries insert rows of data into an existing table. Update queries update specific fields in specified rows in an existing table. Delete queries delete entire rows of data in an existing table, based on specified criteria. As may be surmised, inserting and deleting rows is relatively straightforward. Updating existing data, however, is a more complex endeavor.

A Select query can be easily transformed into any of the four Action queries by merely selecting that query type in the Ribbon. After a few additional adjustments, the new query will be ready to run.

It's important to note that, unlike Select queries, there is a distinct difference in Action queries between the Datasheet View and the Run command. For Select queries, choosing either the Datasheet View or the Run command causes the query to display the data specified in the query. For Action queries, however, the Datasheet View merely displays the data that *will be* affected when the query is run. You must click the Run command to actually execute the query and carry out the desired action.

We'll assume in this chapter that, as a data analyst, any updating you'll be doing will be with internal tables in your Access database. If you should ever find the need to update production data with Access, a number of strategies can be employed to help prevent unintentional blunders. For example, when deleting rows from a table, you can employ a *soft delete* technique. In other words, instead of actually deleting rows, you can denote a special column in a table that marks each row as either active or inactive. Rather than deleting a row, you merely mark a row as being inactive. That way, if a delete is done in error, you can easily reverse it by changing the value of the active/inactive column.

A similar technique can be utilized with inserts. When adding a row, you can mark in a special column the exact date and time of the insert. If it is later determined that the row was added in error, you can find all rows added in a specified time range and delete them.

The problem is more complex when it comes to updating data. Generally, it's advisable to maintain a separate table that holds data on intended update transactions. If any kind of error is made, you can go back to the transaction table to look up the before and after values for modified data, and use that to reverse any earlier mistakes.

These strategies are just a few of the many approaches that can be taken. This topic is well beyond the scope of this book. Just be sure that you are cautious when updating production data. Once an Action query is run, there is no undo command that can reverse the modification.

Make Table Queries

In a perfect world, there would never be a need to save data in an Access database. If data is always available and if historical data can be retrieved just as easily as current data, then one should be able to rerun any query at a later date and receive the same results. Unfortunately, this is not always the case. Temporary data sets are always a factor and there is therefore sometimes a need to save results from queries. One possibility for saving data is simply to export it to Excel after the query is run. However, this can be a cumbersome step, especially if that data may eventually be used as input for future queries. To assist with the process of saving data, Access provides the Make Table query.

Make Table queries serve a dual purpose: They not only allow you to insert data into a table, but they also create the table for you. If the specified table name happens to exist already when the Make Table query is run, it will first delete the table, and then create it again with the new data specified in the query.

Let's illustrate the process with the tables shown in Figures 11.1 and 11.2.

Customers		
CustomerID ▾	CustomerName ▾	State ▾
1	Paul Gordon	WI
2	Warren Winnie	OH
3	Pratul Batra	CA
4	Irena Dunn	WI
5	Fred Winter	NV
6	Stephen Cobbler	OH
7	Indira Watkins	CA
8	Joyce Bentley	NV
9	Carol Swiftly	WI
10	Carmen Garcia	NV

Figure 11.1
Datasheet View of Customers table.

Preferences				
PreferenceID ▾	CustomerID ▾	Email ▾	Mail ▾	Phone ▾
1	3	☑	☐	☑
2	4	☑	☐	☑
3	2	☐	☐	☑
4	6	☑	☑	☐
5	5	☐	☑	☐
6	8	☐	☐	☑
7	7	☑	☑	☑
8	10	☐	☑	☐

Figure 11.2
Datasheet View of Preferences table.

The intent of these two tables is to record preferences from customers as to whether they wish to be contacted by email, mail, or phone. The assumption is that the organization creates a single record in the Preferences table when a customer indicates or changes their preferences. Any old records for that customer are deleted, so there is only one record per customer. Additionally, we'll assume that not every customer necessarily has a preferences record.

The nature of this design is that the history of prior preferences of customers is discarded. With this in mind, an analyst may see a need to store the current preferences of customers on a periodic basis.

One minor note about the Preferences table: The Email, Mail, and Phone fields utilize a Yes/No data type. This means that they can only contain two values: true or false. When you first add a Yes/No field to table, the Display Control property for the field will have a default value of Check Box. This is why these fields appear as check boxes in Figure 11.2. If desired, you can change the properties of this table so the values display as True/False, Yes/No, or On/Off. This is accomplished by modifying the Format and Display Control properties of the field.

Let's begin by creating a Select query for the data we want to save. For illustrative purposes, we'll say that the analyst wants to store preferences only for customers in the state of Ohio. The Select query is shown in Figure 11.3.

Figure 11.3
Design View of a Select query.

To transform this query into a Make Table query, we merely need to click the Make Table command in the Query Type section of the Ribbon. The window shown in Figure 11.4 then pops up asking for the name of a table. We've supplied the name SavedPreferences.

The Design View of the new Make Table query will appear as identical to the Select query shown in Figure 11.3. Our only remaining task is to run the query to create the table. To do this, we click the Run command on the Ribbon. If the table already exists, we see a warning message that the existing table will first be deleted. We then see another warning message saying that x rows are about to be pasted into a new table. After responding Yes to these messages, the table is created. Figure 11.5 shows the data in this new table.

Figure 11.4
Make Table window.

SavedPreferences				
CustomerName ▾	State ▾	Email ▾	Mail ▾	Phone ▾
Warren Winnie	OH	0	0	-1
Stephen Cobbler	OH	-1	-1	0

Figure 11.5
Datasheet View of SavedPreferences table just created.

Notice that the Email, Mail, and Phone fields appear in a format not previously seen. The values of –1 and 0 are the raw values that Access uses to store Yes/No fields. The –1 and 0 values represent true and false, respectively. To format this table to display the data in a more readable format, we merely need to change the Format or Display Control properties for those fields. If we change the Display Control property for these three fields to Check Box, the data appears as in Figure 11.6.

SavedPreferences				
CustomerName ▾	State ▾	Email ▾	Mail ▾	Phone ▾
Warren Winnie	OH	☐	☐	☑
Stephen Cobbler	OH	☑	☑	☐

Figure 11.6
Datasheet View of SavedPreferences table after format modification.

The format of the table has been successfully modified, but if the query is run a second time, it will again have the original format. This is because the Make Table query completely deletes the table before creating it and inserting rows.

See the SQL

The SQL equivalent of the Make Table query, derived from the Select query of Figure 11.3 is:

```
SELECT
Customers.CustomerName,
Customers.State,
Preferences.Email,
Preferences.Mail,
Preferences.Phone
INTO SavedPreferences
FROM Customers
LEFT JOIN Preferences
ON Customers.CustomerID = Preferences.CustomerID
WHERE Customers.State = "OH";
```

Syntax Notes:

■ The INTO clause has been added to the SELECT statement to specify the new table that will be created to hold the results.

■ Other than the INTO clause, this Make Table query is identical to the corresponding Select query.

As mentioned earlier, Make Table queries have the dual purpose of both creating tables and inserting data. This provides an easy way to quickly create a table, even if it is to initially contain no data. To accomplish this, simply set up a Make Table query based on fields from other tables and specify selection criteria that will result in no data being selected. When the query is run, it will then create the desired table without any rows.

Append Queries

In the previous example, we used a Make Table query to insert data from the state of Ohio into a SavedPreferences table. At this point, we may certainly want to add data from other states to the table. This is where the Append query comes in.

To create the Append query, we can start with either the original Select query, or the newer Make Table query, and select the Append command in Query Type section of the Ribbon. After doing this, you'll see a window identical to Figure 11.4, except that it will say Append rather than Make Table on the title bar. To select the desired table name, we can use the drop-down menu to select the existing SavedPreferences table. After doing so, the Design View grid will appear as in Figure 11.7.

Field:	CustomerName	State	Email	Mail	Phone
Table:	Customers	Customers	Preferences	Preferences	Preferences
Sort:					
Append To:	CustomerName	State	Email	Mail	Phone
Criteria:		"NV"			
or:					

Figure 11.7
Design View of an Append Query.

Notice that the Show line of the grid has been replaced by an Append line. The drop-down menu in each column in the Append To line allows you to select the field in the target table that you want that field to go to. For example, the third column indicates that the Email field of the Preferences table should go to the Email field of the target table, which is SavedPreferences.

To append a different state, we'll change the criteria for the State column to NV for Nevada. If we want to check on the data that will be appended to the SavedPreferences table before running the query, we can simply switch to the Datasheet View. The data appears as in Figure 11.8.

Append Query					
CustomerName ▾	State ▾	Email ▾	Mail ▾	Phone ▾
Fred Winter	NV	☐	☑	☐
Joyce Bentley	NV	☐	☐	☑
Carmen Garcia	NV	☐	☑	☐

Figure 11.8
Datasheet View of an Append Query.

See the SQL

The SQL equivalent of Figure 11.7 is:

```
INSERT INTO SavedPreferences
(CustomerName, State, Email, Mail, Phone)
SELECT
Customers.CustomerName,
Customers.State,
Preferences.Email,
Preferences.Mail,
Preferences.Phone
```

FROM Customers
LEFT JOIN Preferences
ON Customers.CustomerID = Preferences.CustomerID
WHERE Customers.State = "NV";

Syntax Notes:

- The INSERT INTO clause has been added to the SELECT statement to specify the new table that will be created to hold the results.

- The column names within the following parentheses list the target columns in an order corresponding to the columns specified after the SELECT.

- Other than the INSERT INTO clause, this Append query is identical to the corresponding Select query.

As with Make Table, executing the query is simple: We simply click the Run command in the Ribbon. After doing so, the SavedPreferences table appears as in Figure 11.9.

Figure 11.9
Datasheet View of SavedPreferences table after an append.

Delete Queries

Deleting data is much simpler than adding it. A Delete query can be set up to delete entire rows of data from an existing table, based on any specified criteria. The simplest and most typical use of the Delete query is to delete rows from the table based on criteria in that same table. To illustrate, let's say that we have a table with information about artists, as shown in Figure 11.10.

The last field, InCollection, will be used when we discuss Update queries. At this point, we want to delete all artists born between 1/1/1920 and 1/1/1930. To create such a query, we simply start with a Select query that selects those artists from the table. We then click the Delete command in the Query Type section of the Ribbon. The query then appears as in Figure 11.11.

To review the artists who will be deleted when the query is executed, we merely need to switch the query to Datasheet View. This is shown in Figure 11.12.

Figure 11.10
Datasheet View of Artists table.

Field:	ArtistName	DateOfBirth
Table:	Artists	Artists
Delete:	Where	Where
Criteria:		Between #1/1/1920# And #1/1/1930#
or:		

Figure 11.11
Design View of a Delete query.

ArtistName	DateOfBirth
Andy Warhol	8/6/1928

Figure 11.12
Datasheet View of a Delete query.

As expected, the Datasheet View shows both columns on the design grid. However, in terms of accomplishing the delete, it's only necessary to include the DateOfBirth column in the query, because that is the only column used in the selection criteria. Delete queries always delete entire rows of data, no matter how many columns are specified in the query. However, there must always be at least one column in the query for the delete to work.

After clicking the Run command, the query will delete the row shown in Figure 11.12 from the Artists table.

This example of a Delete query employs relatively simple selection criteria. It should be noted, however, that more complex criteria can be stipulated. For example, one might want to delete rows in one table based on whether that entity exists in another table. In that situation, one can use a subquery as selection criteria to tie the two tables together.

See the SQL

The SQL equivalent of Figure 11.11 is:

DELETE
Artists.ArtistName,
Artists.DateOfBirth
FROM Artists
WHERE Artists.DateOfBirth BETWEEN #1/1/1910# AND #1/1/1920#;

Syntax Notes:

- ■ The DELETE keyword indicates that this is a Delete query.
- ■ Unlike standard SQL, Access Delete queries require at least one column in a columnlist following the DELETE keyword. The equivalent of the above statement in standard SQL is:

DELETE
FROM Artists
WHERE Artists.DateOfBirth BETWEEN #1/1/1920# AND #1/1/1930#;

You may have noticed that the Delete line of the design grid shows the value "Where". This cell is actually a drop-down menu that allows you to choose between "Where" and "From". The "From" value is used in situations when you want to delete *all* rows from a table. In that situation, you would devise a query that looks like Figure 11.13.

Field:	Artists.*
Table:	Artists
Delete:	From
Criteria:	
or:	

Figure 11.13
Design View of a query deleting all rows in a table.

When run, this query will delete all rows from the Artists table.

Update Queries

Update queries come in many different flavors and levels of complexity. The simplest example is one in which a single column in a table is updated based on criteria derived from that same table. Continuing with the Artists table from our prior queries, let's say we realized that we made a mistake with the birthdate of Jackson Pollock. Instead of 1/27/1912, as is currently in the table, we discover that his real birthdate is 1/28/1912. The Update query shown in Figure 11.14 can be used to make this correction.

Field:	DateOfBirth	ArtistName
Table:	Artists	Artists
Update To:	#1/28/1912#	
Criteria:		"Jackson Pollock"
or:		

Figure 11.14
Design View of an Update Query.

As with Delete queries, the easiest way to create an Update query is to start with a Select query and then click the Update command in the Query Type section of the Ribbon. When the Select query is switched to an Update query, the Sort and Show lines of the design grid are replaced by an Update To line. The first column in the design grid indicates that the DateOfBirth column should be updated to 1/28/1912. The second column of the query specifies that the records to be updated are those with an ArtistName equal to "Jackson Pollock". To see the data that will be updated when this query is run, we simply switch to Datasheet View, as shown in Figure 11.15.

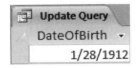

Figure 11.15
Datasheet View of an Update Query.

See the SQL

The SQL equivalent of Figure 11.14 is:

UPDATE Artists

```
SET Artists.DateOfBirth = #1/28/1912#
WHERE Artists.ArtistName = "Jackson Pollock";
```

Syntax Notes:

- ■ The UPDATE keyword indicates that this is an Update query.
- ■ The SET keyword indicates the column or columns to update, along with the new value.
- ■ As in SELECT queries, the WHERE clause specifies the selection criteria.

This example is simple enough, but in the real world, updates tend to be considerably more complex. A more common example of an update involves a situation where data in one table is updated based on data in another table. To illustrate, let's say we have a table named ArtCollection that has information on artworks we own. Using this table, we want to update the InCollection field of the Artists table to indicate that we own at least one piece of art from that artist in our collection. The ArtCollection data appears in Figure 11.16.

ArtCollection		
CollectionID ▾	ArtistID ▾	ArtworkID ▾
1	2	1
2	4	2
3	5	5

Figure 11.16
Datasheet View of ArtCollection table.

In this table, the ArtistID field points to a record in the Artists table. The ArtworkID field points to a record in an Artwork table, which has detailed information on the piece of artwork. For purposes of our update, the data in this table indicates that we own three pieces of art, by artists 2, 4, and 5. Figure 11.17 shows an Update query that updates the Artists table, based on this data in the ArtCollection table.

Field:	InCollection	ArtistID
Table:	Artists	Artists
Update To:	Yes	
Criteria:		In (Select ArtistID from ArtCollection)
or:		

Figure 11.17
Design View of an Update query with a subquery.

See the SQL

The SQL equivalent of Figure 11.17 is:

```
UPDATE Artists
SET Artists.InCollection = Yes
WHERE Artists.ArtistID IN
(SELECT ArtistID from ArtCollection);
```

Syntax Notes:

- This Update query contains a subquery in the WHERE clause.

The tricky part of this query is with the second column. The selection criterion is a subquery that states that the ArtistID of the Artists table must be found in the Art-Collection table. The first column specifies the value of the update to apply. In this case, we want to set the InCollection field to a value of Yes. To see the data that will be updated when the query is executed, we can switch to the Datasheet View, shown in Figure 11.18.

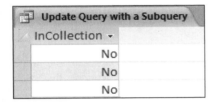

Figure 11.18
Datasheet View of an Update query with a subquery.

Notice that the Datasheet View still shows values of No for the update records. This is because the update has not yet been executed. After the query is run, the Artists table appears as in Figure 11.19.

As expected, the three artists represented in the ArtCollection table have had their InCollection field changed to Yes. As can be inferred, the subject of using subqueries for updates can get quite complex. As such, the topic is generally beyond the scope of this book. However, we've included this example if only to give an idea of some of the complexities involved in data updates.

Figure 11.19
Datasheet View of Artists table after an update.

Focus on Analysis: Fiscal Calendars

Many organizations employ a fiscal year that is different from the normal calendar year. As such, a common problem is with the ability to easily relate real calendar dates to the fiscal quarter or year. One solution is to develop a custom function to translate a date to the appropriate fiscal quarter or year, but such a function can be quite complex. A more straightforward solution is to develop a special table with these three fields: Date, FiscalQuarter, FiscalYear.

To accomplish this, we can start in Excel and create a spreadsheet with a single column with the range of all dates we might ever need, in both the past and future. We would start by entering the value "Date" in the cell A1. We can enter the earliest date in cell A2, and then this formula in A3: =A2 + 1. That formula can then be copied down to as many rows as needed to create the range of dates.

The remaining steps can be carried out in numerous ways. One approach is to first create a table in Access called CalendarDates. This table would contain three columns: Date, FiscalQuarter, and FiscalYear. The Date field is a date/time data type. The other two would be text fields.

We could then import the spreadsheet into that table, appending the data directly into the CalendarDates table. Since the spreadsheet and Access table both have a column or field named "Date", Access is smart enough to determine that the data corresponds.

Now that the CalendarDates table has the range of dates, we can run a series of Update queries against the CalendarDates to populate the FiscalQuarter and FiscalYear columns with appropriate values. As an example, we might enter these three values in such a query:

- In the Criteria row of the Date column: Between #4/1/2011# And #6/30/2011#
- In the Update To row of the FiscalQuarter column: "2011 Q1"
- In the Update To row of the FiscalYear column: "2011"

Looking Ahead

This chapter presented an overview of the various methods of updating data. The mechanics of executing simple inserts, deletes, and updates are relatively straightforward. However, the entire notion of applying updates to data is a demanding exercise, especially if the updates involve production data. With the ability to update thousands of rows of data with a single command comes an admonition to be cautious when performing any type of update. Procedures for reversing any updates should be carefully planned before any data modifications are applied.

With our next chapter, we leave the world of data updates and return to data retrieval. The final query type, the Crosstab query, provides a method of selecting data in a more dynamic fashion. The topic of Crosstab queries leads directly into the more significant topic of PivotTable Views. As will be seen, the PivotTable View is an indispensable tool for data analysts. Just as pivot tables in Excel provide the analyst with a powerful tool for data exploration, the PivotTable View in Access provides similar flexibility and functionality. Additionally, pivot tables serve as a critical bridge to the topic of Business Intelligence, which will be the focus of Part III of this book.

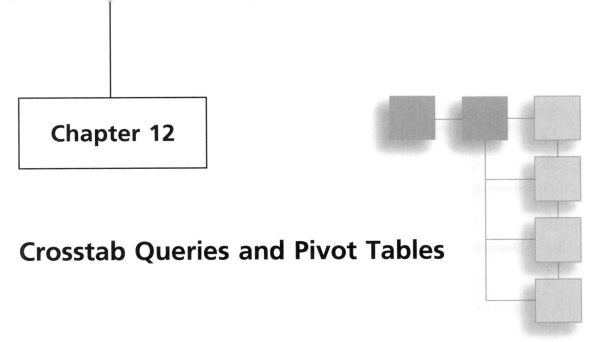

Chapter 12

Crosstab Queries and Pivot Tables

The Select queries discussed in Chapters 4 through 10 have been limited by the functionality of the SQL language underlying those queries. Through graphical means, Access allows the analyst to create queries that utilize basic SQL functionality. This includes the ability to create expressions, combine data into groups, utilize aggregate functions, and apply selection criteria on either individual rows or aggregated groups. However, with crosstab queries and pivot tables, Access provides a new type of technology that allows the user to retrieve data in a more dynamic fashion. As such, this represents a leap in capabilities beyond the functionality of the Select query.

Of the two main topics of this chapter, Crosstab queries and pivot tables, pivot tables are decidedly much more useful. Crosstab queries were introduced with the first version of Access back in 1992. At that time, Crosstab queries provided an innovative solution to a common problem in data analysis: the desire to present data in a crosstab type of format. To pull off this trick, Microsoft added non-standard features to its implementation of SQL. If you've been following our "See the SQL" sidebars, you'll find that Crosstab queries use non-standard SQL keywords.

Pivot tables, on the other hand, weren't part of Access until the 2002 edition appeared. As will be seen, pivot tables allow for the presentation of data in a crosstab format, but with much greater flexibility. As an added bonus, the SQL syntax of queries in PivotTable View is identical to the syntax of the Select queries you've already seen. As such, pivot tables in Access are basically Select queries presented in a special PivotTable View. The PivotTable View allows for all the features of Crosstab queries, but in a more interactive format.

After examining Crosstab Queries and pivot tables, we'll look at why one might want to export an Access pivot table to Excel and how that is accomplished. Finally, we'll close out the chapter with a look at another view option in Access called the PivotChart View.

Crosstab Queries

As mentioned, Crosstab queries have been part of Access since its inception. To illustrate this query type, we'll look at data in three tables that maintain purchases of products stocked by a hardware company. Figures 12.1 and 12.2 show the design and data in these tables.

Figure 12.1
Design View of a Select query.

PurchaseDate ▾	SupplierName ▾	Description ▾	Quantity ▾	PricePerItem ▾
7/11/2011	Measure Up	wood yardstick	5	2
7/11/2011	Pliable Pliers	2 inch needle nose pliers	10	4
7/11/2011	Sam's Screws	1 inch #10 wood screws	3	2
7/12/2011	Pliable Pliers	Glasswork pliers	5	10
7/12/2011	Sam's Screws	1 inch wire brads	8	1.25
7/12/2011	Sam's Screws	2 inch #8 metal screws	12	1
7/13/2011	Measure Up	8 foot tape measure	4	2.25
7/13/2011	Measure Up	metal yardstick	5	3.2
7/14/2011	Measure Up	wood yardstick	3	2
7/14/2011	Pliable Pliers	2 inch needle nose pliers	10	4

Figure 12.2
Datasheet View of a Select query.

As seen, the Purchases table has information on the purchase date, quantity, and price per item. The Products table has a description of the product, and the Suppliers table has the name of the supplier. The data in Figure 12.2 shows ten purchases made between 7/11/2011 and 7/14/2011.

With this data in mind, let's say we want to get information on total purchases by date and supplier. To accomplish this with an ordinary Select query, we need to use aggregation to group sales by both date and supplier. The design for such a query would be as shown in Figure 12.3.

Field:	PurchaseDate	SupplierName	Total Purchase: Sum([Quantity]*[PricePerItem])
Table:	Purchases	Suppliers	
Total:	Group By	Group By	Expression
Sort:	Ascending	Ascending	
Show:	✓	✓	✓
Criteria:			
or:			

Figure 12.3
Design View of a Select query with aggregation.

In this query, we're grouping by PurchaseDate and SupplierName. The summed field is a calculated field, consisting of Quantity times PricePerItem. When run, the results appear as in Figure 12.4.

Select Query with Aggregation		
PurchaseDate ▾	SupplierName ▾	Total Purchase ▾
7/11/2011	Measure Up	10
7/11/2011	Pliable Pliers	40
7/11/2011	Sam's Screws	6
7/12/2011	Pliable Pliers	50
7/12/2011	Sam's Screws	22
7/13/2011	Measure Up	25
7/14/2011	Measure Up	6
7/14/2011	Pliable Pliers	40

Figure 12.4
Datasheet View of a Select query with aggregation.

From this query, we can see that there were $10 of purchases made on July 11 from the Measure Up supplier. Since the results are sorted by date, we can easily add the total purchases amounts from the first three lines to get total purchases on 7/11/2011.

If we wanted to determine total purchases during this time period from Measure Up, we would need to sort by SupplierName.

The problem with this query, and in fact with all Select queries, is that its primary emphasis is on rows. The dynamic aspect of the query lies with how many rows are returned when the query is run. The columns in a Select query merely contain the various bits of information we want to show for each row. In contrast, Crosstab queries allow for a more dynamic structure in which rows and columns are independent elements.

Without explanation as to how it was created, Figure 12.5 shows a Crosstab query with the same data shown in Figure 12.4.

Crosstab Query			
PurchaseDate ▾	Measure Up ▾	Pliable Pliers ▾	Sam's Screws ▾
7/11/2011	10	40	6
7/12/2011		50	22
7/13/2011	25		
7/14/2011	6	40	

Figure 12.5
Datasheet View of a Crosstab query.

In the Crosstab query of Figure 12.5, the dates are shown in rows. The value of each PurchaseDate is in the column on the far left. Likewise, suppliers are shown in columns, with the SupplierName values in the top row. All of the intersecting cells show the total Purchase amount for the corresponding date and supplier. For example, we see that we purchased $10 from Measure Up on 7/11/2011. The blank cells represent combinations for which there were no sales. For example, we can easily see that there were no purchases from Measure Up on 7/12/2011.

The advantage of the crosstab display in Figure 12.5 over the Select query of Figure 12.4 is that it is much easier to quickly find the total purchase amount for any date/ supplier combination. One merely needs to locate the appropriate row and column, and then find the intersecting cell. In contrast, the Select query forces us to scan a list of rows until the desired value is found. Let's now look at the Design View of this crosstab query, to see how it was put together. The design grid for the query is shown in Figure 12.6.

Field:	PurchaseDate	SupplierName	Total Purchase: Sum([Quantity]*[PricePerItem])
Table:	Purchases	Suppliers	
Total:	Group By	Group By	Expression
Crosstab:	Row Heading	Column Heading	Value
Sort:			
Criteria:			
or:			

Figure 12.6
Design View of a Crosstab query.

The chief addition to the design grid for Crosstab queries is the Crosstab row. This row allows four values:

- Row Heading
- Column Heading
- Value
- (not shown)

In our example, PurchaseDate is specified as a Row Heading since the dates appear on rows. Similarly, SupplierName is a Column Heading since these values are in columns. The expression with the column alias Total Purchase is specified as a Value on the Crosstab row. This means that the aggregate expression shown on the Field row will be used to calculate the values in all the intersecting cells.

Note also that the design grid has a Total row. The values in this row indicate how the columns are aggregated. The PurchaseDate and SupplierName columns are Group By columns. The Total Purchase column is an expression with the SUM aggregate function.

The "(not shown)" value for the Crosstab row isn't used in this query. This value would be used only for criteria not displayed in the query.

Several rules apply to the design of all Crosstab queries:

- There must be one or more columns specified as a Row Heading. These columns must have Group By on the Total line.
- There must be exactly one column specified as a Column Heading. This column must have Group By on the Total line.
- There must be exactly one column specified as a Value. This column must have an aggregate function, such as SUM or COUNT, on the Total line.

These rules mean that the columns that would be the Group By columns in a Select query need to be Row or Column Headings in a Crosstab query. There can be only one Value column in a Crosstab query, and this must have an aggregate function specified.

See the SQL

The SQL equivalent of Figure 12.6 is:

```
TRANSFORM SUM (Quantity * PricePerItem) AS [Total Purchase]
SELECT Purchases.PurchaseDate
FROM (Purchases
INNER JOIN Products ON Purchases.ProductID = Products.ProductID)
INNER JOIN Suppliers ON Products.SupplierID = Suppliers.SupplierID
GROUP BY Purchases.PurchaseDate
PIVOT Suppliers.SupplierName;
```

Syntax Notes:

- Crosstab queries use TRANSFORM and PIVOT keywords. These keywords are not part of standard SQL.
- The Crosstab Value column is placed after the TRANSFORM keyword.
- The Crosstab Column Heading column is placed after the PIVOT keyword.
- The Crosstab Row Heading column or columns are placed after the GROUP BY keyword.

Although Crosstab queries can have only one Column Heading or Value column, they can have multiple Row Heading columns. To illustrate, let's modify the query of Figure 12.6 so the SupplierName and Description are both Row Headings. We'll use PurchaseDate as the Column Heading. The query now appears as in Figures 12.7 and 12.8.

Field:	SupplierName	Description	PurchaseDate	Total Purchase: Sum([Quantity]*[PricePerItem])
Table:	Suppliers	Products	Purchases	
Total:	Group By	Group By	Group By	Expression
Crosstab:	Row Heading	Row Heading	Column Heading	Value
Sort:				
Criteria:				
or:				

Figure 12.7
Design View of a Crosstab query with two Row Headings.

Crosstab with Two Row Headings					
SupplierName ▾	Description ▾	7/11/2011 ▾	7/12/2011 ▾	7/13/2011 ▾	7/14/2011 ▾
Measure Up	8 foot tape measure			9	
Measure Up	metal yardstick			16	
Measure Up	wood yardstick	10			6
Pliable Pliers	2 inch needle nose pliers	40			40
Pliable Pliers	Glasswork pliers		50		
Sam's Screws	1 inch #10 wood screws	6			
Sam's Screws	1 inch wire brads		10		
Sam's Screws	2 inch #8 metal screws		12		

Figure 12.8
Datasheet View of a Crosstab query with two Row Headings.

As shown, there are now two columns that function as Row Headings: SupplierName and Description. The values in the intersecting cells apply to the values in the column heading and in both row headings. For example, the crosstab shows $16 of purchases of metal yardsticks from the Measure Up supplier on 7/13/2011.

The PivotTable View

One of the great innovations of Microsoft Excel was the introduction of Pivot Tables in Excel 5, which was released in 1993. Similar functionality was added to Access in its 2002 version by way of the PivotTable View.

To illustrate how the PivotTable View works, we'll start with the Select query shown in Figure 12.1. One modification will be needed. Rather than having separate columns for Quantity and PricePerItem, we'll need a column with an expression that computes a total purchase amount. Such a design is shown in Figure 12.9.

Field:	PurchaseDate	SupplierName	Description	Total Purchase: [Quantity]*[PricePerItem]
Table:	Purchases	Suppliers	Products	
Sort:	Ascending	Ascending	Ascending	
Show:	☑	☑	☑	☑
Criteria:				
or:				

Figure 12.9
Design View of a Select query.

The Datasheet View of this query is identical to Figure 12.2, except that there would be only a single Total Purchase column in place of the Quantity and PricePerItem columns. To switch this query to a Pivot Table, we merely select PivotTable View from the View command under the Design tab on the Ribbon. The screen then appears as in Figure 12.10.

Figure 12.10
PivotTable View of a Select query.

Notice that a new Design tab appears on the Ribbon under a PivotTable Tools heading. This Ribbon has all the commands pertinent to the manipulation of pivot tables. At this point, the pivot table itself is empty. The work area shows the four areas of a pivot table:

- Row Area
- Column Area
- Filter Area
- Data Area

Since the pivot table contains no data, we see four corresponding sets of instructions:

- Drop Row Fields Here
- Drop Column Fields Here
- Drop Filter Fields Here
- Drop Totals or Details Fields Here

Comparing the areas of the PivotTable View to the components of an Access Crosstab query, the Column and Row Field areas correspond to Crosstab Column and Row Headings. The Data Area corresponds to the Values column of a Crosstab query. The Filter Area is an added feature of pivot tables not found in Crosstab queries.

We also see a PivotTable Field List window at the far right of the screen. This window can be shown or hidden by clicking the Field List command button on the Ribbon. This field list contains all fields originally selected in the underlying Select query, as well as additional fields calculated entirely within the PivotTable View.

As an interactive tool, the pivot table allows you to drag fields in the PivotTable Field List to any of the four areas of the pivot table. Alternatively, one can select a field in the PivotTable Field List and click the Add To button to add the field to a desired area. If you should decide to use the Add To button to move fields to the work area (rather than dragging fields), you'll find that it actually offers five choices for target areas, rather than the expected four:

- Row Area
- Column Area
- Filter Area
- Data Area
- Detail Data

The Data Area and Detail Data selections both refer to the Data Area. When you move fields to Detail Data, it keeps the data at the detail level, which allows you to later aggregate the data within the Pivot Table by various means such as Sum, Count, and Average. However, when you specify that you want to move data to the Data Area, you're essentially losing the detail. It immediately aggregates the data by Sum. That means you can no longer perform other aggregations on the data such as Count or Average.

We recommend always specifying Detail Data when you use the Add To button to move fields to the Data Area of a pivot table. Note that if you forgo the Add To button and simply drag fields to the Data Area of a pivot table, it is always moved as Detail Data. For that reason, we recommend simply dragging fields to and from the pivot table rather than using the Add To button. This reduces confusion. The forthcoming example will clarify the distinction between the Data Area and Detail Data.

To create the equivalent of the Crosstab query shown in Figure 12.5, we merely need to move the PurchaseDate field to the Row Area, the SupplierName field to the Column Area, and the Total Purchase field to the Data Area. We'll drag the fields directly from the PivotTable Field list to the appropriate areas of the work area. The PivotTable View then appears as in Figure 12.11.

PivotTable View				
	SupplierName ▾			
	Measure Up	Pliable Pliers	Sam's Screws	Grand Total
	+ −	+ −	+ −	+ −
PurchaseDate ▾	Total Purchase ▾	Total Purchase ▾	Total Purchase ▾	No Totals
7/11/2011	10	40	6	
7/12/2011		50	10	
			12	
7/13/2011	9			
	16			
7/14/2011	6	40		
Grand Total				

Figure 12.11
PivotTable View of a Select query, with detail data.

At this point, we're still seeing a detail view of our data. For example, if you look at the cell that intersects 7/12/2011 with Sam's Screws, it shows two separate purchases of 10 and 12. It doesn't sum them to 22, as would normally be the case in a pivot table. Similarly, the Grand Total rows and columns don't yet show any values. That is because we have not yet specified how we want to aggregate the detailed data.

To add aggregation to the PivotTable View, we merely need to click any cell in the Data Area of the pivot table, and then the AutoCalc command in the Tools section of the Ribbon. This command can be seen in Figure 12.10. One is then presented with these aggregation options:

■ Sum

■ Count

■ Min

■ Max

■ Average

■ Standard Deviation

■ Variance

■ Standard Deviation Population

■ Variance Population

After selecting Sum, the PivotTable View appears as in Figure 12.12.

Figure 12.12
PivotTable View of a Select query, with detail and total data.

We now see both the detail data and total data, with aggregation by Sum. We also see values in the Grand Total column and row. For example, we can see that the purchases on 7/12/2011 from Sam's Screws of 10 and 12 now sum up to 22. However, the combination of both detail and total data is somewhat difficult to look at and decipher. To alleviate the problem, we'll click the Hide Details button on the Ribbon. We'll also click the Drop Zones button on the Ribbon so we don't see the "Drop Filter Fields Here" message in the Filters Area of the pivot table. The result is shown in Figure 12.13.

Figure 12.13
PivotTable View of a Select query, with total data.

We now see only total data. Let's now take another look at the PivotTable Field List window, shown in Figure 12.14.

Figure 12.14
PivotTable Field List.

Notice that the Field List now includes a new Sum of Total Purchase field. This field was added automatically when we selected the Sum aggregation on the AutoCalc button. Notice also the PurchaseDate By Week and PurchaseDate By Month fields. These fields are provided automatically because Access recognizes the PurchaseDate field as a Date/ Time field.

Another important piece of functionality available in the PivotTable View is the ability to select specific values of the row and column fields for display. For example, one can click the down arrow in the PurchaseDate cell, and be presented with a list of all dates, as shown in Figure 12.15.

Figure 12.15
Selection for the PurchaseDate field.

One can then check or uncheck individual dates to remove them from the display. This doesn't affect the underlying Select query; it only affects what's currently seen in the PivotTable View.

One of the major advantages of pivot tables over Crosstab Queries is that they are much more interactive. With a few keystrokes, one can transform this query by selecting different fields from the Field List, or by arranging them in a different format. As an example, let's modify the query by placing the PurchaseDate in the columns and the SupplierName in rows. We'll also change the Sum of Total Purchase to a count. This is done by dragging the fields to their new positions, and adding a new Count AutoCalc field. Finally, we'll also utilize the selection pane shown in Figure 12.15 to deselect 7/13/2011 and 7/14/2011. The results are shown in Figure 12.16.

PivotTable View Modified			
PurchaseDate ▾			
	7/11/2011	**7/12/2011**	**Grand Total**
	+ −	+ −	+ −
SupplierName ▾	Count of Total Purchase	Count of Total Purchase	Count of Total Purchase
Measure Up	1		1
Pliable Pliers	1	1	2
Sam's Screws	1	2	3
Grand Total	3	3	6

Figure 12.16
PivotTable View of a Select query.

The next piece of pivot table functionality we'll discuss is their ability to let the user perform *drill down* and *drill up* operations on data. The term *drill down* refers to a hierarchical movement through data, from summary to more detailed data. For example, one might want to drill down from a calendar month to a day in that month. The term *drill up* is the reverse process. To illustrate, we'll add the Description field to the Row Area of our most recent PivotTable View. We'll also switch our aggregation from counts back to sums. Since products are related to the supplier name, this is a natural hierarchy, in the sense that each product belongs to one and only one supplier. After adding the Description field to the pivot table of Figure 12.16, we see the PivotTable View of Figure 12.17.

Notice how we now see a hierarchical structure in the Row Area, leading from each supplier to the products they provide. Subtotals are provided automatically for each supplier. What may not be obvious in Figure 12.17 is that there is now an added layer of interactive functionality in this data. One can double-click on any supplier to collapse the products shown under that supplier. This is the drill up functionality. One can also double-click on collapsed cells to drill back down again.

For example, if we double-click on the Pliable Pliers cell in Figure 12.17, we see results as in Figure 12.18.

PivotTable View with Drill Down					
			PurchaseDate ▼		
			7/11/2011	7/12/2011	Grand Total
			+|-|	+|-|	+|-|
SupplierName ▼	Description	▼	Sum of Total Purchase	Sum of Total Purchase	Sum of Total Purchase
⊟ Measure Up	wood yardstick	+−	10		10
	Total	+−	10		10
⊟ Pliable Pliers	2 inch needle nose pliers	+−	40		40
	Glasswork pliers	+−		50	50
	Total	+−	40	50	90
⊟ Sam's Screws	1 inch #10 wood screws	+−	6		6
	1 inch wire brads	+−		10	10
	2 inch #8 metal screws	+−		12	12
	Total	+−	6	22	28
Grand Total		+−	56	72	128

Figure 12.17
PivotTable View of a Select query, with two fields in the Row Area.

PivotTable View with Drill Down					
			PurchaseDate ▼		
			7/11/2011	7/12/2011	Grand Total
			+|-|	+|-|	+|-|
SupplierName ▼	Description	▼	Sum of Total Purchase	Sum of Total Purchase	Sum of Total Purchase
⊟ Measure Up	wood yardstick	+−	10		10
	Total	+−	10		10
⊞ Pliable Pliers		+−	40	50	90
⊟ Sam's Screws	1 inch #10 wood screws	+−	6		6
	1 inch wire brads	+−		10	10
	2 inch #8 metal screws	+−		12	12
	Total	+−	6	22	28
Grand Total		+−	56	72	128

Figure 12.18
PivotTable View of a Select query, after a Drill Up operation.

All the detail for Pliable Pliers has been collapsed up to the SupplierName level. If we double-click on Pliable Pliers one more time, we'll again see the detail in Figure 12.17. As a side point, note that the drill up and drill down operations can also be accomplished by clicking on the small plus and minus signs shown in these cells.

The power of drill down and drill up operations cannot be overemphasized. One of the primary attractions of pivot tables is their ability to drill into data in a literal sense, letting users move from summary data to underlying data with a simple click.

The final piece of functionality we'll demonstrate is the ability to use the Filter Area of the pivot table to add additional selection criteria. The PivotTable View of Figure 12.18 shows two different dates in the Columns Area: 7/11/2011 and 7/12/2011. Let's suppose that we want to select on only those two dates, but don't need to see a breakdown of purchases by day. To accomplish that, we can drag the PurchaseDate field from the Column Area to the Filter Area. The result is shown in Figure 12.19.

PivotTable View with a Filter		
PurchaseDate ▾		
(Multiple Items)		
SupplierName ▾	Description ▾	Sum of Total Purchase
⊟ Measure Up	wood yardstick	10
	Total	10
⊟ Pliable Pliers	2 inch needle nose pliers	40
	Glasswork pliers	50
	Total	90
⊟ Sam's Screws	1 inch #10 wood screws	6
	1 inch wire brads	10
	2 inch #8 metal screws	12
	Total	28
Grand Total		128

Figure 12.19
PivotTable View of a Select query with a filter.

The PurchaseDate field is now in the Filter Area. This dictates that all data shown in the rest of the pivot table reflects the exclusions specified in the filter. The "(Multiple Items)" description means that multiple dates have been selected. If the down arrow in the PurchaseDate cell is clicked, the drop-down pane will display the data shown in Figure 12.15, except that only 7/11/2011 and 7/12/2011 will be checked. Note that this PivotTable View has nothing in the Column Area. Unlike Crosstab queries, there is no requirement in pivot tables that data must be present in both rows and columns.

One final point to emphasize in all of the PivotTable View transformations we've seen is that nothing we've done has altered the original Select query. If, at any point, we switch our view back to Design View, we'll see the same query shown in Figure 12.9. Likewise, if you've been following our "See the SQL" sidebars, nothing in the underlying SQL has changed. All of the transformations shown in Figures 12.10 through   12.18 have affected only the PivotTable View. Since pivot tables are completely interactive, the PivotTable View always shows the most recent state of the pivot table.

Let's recap the main features of the Access PivotTable View, focusing on those features of PivotTable Views that aren't available in Crosstab Queries:

- **Interactivity.** Unlike Crosstab queries, PivotTable Views are completely interactive. One can drag fields around, double-click on cells to drill down, and select specific values.

- **Flexibility.** PivotTable Views allow for any number of fields in the Row, Column, or Data areas. In contrast, Crosstab Queries require exactly one field in the Column and Data areas, and at least one field in the Row Area.

- **Filtering.** PivotTable Views permit any number of fields to be used as filters. This doesn't affect selection in the underlying Select query.

- **Drill Down.** When multiple related fields are placed side by side in either the Row or Column Area, one can drill down and up from one field to the next.

- **Detail Data.** Unlike Crosstab queries, which only show aggregated values, PivotTable Views can display the underlying detailed data beneath aggregations. One has the option to display or hide detail data.

- **Data Selection.** In addition to the Filter area, PivotTable Views allow one to select specific values to display in the Row or Column areas. Additionally, one can select specific values for fields in the Data Area at the detail level.

Even with all these features, we haven't hit all the capabilities of Access pivot tables. More functionality can be discovered by exploring the various commands in the Tools section of the Ribbon under the PivotTable Tools Design tab.

Exporting to Excel Pivot Tables

Once a PivotTable View is created and manipulated to the desired layout, one has the option of exporting that pivot table to Excel. As will be seen in Chapter 16, "Excel Pivot Tables," there are quite a number of differences between Access and Excel pivot tables. Excel pivot tables offer substantially more options in the way of formatting. Whereas Access offers one Ribbon with commands specific to its PivotTable View, Excel has two full Ribbons with commands for its pivot tables. Additionally, the pivot table interface in Excel is generally easier to work with and clearer in its design. Specifically, Excel tends to be much more understandable with reference to showing detail and totals in its pivot tables. Whereas Access allows you to view detailed and summarized data simultaneously, Excel separates it out so that detailed data is visible only via a separate *drillthrough* operation. These differences will be covered in Chapter 16.

The process of exporting an Access PivotTable View to Excel is simple. While in PivotTable View, you'll find a command named Export to Excel in the Data area of the PivotTable Tools Design Ribbon. After clicking this command, Access will instantly open an Excel worksheet with a Pivot Table that corresponds to the current state of your PivotTable View. To illustrate, Figure 12.20 shows the Excel file that is generated after clicking the Export to Excel command while in the PivotTable View shown in Figure 12.19.

	A	B	C
1	PurchaseDate	(All)	
2			
3	Sum of Total Purchase		
4	SupplierName	Description	Total
5	⊟ Measure Up	wood yardstick	10
6	Measure Up Total		10
7	⊟ Pliable Pliers	2 inch needle nose pliers	40
8		Glasswork pliers	50
9	Pliable Pliers Total		90
10	⊟ Sam's Screws	1 inch #10 wood screws	6
11		1 inch wire brads	10
12		2 inch #8 metal screws	12
13	Sam's Screws Total		28
14	Grand Total		128

Figure 12.20
Excel Pivot Table after an export from a PivotTable View.

After the export to Excel has been done, the created HTM web page needs to be saved manually in the desired Excel format. The normal procedure would be to save it as an Excel worksheet with an XLSX suffix.

It should also be noted that this operation to save PivotTable Views as an Excel pivot table is available only as a manual step within the PivotTable View. Unfortunately, Access doesn't provide a macro with similar functionality. The Export macro in Access only exports data in the Datasheet View format.

The PivotChart View

We now turn to a topic related to pivot tables: the PivotChart View. Like the Pivot-Table View, the pivot chart provides another way to view data in a way that can't be accomplished within the Datasheet View. Although the focus of this book is not on charts and graphs, we'll provide enough basic information on the PivotChart View to get you started with its functionality.

The PivotChart View is related and tied to the PivotTable View. Any changes made to the PivotTable View cause corresponding changes to the PivotChart View, and vice versa. As we have seen, the PivotTable View allows users to interactively place fields in one of four areas: Filter, Data, Rows, and Columns. The PivotChart View has these four areas:

■ Filter Area

■ Data Area

■ Category Area

■ Series Area

The Filter and Data areas correspond to the Filter and Data areas of the PivotTable View. The Category Area corresponds to the Row Area of the PivotTable View. The Series Area corresponds to the PivotTable Column Area. On top of these four layout areas, the PivotChart View also allows the user to select between 12 different chart types. For each of these chart types, there are any number of sub-types that refine the chart appearance. The basic chart types are:

■ Column

■ Bar

■ Line

■ SmoothLine

■ Pie

■ XY (Scatter)

■ Bubble

■ Area

■ Doughnut

■ Radar

■ Stock

■ Polar

Let's begin by creating a basic Bar chart from the PivotTable View shown in Figure 12.13. This query had PurchaseDate in the Row area, SupplierName in the Column area, and TotalPurchased in the Data Area. TotalPurchased was aggregated by SUM. To convert this to a PivotChart, we merely go to the View command in the Ribbon and switch it to

PivotChart View. After doing so, we see a Column chart appear, along with a new Ribbon, named PivotChart Tools Design. Additionally, we'll click the Legend command in the Show/Hide section of the Ribbon, which causes the SupplierName values to appear. We then see the chart shown in Figure 12.21.

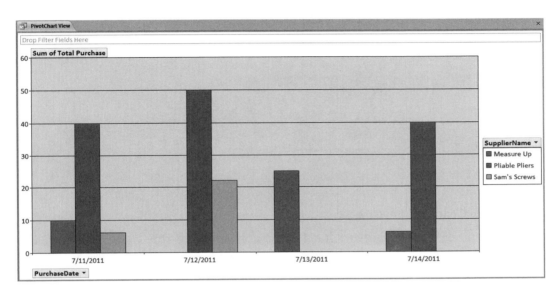

Figure 12.21
PivotChart View of a Select query, with a Clustered Column chart.

A few items to point out: First, since this is our first use of a PivotChart for this query, Access automatically selected a Clustered Column chart. This is the default chart type. Since the PurchaseDate was in the Row Area of the PivotTable, it now appears in the Category Area of the PivotChart. This means that the PurchaseDate values are shown along the bottom horizontal axis. Similarly, since SupplierName was in the Column Area of the PivotTable, that field now appears in the Series Area of the PivotChart. As a result, the SupplierName values are shown in the Legend on the far right. The TotalPurchased sums appear in the Data Area of the PivotChart. There is no filter.

This chart shows a breakdown of SupplierName within PurchaseDate. Since each supplier is shown in a separate column, this provides an easy way to see which supplier provided the most goods on any particular date.

Let's take a quick look at two areas of the PivotChart Tools Design Ribbon to see some of the other design options. These are shown in Figures 12.22 and 12.23.

Figure 12.22
Left side of the PivotChart Tools Design Ribbon.

Figure 12.23
Right side of the PivotChart Tools Design Ribbon.

Of prime importance is the Change Chart Type command in the Type section of the Ribbon. This allows you to instantly change the chart to any of 12 chart types and numerous additional sub-types. Including all the sub-types, there are over 60 available charts. The Property Sheet command allows you to specify all the normal formatting for charts. The Drop Zone command in the Show/Hide section is a toggle that causes the areas of the PivotChart to be visible or hidden. Likewise, the Field List command is a toggle that causes the Chart Field List to appear. As with the PivotTable View, you can drag fields from the Chart Field List directly to any PivotChart area to change the configuration of the chart. Another important capability is provided by the Switch Row/Column command in the Active Field section of the Ribbon. This allows you to quickly switch the Row and Column fields, which correspond to the Category and Series areas of the chart. For example, if we were to select this command, the PurchaseDate would become the Series, and the SupplierName would become the Category.

Coverage of the more than 60 chart types is well beyond the scope of this book. However, we'll make a few remarks about appropriate use of Column, Bar, and Pie charts. First, it should be noted that Column and Bar charts are basically identical except for the fact that Column charts run vertically, while Bar charts are horizontal. Aside from the 3D variants of Column (or Bar) charts, there are three basic types of Column charts:

- Clustered Column
- Stacked Column
- 100% Stacked Column

The Clustered Column chart was shown in Figure 12.21. By clicking the Change Chart Type command, one can easily switch to the other two types of Column charts. Figure 12.24 shows the Stacked Column variation.

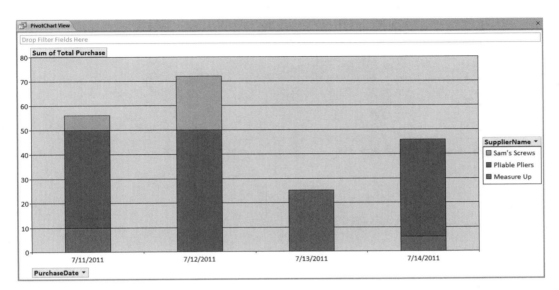

Figure 12.24
PivotChart View of a Select query, with a Stacked Column chart.

Unlike the Clustered Column chart, the Stacked Column chart has only one column per category, which in this example is the PurchaseDate. The values for each SupplierName in the series are proportionately allocated in each column. This allows us to easily compare the total purchases for each day, as well as see a relative breakdown of each day's purchases by supplier. Figure 12.25 shows another variant, the 100% Stacked Column chart.

The 100% Stacked Column of Figure 12.25 is identical to the Stacked Column of Figure 12.24, except that all data is now shown as a percentage. Each column now has an equal length, so we can no longer compare the total purchases for each day. However, we can now more easily comprehend the relative contributions of each supplier to the day's purchases. In a way, the 100% Stacked Column chart is directly comparable to the traditional Pie chart, in that it expresses values in terms of percentages of the total column or pie. Unlike the Pie chart, however, a series of columns can be shown so one can see, for example, how relative percentages change over time.

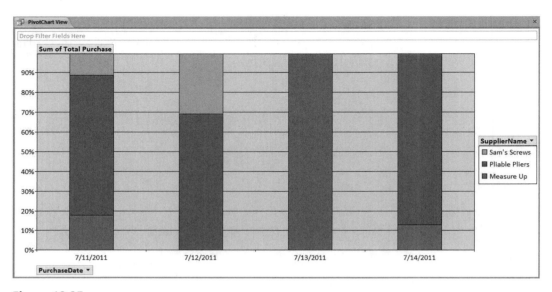

Figure 12.25
PivotChart View of a Select query, with a 100% Stacked Column chart.

Focus on Analysis: Histograms

The histogram is a standard graphical tool used in statistics to get a sense of the distribution of a set of data. When analyzing data, the AVG aggregation can provide a single statistic that indicates the center of a set of data. However, it's often useful to assess how values are distributed. Histograms can be easily generated in Access for numeric data, using the PARTITION function and the PivotTable and PivotChart Views. We've encountered the PARTITION function already in Chapter 9, but we'll now see how data from that function can be converted into a graphical format.

To create a Histogram, we need to start with a query with two essential columns. One column will have numeric values to be evaluated. The second column will use the PARTITION function to create a label describing the range of numbers to which the value belongs. As seen in Chapter 9, the template for the PARTITION function is:

Partition («number», «start», «stop», «interval»)

The Number parameter is the name of the field to be evaluated. Start and Stop are the beginning and ending numbers of the total range. Interval is the desired interval for each individual range. To illustrate, for a table of student grades ranging from 1 to 100, one can use this expression to create range labels:

Range: PARTITION (Grade, 1, 100, 5)

In this example, Range is the column alias. Grade is the name of the column being evaluated. The lowest possible grade is 1 and the highest is 100. We want to report grades in ranges with increments of 5. As an example, for grades between 86 and 90, the PARTITION function will return this value: 86:90. In the Datasheet View, our query will have two relevant columns: Grade and Range. The Grade column will be the individual grade, and the Range will have the label for the range.

The next step is to view this query in PivotTable View. After doing so, we'll move the Grade to the Data area and the Range to the Row area. We'll also use the AutoCalc command to create a Count of the Grade field. We need to apply a COUNT rather than a SUM, because histograms are a count of individual values.

The final step is to view this query in PivotChart View. Since we already set up our data in the PivotTable, we should see the Grade in the Category area and the Range in the Data area. The default Clustered Column chart type works best for a histogram. The result will look like the following:

Grades histogram.

Looking Ahead

We began this chapter with a look at Crosstab queries, Microsoft's first attempt to add crosstab capabilities to ordinary Select queries. Crosstab queries provide some solid advantages over Select queries. However, the newer PivotTable technology offers similar analysis capabilities with much greater flexibility. As a completely interactive tool, the PivotTable View offers many possibilities for interacting with your data. Capabilities of the PivotTable View include drill down, filtering, and the ability to view data at both detail and summary levels.

We also made special mention of the ability to export the Access PivotTable View directly into Excel pivot tables. This is actually quite an important feature, and one that will be made use of in our discussion in subsequent chapters on Business Intelligence strategies.

PivotChart Views are another tool that allows you to view data in a purely visual way. Some chart types, such as the basic Pie chart, are geared toward making a simple and obvious point for a presentation. However, more sophisticated chart types, such as Line and Scatter charts, offer greater opportunity for gaining insight by observing patterns in your data.

The coverage of pivot tables in this chapter leads directly to our discussion of Business Intelligence topics in the upcoming chapters. As it turns out, a significant aspect of the user interface commonly utilized in Business Intelligence applications is directly related to the structure of pivot tables. Thus, our understanding of pivot tables gained in this chapter will prove relevant to Business Intelligence concepts.

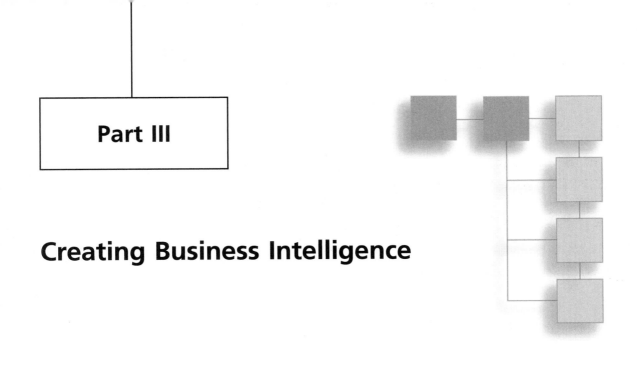

Part III

Creating Business Intelligence

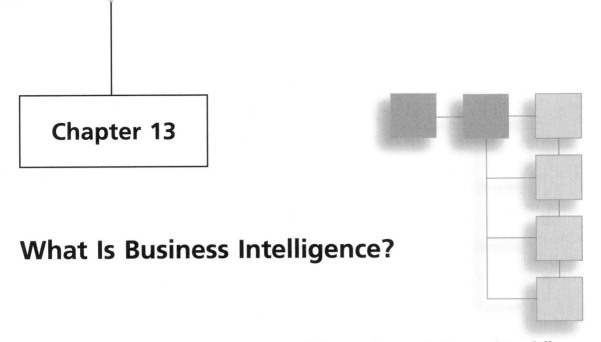

Chapter 13

What Is Business Intelligence?

In Chapter 1, we explored the meaning of data analysis and discussed its different aspects: data, visual, and quantitative. We'll now broaden that discussion to include the topic of business intelligence.

If you were to pick up ten books on business intelligence (or BI) and look at how the authors define the subject, you will surely find ten distinct explanations. Business intelligence is one of those terms that means different things to different people. Additionally, its meaning has evolved over time as the capabilities of actual BI software have changed.

In many ways, business intelligence is strictly a marketing label, and it's a very good one. The key word is *intelligence*. Many years ago, when mainframes ruled the world of computerized systems, the field of computing was known as *data processing*. The main currency of the machines was data, which was said to be processed by complex computerized systems. As time went on, the crassness of mere data was replaced by the search for *information*. Departments of Data Processing were renamed Information Systems, and computerized systems were seen as a source of information for the business. With the advent of business intelligence, information has been replaced with true *intelligence*, and as if intelligence weren't enough, these BI systems are also sometimes referred to as a component of *knowledge* management.

So yes, there is a bit of marketing hyperbole that occurs when terms like business intelligence are thrown around to describe systems and software. However, there is also an underlying reality to the hype, and that's what we want to explore.

Just as data analysis represents the desire to foster greater understanding of the data underlying business processes, business intelligence also starts with a desire for greater analytical understanding. The difference, however, is that there are major software companies offering specific products in the business intelligence realm. Thus, unlike data analysis, BI tends to be more product specific. It therefore makes sense to include in our exploration of business intelligence a look at a few products that carry the label. After looking at the capabilities of those products, we'll be able to infer a definition as to what the term really means.

It is the contention of this book that business intelligence can be seen as a natural extension of traditional data analysis. Additionally, as we look at the various components of business intelligence, we'll emphasize those aspects relevant to Microsoft Access. Our goal will be to find ways to implement a form of business intelligence in Access.

Data Warehouses

Business intelligence can refer either to the capabilities of specific software tools, or to a general process that involves using data to gain intelligence for an organization. However, before we can talk about what business intelligence means, it's helpful to focus on the underlying physical reality. Behind any software system, there always lies data. Moreover, the specifics of how that data is organized always affect the resulting processes that utilize the data. In the case of business intelligence, the underlying data structure is usually referred to as a *data warehouse.*

Depending on one's definition, some aspects of business intelligence can be said to exist without an underlying data warehouse. However, for purposes of discussion in this book, we'll assume that BI always requires some sort of data warehouse in order to function.

In many ways, data warehouses were the precursor to today's business intelligence systems. Back in 1992, Bill Inmon published the influential book, *Building the Data Warehouse*, which presented his findings on this relatively new subject. In that book, he proposed the building of a data warehouse as a way to capture business information for further analysis. In a later book, *Using the Data Warehouse* by Inmon and Hackathorn (1994), the main characteristics of a data warehouse were identified as it being:

- Subject oriented
- Integrated
- Time variant
- Nonvolatile

The subject orientation of a data warehouse means that it is aligned with the subject matter of the business rather than individual applications. The integrated characteristic means that the data warehouse contains a single view of organizational data. Rather than store data as referenced in the myriad applications an organization may use, it is standardized and made consistent. The time variance of a data warehouse is a key component. Unlike operational systems, which tend to offer a current view of data, the data warehouse is organized along time dimensions, allowing data to be analyzed as of any moment in time. Finally, the nonvolatility of a data warehouse means that it's a stable, non-changing environment. Since data in a data warehouse isn't generally updated once it's been inserted into the database, it can be counted on producing consistent results, no matter when the analysis is done.

The reasons for building a data warehouse, as made clear by Inmon, presented organizations with a powerful incentive to initiate this type of undertaking. However, it took a while for technology to catch up to the desire. Many of the techniques for building a data warehouse in the early nineties would not be applicable today. In fact, the entire notion of what a data warehouse entails has changed as the software for building and maintaining a data warehouse has evolved.

Even today, there are many ways in which data can be organized into something that can be referred to as a data warehouse. We'll review some of the software used for this purpose later in this chapter. For now, however, we'll simply state that, in physical terms, there are two basic types of data warehouses:

- Relational databases
- Multidimensional cubes

A data warehouse stored as a relational database is one that can be accessed via SQL. Microsoft Access can be used to retrieve data from such a database, since Access uses SQL as the underlying mechanism to view data. This type of database consists of numerous tables, which can be joined together in the usual way. In the early days of data warehousing, a relational database would commonly be designed with a normalized data structure, as discussed in Chapter 6. However, one of the more recent advances in data warehouse thinking has emphasized a special design structure known as a *dimensional model*. This approach has been championed by Ralph Kimball, who, along with Bill Inmon, is generally acknowledged as one of the chief architects of the modern data warehouse. Ralph Kimball's book, *The Data Warehouse Toolkit*, first published in 1996, has been instrumental in this regard.

What is a dimensional model? In essence, a dimensional model is a broader term for the star schema design briefly discussed in Chapter 6. We'll explore dimensional models in detail in our next chapter, but for now we can reiterate that this type of model is primarily about organizing data into one or more central fact tables surrounded by any number of dimension tables. Dimension tables contain information about basic organizational entities, such as customers or products. One particular dimension that is ubiquitous in all dimensionally designed data warehouses is the time dimension. This special dimension allows users to perform analysis against time. Fact tables contain additive fields, also known as *measures*, that can be summed up across any number of dimensions. An example of a measure would be an Order-Amount field.

One of the key design elements stressed by Kimball was the need for *conformed dimensions*. This essentially means that, if properly designed, dimensions can be used in multiple data warehouses within an organization. Whereas Inmon tended to emphasize a structure with a single data warehouse, Kimball advocated the development of multiple data warehouses for an organization. The presence of conformed dimensions guarantees that a customer dimension in one data warehouse will have the basic structure as a customer dimension in another data warehouse, thus adding both conformity and flexibility.

The whole idea of dimensional modeling is actually quite analogous to the pivot table technology discussed in the previous chapter. The fact tables of a dimensional model contain data that is appropriate for the data area of a pivot table. The dimension tables of a dimensional model contain data that can be used in the row, column, or filter areas of a pivot table.

What all this means is that, in today's world, data warehouses created as relational databases tend to use the dimensional model for their design.

At this point, let's review the major benefits of creating a dimensionally designed relational data warehouse from an underlying operational database. The first advantages are those initially identified by Inmon: that it is subject oriented, integrated, time variant, and nonvolatile. These benefits apply to any type of data warehouse. However, a relational database with a dimension design has these additional advantages:

- **Intuitive.** Since data has been organized into a dimensional design, retrieval is more understandable. There are fewer tables to be joined, and the analyst can more readily comprehend the data structure. The dimensional structure implies that the organization of the data corresponds to typical business entities, such as customers, products, and suppliers.

- **Quick Retrieval.** A simplified structure with fewer tables means that data retrieval tends to be quicker, since there are fewer tables to be joined together.

■ **A Time Dimension.** Dimensional designs typically include an explicitly defined time dimension. This allows the analyst to more easily compare data across different periods of time, and also take the unique time attributes of the organization, such as the fiscal year calendar, into consideration.

The second main type of data warehouse is the *multidimensional cube*. This special data structure stores dimensionally modeled data in an extremely efficient manner for subsequent data retrieval. In common usage, multidimensional cubes are also known as *OLAP cubes*. OLAP stands for "online analytical processing" and is meant to be contrasted with OLTP databases, where OLTP stands for "online transactional processing." Whereas OLTP databases are standard operational relational databases, suitable for general retrieval or updating, OLAP cubes are specifically designed for retrieval along dimensional lines.

Unlike data warehouses physically stored as a relational database, multidimensional cubes (or OLAP cubes) have a more proprietary structure that varies by vendor. Due to their unique structure, SQL cannot be used to retrieve data from a cube. Instead, cubes rely on a language known as MDX (multi-dimensional data expressions) to retrieve their data. The proprietary structure of cubes means that an analyst cannot simply open up a database and view the OLAP cube as can be done in a traditional DBMS (database management system) such as Microsoft SQL Server. In other words, a cube doesn't contain anything like the tables found in traditional databases. Instead, one needs to first design the cube, usually based on data that resides in a relational database, and then generate it with the provided cube software. Once it is created, MDX can then be used to access its contents.

This means that software such as Microsoft Access can't be employed to access a cube. However, all vendors of software that create cubes also provide software that can be used to access data in the cube. For example, Microsoft allows users to connect to and retrieve data from cubes with Excel pivot tables.

It should also be noted that, although MDX is often used behind the scenes to retrieve data from cubes, the ordinary user would not typically need to utilize MDX statements. As an order of difficulty beyond SQL, MDX presents challenges that the average analyst probably would not want to tackle. Fortunately, with appropriate software, data retrieval from cubes is generally more intuitive than from relational databases, and therefore reduces the necessity of using MDX.

In some regards, the development of OLAP cubes can be considered an optional step. Many organizations create a relational data warehouse and stop there. There are many advantages to simply having a relational data warehouse with a dimensional design. However, there are also some specific reasons why the leap to a cube structure is greatly beneficial. Some of the advantages of multidimensional cubes over dimensional relational databases include:

- **Extremely quick retrieval.** The process of building a cube typically involves a step in which the data is scanned to create *aggregations*. This means that the cube will contain pre-aggregated quantities that provide quick answers to the most commonly requested combinations of data. These aggregations can be calculated in advance. For example, when a cube contains pre-aggregated values, if a user requests total sales from June 2011 for customer x, involving product y, the cube might already contain the answer to that question without having to run a query. If a user asks for sales for June and July 2011 for that same customer and product, the cube merely needs to add up the pre-aggregated numbers for June and July to get the answer. In addition to these aggregations, the proprietary nature of the cube means that data is stored in a highly compressed structure designed for efficient data retrieval. As a result, data retrieval from a cube tends to be much quicker than from SQL-based relational databases.

- **Interactivity.** As with pivot tables, the interface to a cube can be completely interactive, giving the user complete control over the data and layout of the retrieved data.

- **Hierarchical structures.** In cubes, dimensions can be designed with built-in hierarchical structures. For example, a time dimension can be designed to automatically drill down from year to month to day. A customer dimension can be designed to drill down along geographic lines from country to state to zip to the individual customer. The ability to drill down or drill up through dimensions is related to these hierarchical structures. Additionally, hierarchical structures typically include the ability to handle parent–child relationships, which allow for an unlimited number of levels in the hierarchy.

- **Drill-through capabilities.** Similar to pivot tables, cubes typically allow one to perform a drill-through operation, so one can view the detailed data underlying summarized values.

- **Semi-additive measures.** Certain types of dimensions have special requirements as to how drill-down functionality works in those dimensions. For example, financial dimensions that model a company's general ledger typically have special requirements as to how drill down works for different types of accounts. Cube functionality typically has provisions for these types of special situations.

- **Write-back capabilities.** When write-back functionality is enabled for a cube, users can drill down to a desired cell, and then write a value to the cube itself.

This scenario can be useful for applications such as a budget cube, where financial analysts may want to update a budget with their own values.

Now that we've discussed some of the characteristics of relational data warehouses and multi-dimensional cubes, the next issue to examine is how these two structures are created. There are as many ways to create a data warehouse as there are organizations, but in general, a number of procedures are usually followed.

In building a data warehouse, one begins with one or more production databases with operational data. The first step is to somehow move data from these databases into one or more data warehouses. The simplest case is one in which an organization has a single operational database with all necessary information stored in a well-designed normalized structure. More typically, one faces a situation with multiple databases and additional organizational knowledge stored informally in spreadsheets. In more complex situations, one typically wants to first create replicated copies of operational databases so that subsequent queries don't adversely affect performance. Second, one usually wants to create special databases that serve as a bridge between the operational database and the relational data warehouse. Such databases are commonly referred to as *staging databases*. Staging databases are often needed to clean up and transform data prior to its being inserted into a data warehouse. The entire process of moving data from operation databases to a relational data warehouse database is generally known as ETL—or extract, transform, and load. Most BI vendors provide software to assist in this process.

Whether the data comes directly from an operational database or a staging database, the next step is to move data from that database to the relational data warehouse. The main emphasis in this process is in transforming the normalized data in an operational database to a dimensional design. We'll talk about this process in detail in Chapter 15, "The Data Warehouse."

Once the dimensional data warehouse is created, the next step is to create a multi-dimensional cube from that relational database. The process of building a cube from a relational database is usually handled by vendor-specific software. In general, there are four steps to the process:

1. **Identify the source data.** A connection needs to be made to the relational data warehouse and to any auxiliary sources of data.

2. **Define the cube structure.** If the relational database already has a dimensional design, this is fairly easy. The dimensions of the cube will correspond to dimension tables in the relational data warehouse. The cube measures will correspond

to fields in the fact tables. However, certain structures specific to a cube need to be added, such as dimensional hierarchies and custom measures.

3. **Define aggregations.** As mentioned, one of the benefits of a cube is that it allows the designer to create pertinent aggregations in advance. Sophisticated cube software is able to look at the queries that users have previously issued in order to determine an optimal set of aggregations for the cube.

4. **Create the cube.** After aggregations are defined, the cube needs to be processed to actually create the cube from the specified design definitions. After the cube has been successfully created, queries can be issued against the data.

Survey of Microsoft BI Software

Now that we've acquired an initial understanding of data warehouses, we can return to our original question: What is business intelligence? We'll begin by looking at some of the software offerings in the BI world to get a better sense of what it's all about. In doing so, we'll want to look at software that allows developers to build data warehouses, and also software utilized by end users to browse through relational data warehouses or cubes.

We'll keep our overview focused on Microsoft software, as it's most applicable to Access users. Since Access databases can be easily migrated to the more fully featured Microsoft SQL Server, it helps to be aware of some of the complementary BI offerings from Microsoft. In our brief survey, we'll include a few screenshots to give a sense of what the software looks like. After presenting this overview of Microsoft software, we'll follow up with a few comments about some of the other major BI vendors.

Microsoft Business Intelligence software revolves around three products:

- SQL Server
- Excel
- Sharepoint Server

The primary product is SQL Server, the current version of which is SQL Server 2008 R2. In addition to its database management capabilities, the Standard and Enterprise versions of SQL Server include three major components specific to business intelligence:

- Reporting Services
- Analysis Services
- Integration Services

The Reporting Services component allows for the creation of reports that can retrieve data from either a relational database or a cube, via SQL or MDX, respectively. In addition to creating reports, Reporting Services can also be used to configure a Reporting Server that holds all these reports and allows user access. The reports can be organized in a custom directory structure. A great number of interactive features can be designed into the reports, allowing such things as parameter selection, drill down, and links to other reports or web pages. Reports can be designed in either a tabular or a matrix structure, and can also include embedded charts. The matrix structure is similar to the crosstab reports we have already seen. In addition to providing the ability to run reports in an interactive fashion, Reporting Services also permits users or administrators to set up report schedules, allowing reports to be run automatically and delivered via email or placed in an appropriate directory for future user access.

The Analysis Services component allows for the creation of OLAP cubes from any source data. Although Analysis Services includes a built-in browser for developer use, end users will typically use other software to access the data in cubes after they're created.

Integration Services is an ETL tool (extract, transform, and load) with numerous elements that organize, merge, and filter data. This sophisticated visual tool can accomplish much of what would normally require complex SQL statements. Integration Services can be used to apply complex transformations of data from the operational source to the data warehouse.

Excel is put forth as the key tool for access to OLAP cubes built via Analysis Services. Excel pivot tables serve as the primary user interface for user access to cubes. When connected to cubes, pivot tables exhibit additional functionality that isn't available when pivot tables are based on non-cube data. Additionally, Microsoft recently released a newer product called PowerPivot. This add-on to Excel extends pivot table functionality beyond what is possible with standard pivot tables. The capabilities of Excel pivot tables, along with some additional information on PowerPivot, will be covered in Chapter 16, "Excel Pivot Tables."

The Sharepoint Server applies to applications other than business intelligence but is basically a tool for allowing web-based collaboration of documents. This can include Excel worksheets with pivot tables connected to cubes.

To provide a better picture of what this software can accomplish, we'll look at a few representative screenshots. Starting with Reporting Services, Figure 13.1 shows the Design View of a basic query.

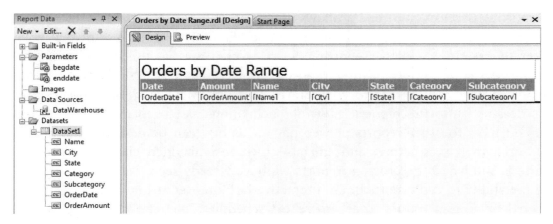

Figure 13.1
Design View of a report in Reporting Services.

The Report Data pane on the left lists some of the elements of the report. This includes the parameters of the report, along with the *dataset*, which is basically just the SQL query on which the report is based. The main pane on the right shows a report title, along with the fields that will be displayed on the report. Just as the Microsoft Access Design View is a graphical view of a SQL statement, this Design View also relies on an underlying SQL statement. The SQL can be seen by opening up the dataset as a query, as shown in Figure 13.2.

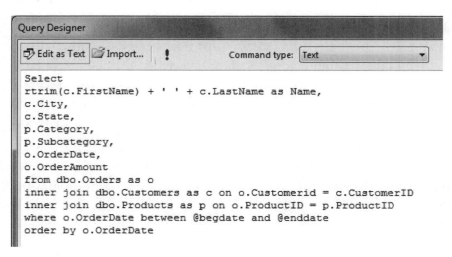

Figure 13.2
Dataset query of a report in Reporting Services.

This dataset happens to consist of a single SQL statement, but Reporting Services also allows developers to build more complex procedures, with multiple SQL statements, as the basis of the datasets that lie behind reports. Notice that the second-to-last line refers to two parameters, @begdate and @enddate. These parameters will be seen when the report is run. Just as in Access, datasets can be set up with parameters. In Reporting Services, parameters can be easily associated with additional SQL statements, allowing you to display currently allowable values for parameters in a dynamic fashion.

To view the report, one simply clicks on the Preview tab seen in Figure 13.1. When this is done, we see the screen shown in Figure 13.3.

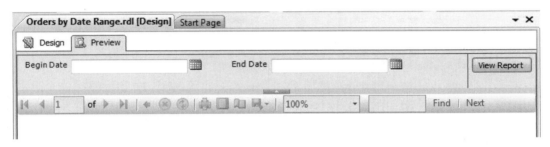

Figure 13.3
Parameter prompt for a report in Reporting Services.

At this point, we're prompted to enter the two parameters, Begin Date and End Date. After entering appropriate values and clicking the View Report button, we see the screen in Figure 13.4.

Everything we've seen so far has been in using Reporting Services as a design tool. Once a report has been tested and ready to use, it is typically deployed to a Report Server, where users can access and run the report. After the report has been deployed, a user might sign on to the Report Server and see a screen such as shown in Figure 13.5.

This figure shows the reports in an Orders Reports directory. An administrator can set up any number of directories in a hierarchical structure. Windows-based security can be applied so that different users will see only those directories appropriate for their use. After selecting the desired report in this directory, the user enters any required parameters and then executes the report. If the Orders by Date Range report is selected, the results would be the same as shown in Figure 13.4.

Reporting Services offers a great deal of flexibility when it comes to report design. In addition to the tabular report seen in Figure 13.4, reports can be designed with a matrix or drill-down structure, and include charts and graphs, links to other reports and subtotals. The number of available features is substantial. Just to give two final examples, Figures 13.6 and 13.7 show similar queries presented in drill-down and matrix formats.

Figure 13.4
Testing a report in Reporting Services.

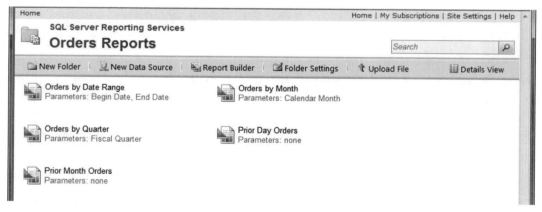

Figure 13.5
Reporting Services report directory.

The reports in Figures 13.6 and 13.7 have transformed the data into a completely different presentation. One of the strengths of Reporting Services is in its layout options and ability to present data in interesting ways. In fact, the SQL statements used in Figures 13.4, 13.6, and 13.7 are all identical. Only the design of the layout differs.

Figure 13.6
A report with drill down in Reporting Services.

Figure 13.7
A matrix report in Reporting Services.

Turning to Analysis Services, we'll run through a similar exercise by connecting to the same data and then using the software to create a cube. Figure 13.8 shows a portion of a screen in Analysis Services that is used to design a cube.

The right pane in Figure 13.8 shows the Solution Explorer for the project being worked on. The name of the project is Chapter 13 Cube. There are four important components to the project: Data Sources, Data Source Views, Cubes, and Dimensions. The Data Source has information about the connection to the underlying database. The Data Source View shows all the relevant tables in that database and the relationships between the tables. The three Dimensions shown are Products, Customers, and Time. Finally, the Orders Cube defines the cube itself. A graphical view of this cube is shown in the Data Source View pane, seen on the left side of Figure 13.8.

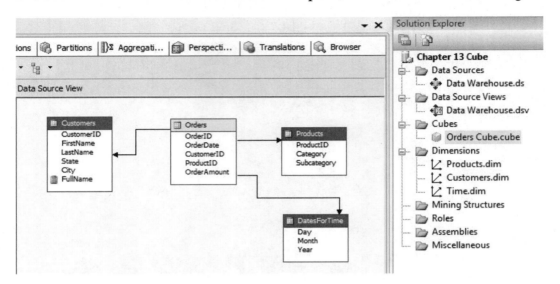

Figure 13.8
Analysis Services Solution Explorer and Data Source View of a cube.

Once the cube is designed, the next step is to create the cube and deploy it to a server. Once that is done, the cube can be viewed via any appropriate software. Microsoft provides both Reporting Services and Excel as tools that can connect to their cubes. When using Reporting Services, specific reports can be designed, but Excel is a more general structure that allows full interactivity with the cube via its pivot table interface. Figure 13.9 shows an Excel pivot table connected to a cube created from the design shown in Figure 13.8.

The left pane in Figure 13.9 shows the PivotTable Field List. The right side of the figure shows the actual pivot table. Notice that the PivotTable Field List breaks down the fields into measures, dimensions, and hierarchies. For example, the Customers dimension of the cube design is now clearly marked as a dimension. Within the Customers dimension, we see a Geographic Hierarchy consisting of State, City, and Customer Name. This dimension and hierarchy was created in Analysis Services. Similarly, the Products dimension has a hierarchy consisting of Category and Subcategory. The Time dimension has a Year-Month-Day hierarchy that allows for drill down from year to month to day. As with all Excel pivot tables, any elements in the PivotTable Field List can be moved into the rows, columns, filter, or data areas of a pivot table, and additional filtering can be applied.

PivotTable Field List

Choose fields to add to report:

- ☐ Σ **Orders**
  - ☑ Order Amount
  - ☐ Orders Count
- ☐ 🗂 **Customers**
  - ☐ ☑ **Geographic Hierarchy**
    - State
    - City
    - Customer Name
  - ⊞ 🗂 More fields
- ☐ 🗂 **Products**
  - ☐ ☑ **Product Hierarchy**
    - Category
    - Subcategory
  - ⊞ 🗂 More fields
- ☐ 🗂 **Time**
  - ⊞ 🗂 Year-Month-Day
  - ⊞ 🗂 More fields

	A	B	C	D	E	F	G
1	Order Amount			Category			
2	State	City	Customer Name	Accessories	Paint	Paper	Pens
3	AZ	Phoenix		20			
4	CO	Denver	Elizabeth Salt	5			
5			Thomas Knull	15	22		16
6	FL	Miami	Alison Cooper		5		4
7			Sara Durkin		10		
8		Tampa	Jose Sanchez	19	4		
9	IL	Chicago	Astoria Grant				15
10			Sandy Nesbitt			5	
11		Urbana	Alice Kanter			26	
12	VT	Burlington	Bob Lesser	20			
13							
14							
15							
16							
17							
18							
19							
20							
21							

Figure 13.9
An Excel Pivot Table connected to a cube created in Analysis Services.

With our survey of Microsoft BI software complete, let's mention some of the business intelligence offerings from a few other vendors. We'll limit this discussion to these companies: Oracle, IBM, SAP, SAS, and MicroStrategy. Since software products are always changing, you may want to refer to appropriate websites for current information about these products. The current websites for the business intelligence offerings from Microsoft and these other vendors are:

- Microsoft: microsoft.com/bi
- Oracle: oracle.com/bi
- IBM: ibm.com/software/data/businessintelligence
- SAP: sap.com/solutions/business-intelligence
- SAS: sas.com/technologies/bi
- MicroStrategy: microstrategy.com

Oracle has a multitude of BI products, including a version of its mainstay database, known as OBIEE (Oracle Business Intelligence Enterprise Edition). Like SQL Server, this database has a full range of reporting and OLAP cube features. OBIEE is a direct descendant of Siebel Analytics, which was acquired when Oracle purchased Siebel Systems in 2006. A second notable offering from Oracle is its Essbase database, one of the earliest OLAP cube products in the market. Oracle acquired Essbase when it purchased Hyperion in 2007. Oracle provides Excel add-ins for end user access for both Essbase and the Oracle OLAP cube.

IBM's business intelligence offerings stem largely from its 2007 purchase of Cognos, a major developer of BI products. Aside from Cognos business intelligence software, which includes a complete suite of BI tools, IBM also offers several complementary products. Cognos Express is a lower-end version geared toward midsized organizations. Cognos TM1 is an analytical tool designed specifically for budgeting and forecasting. Cognos Analytic Applications offers focused analysis packages for areas such as sales, workforce performance, and supply chain. Another notable offering from IBM related to the BI space is SPSS Statistics, a fully functional set of statistical software.

Just as IBM bought Cognos in 2007, SAP purchased Business Objects during that same year. As such, SAP's BI offerings come largely from that acquisition. SAP's main BI offering is their BusinessObjects Business Intelligence Platform, a fully featured BI product. One notable component of SAP's offering is Crystal Reports, a complete reporting solution, comparable to Microsoft's Reporting Services.

SAS's BI offerings include the full range of reporting and OLAP capabilities. Their main products are Enterprise BI Server and Business Visualization software. SAS stresses its leadership in the business analytics field as one of its strengths. They emphasize that their Business Analytics software enhances their BI products by providing a view into the future, to complement BI's emphasis on past history.

Finally, MicroStrategy is unique among the companies we're mentioning in that it is solely focused on business intelligence. Their products include MicroStrategy Report Services, MicroStrategy OLAP Services, MicroStrategy Office, and MicroStrategy Desktop.

Business Intelligence Revisited

Our survey of business intelligence software has hopefully provided a general idea of the various claims and capabilities of BI tools. As a marketing label, business intelligence is often defined very broadly and overlaps other similar concepts and labels such as:

- Data Warehouses
- Decision Support Systems
- Knowledge Management

- Analytics
- Data Mining

We've already mentioned that there is a strong connection between data warehouses and BI. Whereas business intelligence represents specific software or processes, data warehouses tend to refer to the associated data structures.

Decision Support Systems (or DSS) is an older term that predates both data warehouses and business intelligence. DSS refers to software systems that assist with business decision making. In many ways, this concept is a more academic variant of the business intelligence label. The decision support systems literature tended to emphasize the importance of model selection and the user interface as being equally important to the data and database itself. Influential books in this area have included *Building Effective Decision Support Systems* by Ralph Sprague and Eric Carlson, published in 1982.

Knowledge management is a much newer concept. It tends to emphasize the knowledge generated from business intelligence systems, and the subsequent generation of additional knowledge. The field is not as software specific as BI, and focuses more on the social interactions necessary for maintaining a knowledge-aware organization.

On the quantitative side of the spectrum, we have concepts such as *analytics* and *data mining*. Analytics is a relatively new approach—popularized by Thomas Davenport and Jeanne Harris's *Competing on Analytics*, published in 2007—and emphasizes the application of quantitative modeling to business problems. Data mining is a more specific quantitative technique that has found its home in several business intelligence products. For example, Microsoft's Analysis Services has a feature that allows for the creation of data mining models. You may have noticed a Mining Structures component in Figure 13.8. Analysis Services allows you to create data mining models based on data contained within a cube or relational database. In brief, data mining employs advanced statistical procedures to discern patterns with a dataset. Microsoft, for example, offers nine basic types of quantitative techniques with which to explore data, including Decision Trees, Clustering, and Time Series Analysis.

As seen in these comparisons, business intelligence is a concept that can defined in a very broad sense. It can be compared with more esoteric concepts such as knowledge management, and also overlaps the complex quantitative techniques used in data mining. However, we now want to focus on those aspects of business intelligence that directly relate to what can be done with Microsoft Access.

In thinking about what distinguishes business intelligence from other analytical processes, one can certainly make the case that it has much to do with the crosstab presentation of data popularized by Excel pivot tables. The ability to view data across multiple categories, or dimensions, allows patterns to be seen that might otherwise escape attention.

A second and equally significant aspect of business intelligence has to do with its adoption of the dimensional model. Whether the data is stored in a relational database or in an OLAP cube, the organization of data into measures and dimensions is a significant aspect of the BI experience. As noted, several aspects of multidimensional cubes exceed the capabilities of relational databases, but either way, the dimension structure is key. Certainly, a significant feature of the dimensional model is that it is simpler and easier to comprehend than the traditional normalized model. As such, the dimensional model, with its categorization of data into streamlined dimensions, such as Customer, Product, and Time, allow the business analyst to view data in a more intuitive manner.

In terms of the general applicability of BI to Access, we can also note that business intelligence tends to be non-quantitative by nature. In our narrow definition of BI, we can exclude the quantitative pursuits of data mining, analytics, and statistics, and still be left with valuable techniques that assist with data exploration.

To sum up, our narrow definition of business intelligence includes these features:

■ Organization of data along the lines of a dimensional model

■ Presentation of data in a crosstab, matrix, or pivot table structure

What really makes business intelligence work as a unified software system is that the dimensional modeling concepts neatly complement pivot table and cube technology. In other words, the capabilities of the available technology are sufficient to handle theoretical concepts and designs.

Access and Business Intelligence

The next question to be asked is how Microsoft Access fits into the BI picture. Our contention is that Access complements the main concepts and goals of business intelligence in several significant ways. First, Access is a tool for managing data. The ability of Access to manipulate data via SQL-based queries means that it can transform any data set into a format appropriate for business intelligence analysis. In the next two chapters, we'll explore the concepts of dimensional modeling and learn how Access can be used to transform data into a dimensional design.

Secondly, by providing a PivotTable View for Select queries, Access allows the analyst to easily transform data into this useful structure. Just as Excel can be used to connect pivot tables to OLAP cubes, Access pivot tables can yield a similar type of experience for the end user. Furthermore, if one prefers to use Excel pivot tables, Excel pivot tables can be set up to connect to Access databases.

In the early part of this chapter, we identified the two basic types of data warehouse as:

- Relational databases
- Multidimensional cubes

In terms of creating data structures, Access can certainly be used to create a relational database. This is true of both normalized databases and databases with a dimensional design. Additionally, the Relationship Manager of Access can be used to relate all tables so subsequent queries utilize relationships properly. It should be stressed that the ability of Access to create Linked Tables means that no data need actually reside in an Access database. As such, Access can be seen as an effective *organizer* of data. By linking to production tables and then reorganizing them into a dimensional model, Access can, in effect, create a sort of virtual data warehouse.

With regard to multidimensional cubes, Access can't create OLAP cubes, but with the PivotTable View, it can create a pivot table structure that contains many of the features of OLAP cubes. Additionally, as will be demonstrated in Chapter 16, one can also use Excel pivot tables to connect directly to data in Access databases.

However, business intelligence is not just about organizing data, but also about providing a useful user interface to access that data. On that front, Access has some very nice capabilities. While not as sophisticated as a full-featured reporting tool like Reporting Services, Access does allow for the creation of a complete reporting application. Although not emphasized in this book, Access forms and macros allow developers to create complete client-based applications. One can develop any number of queries and organize them in any desired manner. Access files can even be turned into a standalone application that can be initiated from the Windows Start menu.

Even with these capabilities of Access, there are a number of significant limitations. As a tool for managing data, Access can't match the sophistication of a full-fledged server database such as SQL Server. Although Access can be used to query production data via Linked Tables, few organizations would want to store their production data in an Access database. In addition to the their security and backup capabilities, software such as SQL Server offers much greater flexibility and power in terms of creating procedures for accessing and maintaining data.

As a reporting tool, a significant limitation of Access is that is client based. Access databases are generally distributed as individual files on a PC. Unlike newer tools like Microsoft's Reporting Services, Access queries can't be deployed to a Reporting Server, allowing web-based access.

As such, Access would not generally be recommended as a production database or as a general reporting tool for a larger organization. However, even with these limitations, Access does still have one very important practical advantage over these more powerful server solutions: it resides on the desktop of many analysts. As such, it can be easily used for smaller development efforts, without affecting or interfering with production systems. Also, its ability to interact with Excel lends importance to its use as an analytical tool.

Additionally, since it is SQL based, queries developed in Access can be easily transferred to other production environments. In fact, entire Access databases can also be migrated to SQL Server.

With these qualities in mind, Access is a flexible development tool, both for analysts and systems professionals. In essence, aside from building cubes, Access can accomplish much of what server-based BI products can accomplish. At the very least, Access can be used as a low cost development or learning tool for BI products, allowing the analyst to later migrate queries and data to more sophisticated software environments.

Looking Ahead

This chapter has taken a long and leisurely detour from Microsoft Access to discuss business intelligence, with an eye toward explaining its relevance to Access and data analysis. The main thrust of our argument is that business intelligence can be seen as a natural extension of the data analysis process. To the many varied techniques and goals of data analysis, business intelligence adds a certain sense of structure to the pursuit.

We began the chapter with an exploration of data warehouses, a necessary precursor to business intelligence software. We emphasized that there are two types of data warehouses: relational databases and multidimensional cubes. For data warehouses built as relational databases, there are two variants: those that use a normalized structure and those that rely on a dimensional model. The dimensional model is seen as increasingly relevant, as it nicely complements the capabilities of BI software. We also discussed some of the advantages of multidimensional cubes over relational databases.

We then took a slight detour into Microsoft BI software, showing examples of Reporting Services and Analysis Services. In our brief tour, we demonstrated both the design and user interfaces of those products. Hopefully, this provided some additional insight into the capabilities of BI software.

After presenting additional definitions of business intelligence and some competing concepts, we discussed the applicability of BI concepts to Microsoft Access. Emphasizing its role as an organizer of data, and also its PivotTable capabilities, we outlined a number of ways in which Access can be used to extend data analysis concepts into the business intelligence realm.

In our next chapter, we'll take another brief detour from Access to go over the dimensional model in greater detail. This chapter can be seen as a complement to Chapter 6, which covered normalization in relational database design. The design techniques learned in our next chapter will then be applied in Chapter 15, "The Data Warehouse." In that chapter, we'll run through the steps that can be used to create a data warehouse in Microsoft Access.

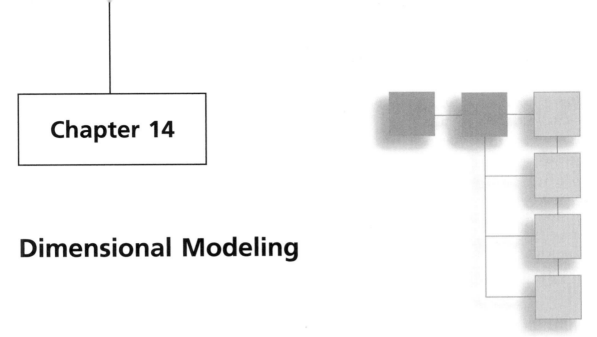

Chapter 14

Dimensional Modeling

In Chapter 6, we discusssed the basics of relational database design, with special attention given to the process of normalizing data. For the majority of operational systems, sometimes referred to as OLTP systems (online transactional processing), normalization is the gold standard of how data should be organized. To be more specific, normalization is essential in reducing the effort involved in updating data. When data is properly normalized, changes to a customer address should only affect a modification to a single row in a Customer table. If a product now costs an organization four dollars instead of three, that should affect only a single row in a Product table.

In contrast to the world of OLTP systems, however, business intelligence systems are primarily about retrieving data. From a retrieval perspective, the ability to reduce the number of tables that must be joined together in a query contributes to the simplicity of the process. Simplicity also helps when presenting a data structure to a data analyst. Thus, in the world of business intelligence, the *denormalization* of data is often seen as a strategic benefit. This is where dimensional modeling comes in.

In our last chapter, we tossed around a number of terms related to dimensional modeling: dimension tables, fact tables, measures, and hierarchies. Before applying these concepts to Microsoft Access queries, let's take some time to explore these concepts in greater detail, and outline some of the basic design principles of dimensional modeling.

Star and Snowflake Schemas

In the final section of Chapter 6, we presented a brief "alternative to normalization" that showed how to turn a normalized design for a Grades database into a dimensional model. The dimensional model shown in Figure 6.8 is often referred to as a *star schema*. In common usage, star schemas are given the same meaning as dimensional models, but there is one small difference. Whereas dimensional modeling is the more general and inclusive term, star schemas refer to a specific type of dimensional model in which there are one or more fact tables at the center of the schema, surrounded by any number of dimension tables. In a star schema, each dimension must be represented by only one table. One common variation of the star schema, known as a snowflake schema, will be discussed later in this chapter.

Let's begin our discussion of star schemas with an example of what such a design looks like, shown in Figure 14.1.

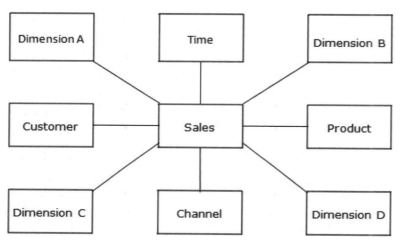

Figure 14.1
A typical star schema.

In the simplest case, star schemas consist of a single central fact table, surrounded by and connected to dimension tables. In this example, the Sales table is the fact table. In a dimensional model, fact tables usually contain numeric fields that are additive in nature. These numeric fields are often referred to as *measures*. They are also sometimes simply called *facts*. In a Sales table, the measures (or facts) might include fields such as SalesAmount and OrderQuantity. These fields are additive in the sense that if one selects 100 records and adds up the quantities in these fields, the resulting sum is a meaningful number. Likewise, one can apply other numeric aggregate functions to these numbers, such as average or count and have a useful result.

Another key concept relevant to fact tables is *granularity*. The granularity of a fact table refers to the level of detail applicable to each individual row. For example, a Sales table might be designed such that there is one row per order, or perhaps one row per line item in an order. In general, it's advisable to keep the grain of a fact table as low as possible, so that details aren't lost.

Of the eight dimension tables shown in Figure 14.1, four have been given names: Time, Customer, Product, and Channel. Since all analysis includes a time element, all dimensional models include a Time dimension. Customer and Product dimensions are also common among star schemas with a Sales fact table. In this example, the Channel dimension refers to the channel in which the sale took place, such as Internet or retail. The four unnamed dimensions in Figure 14.1 represent any other applicable dimensions. For example, one might have a Contract dimension if most sales are associated with a contract. Or, one might have a Salesperson dimension if sales are associated with specific salespeople.

The dimensions are the key entities of the business that relate to the measures in the fact table. In this example, we've indicated a few dimensions that are generally associated with sales facts. However, dimensional modeling applies to many scenarios other than sales. For example, one might have a model where the central fact table contains airline flight data. In that case, the applicable dimensions might include Airports, Aircraft, Customers, Seats, and so on. Measures in the fact table might include miles flown, fare paid, and baggage weight.

In a star schema, each row in the fact table is associated with exactly one row in each of the dimension tables. For example, one row in the Sales fact table might represent sales for one particular customer, regarding one particular product on a specific day, and through a specified channel. The dimensions provide a path into the facts. If an analyst specifies that he or she wants to retrieve data for customer x on day y, then all associated fact rows for that customer and day will be retrieved. The measures for those fact rows will be summed to yield the total sales for that customer on that day.

Just as fact rows are stored at a particular level of granularity, the same is also true of dimensions. For example, a specific row in the Product dimension might represent one specific product. However, that product may be categorized as belonging to a product subcategory, which in turn belongs to a product category. For example, if a product represents a specific pencil, the subcategory might be "writing instruments" and the category might be "office supplies." This brings us to the concept of a hierarchy. In a star schema, the hierarchy of a dimension is stored entirely within one dimension table. For our product/subcategory/category example, separate fields would be set up in the dimension table to hold the subcategory and category values associated with the specific product.

In one common variant of the star schema design, the tables that define the hierarchy of a dimension are stored in separate tables. This is referred to as a *snowflake schema*. Figure 14.2 shows a snowflake schema for the tables shown in the star schema of Figure 14.1. In the snowflake schema, the Product dimension has been expanded to include two additional tables that define the product/subcategory/category hierarchy.

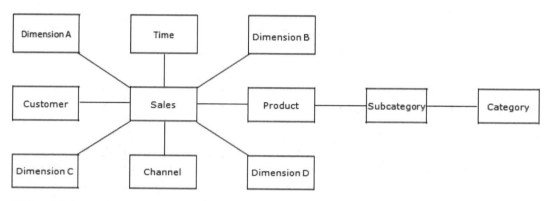

Figure 14.2
A snowflake schema.

Whereas the star schema shown in Figure 14.1 is completely denormalized, the snow-flake schema of Figure 14.2 is partially normalized, by virtue of the expanded Product dimension. It would be typical for an operational system to store codes for product categories and subcategories in separate tables. Such tables would normally contain two columns—one for the code and one for the description. The snowflake schema makes use of the same design, with a code field in the Product table pointing to the Subcategory table, where the descriptions can be found. Similarly, a code field in the Subcategory table points to the Category table.

Fact Tables

Let's now focus a bit more on some of the design possibilities for fact tables. Fact tables can contain three types of fields:

■ Foreign Keys

■ Measures

■ Attributes

To take a specific example, let's examine the details of the Sales fact table shown in Figure 14.1. We'll imagine that this star schema has just three dimensions: Time, Customer, and Product. We'll also say that this table stores rows at the order line level grain. In other words, there is one row per order line item in each order. Figure 14.3 lists the fields in the table.

Sales
TimeDate
CustomerID
ProductID
SalesAmount
SalesQuantity
OrderNumber

Figure 14.3
Fields in a Sales fact table.

The first three fields are foreign keys. These fields relate the row in the Sales table to a corresponding row in each dimension table. For example, the Time table will have a primary key field named TimeDate. The Customer table will have a primary key of CustomerID, and the Product table will have a primary key of ProductID.

The next two fields are the measures in the table. SalesAmount and SalesQuantity are additive measures that can be summed up for any set of data retrieved. If, for example, one retrieves all data from August 1, 2011, the SalesAmount field for those rows can be summed up to give the total sales for that date. Additional aggregate functions can also be applied to additive measures. For example, one can obtain a count of the rows to get a count of number of order lines.

The SalesAmount and SalesQuantity measures in this example are fully additive, which makes them easy to work with. In addition to fully additive measures, dimensional design also allows for *semi-additive* measures. These measures are only additive in certain situations. For example, if one has a fact table that stores inventory levels, those inventory values can't simply be summed up to produce a meaningful number. Inventory values can be averaged to yield an average inventory level, but even then, care must be taken that they are averaged correctly, with precisely one row per period of time.

The final field shown in Figure 14.3, OrderNumber, is an attribute field. The order number is not a key to another dimension, nor is it an additive measure. It is simply a value associated with the row in the fact table. There are basically two ways that attribute fields can be utilized. First, they can be used simply to provide additional information at a detailed level. For example, if one is viewing a summary of total order amounts for a customer, one may want to perform a *drill-through* operation to see the details for that total. In a pivot table, one can double-click on a cell to drill through to all rows for that piece of information. In that situation, the user would then be able to see the order numbers associated with the total order amount.

The second use of attribute fields in a fact table is more interesting and useful. Let's say we had another attribute field in the Sales table named Salesperson. This field would contain the name of the salesperson associated with this order. We might, in fact, have a Salesperson dimension, in which case the Salesperson field would merely be a foreign key pointing to the proper row in the Salesperson table. But it isn't strictly necessary to have a Salesperson dimension or table. We can simply include a Salesperson field in the Sales fact table without a matching dimension. This is referred to as a *degenerate dimension*. Rather than being a foreign key to another table, the Salesperson field can simply contain a value with the name of the Salesperson. When viewing the data in a pivot table, one can utilize the Salesperson field as if it were a dimension, and place it in the Rows or Columns area to see sales by those values.

We'll mention one additional design possibility for fact tables. It's entirely possible that a star schema might utilize more than one fact table. In this situation, the fact tables will be at different grains, and thus not tied to every dimension. For example, we may want to separate the Sales fact table into two separate tables—one to handle measures at the order line level, and one to handle measures at the order level. Figure 14.4 shows such a design.

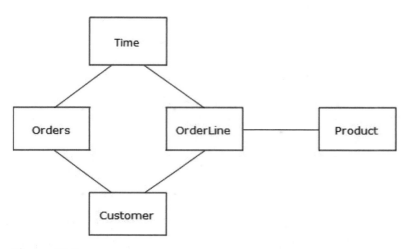

Figure 14.4
Star schema with two fact tables.

In this design, the OrderLine fact table would have those measures that pertain to the order line, such as OrderQuantity and OrderAmount. The Orders fact table would contain measures applicable to the entire order, such as SalesTax and Freight. Since the Orders fact table doesn't contain any order line information, it can't be tied to the Products dimension. This is because rows in the Orders table only relate to the entire order and not to any individual products sold.

Dimensions and Hierarchies

In a dimensional model, dimension tables are the main focus of analysis. In common language, dimensions provide the "by" elements of a query. If an analyst wants to view sales *by* customer and *by* product, then Customer and Product are suitable as dimensions for this purpose. Dimensions serve as the entry point to the desired measures in a fact table. If someone wants to see total sales by customer and month, they can use the Customer and Time dimensions to retrieve aggregate sales amounts from the fact table.

There are two types of fields in dimension tables:

- Primary Keys
- Attributes

To illustrate, we'll start with an example of a Customer dimension. Figure 14.5 shows a Customers table with a few sample fields.

Customers
CustomerID
FirstName
LastName
City
Zip
State
Country

Figure 14.5
Fields in a Customers dimension table.

In this simplified example of a Customers table, the first field, CustomerID, is the primary key. The value in this field will correspond to a CustomerID foreign key field in the fact table. All the foreign keys in the fact table will point to a primary key in a dimension table. All the other fields in the Customers table are attributes of the customer. In a normalized operational database, this information would probably be split among several tables, but in a star schema design, all information about the customer is placed into a single table.

The power of dimensions is enhanced by the fact that attributes in the dimension can be combined at will into any number of hierarchical structures. In this example, one might want to create a hierarchy that allows drill down from country to state to city to customer. Alternatively, one may want a hierarchy of country to zip to customer. In most cases, the lowest level of the hierarchy will be what's referred to as the *leaf* level, or an individual row in the table. There are many other possibilities for hierarchies. For example, an organization might have a structure of large sales regions comprised of individual states. In that case, one might want a hierarchical structure that allows drill down from a sales region to state to customer. The applicable hierarchies in a dimension are intimately related to the analytical needs and structure of the organization.

The way in which hierarchies are actually created depends on the specific technology used to access the data in the dimensional model. If Microsoft Access is used to retrieve data from a dimensional model, the data can be turned into a PivotTable view. Once in a pivot table, any fields in a hierarchy can be used in a drill-down operation, as long as the data itself supports the intended hierarchy. The hierarchy doesn't need to be defined anywhere. It's the pivot table itself that allows for drill down with these fields.

With more sophisticated reporting software, hierarchies can be specifically designed into a report. For example, if using a reporting tool such as Microsoft Reporting Services against a relational database, then drill-down elements can be added to the report based on any fields in a dimension table. This was illustrated in the prior chapter in Figure 13.6. Using a cube-building tool such as Microsoft Analysis Services, hierarchies can be created as elements within a dimension. When that dimension is later viewed in an Excel pivot table connected to the cube, the hierarchical structures will be shown explicitly. This was illustrated in Figure 13.9.

In the prior section about fact tables, we mentioned that attribute fields can be thought of as degenerate dimensions, meaning that the value of the attribute is another way of presenting a simplified dimension with only a single field. The example was given of the Salesperson field, which represents a type of virtual Salesperson dimension. Assuming that there are a small number of salespersons in the organization, it's reasonable that an analyst may want to use these values to filter or organize data. In addition to the Salesperson field, we also discussed another attribute field, OrderNumber. We didn't call OrderNumber a degenerate dimension, but in truth, it's just a matter of degree. The problem with thinking of OrderNumber as a dimension is that there are a great number of values. It would be difficult to filter or organize data by order number, since there are so many values from which to select.

This brings us to a critical observation about fact and dimension tables. In practice, it's important to design dimensions with a limited number of rows, relative to the data in fact tables. Due to the drill-down function often utilized with dimensional data, it's necessary that the number of rows presented in a drill-down situation is a reasonably small number. This consideration directly affects the design of hierarchies. If an organization has a large number of customers, hierarchies in the Customer dimension need to be designed so that one can drill down from top to bottom in a straightforward manner. One wouldn't want to select a customer from 10,000 rows. One must allow the user to drill down from 10 countries to 50 states to cities and then to individual customers.

With reference to the OrderNumber and Salesperson fields, it wouldn't be advisable to design a dimension based on order numbers. There are simply too many of them, with no meaningful hierarchical levels that can be applied. On the other hand, it would be perfectly reasonable to create a Salesperson hierarchy, since the number of salespeople is probably more manageable.

One additional note about dimensions: We mentioned previously that every record in the fact table must relate to one particular row in each dimension. In an ideal world, this would always be possible. But in the real world, there exists the possibility that a fact may not relate correctly to a dimension record. For example, one might find that an order was placed with an invalid product number. The order needs to be stored in the data warehouse even if the product is at present unknown. To resolve these types of issues, it is usually advisable to have a row in each dimension that represents an unknown condition. This allows all facts to be stored, even if some information is temporarily missing.

Slowly Changing Dimensions

The issue of changing values in dimension tables, or *slowly changing dimensions*, as it is referred to in the literature, is one that trips up the efforts of many data warehouse designs. In our last section, we glossed over the fact that dimensions contain a primary key field that relates dimension records to the foreign keys in a fact table. In fact, however, the primary key in dimension tables is a somewhat problematic field. This has to do with the fact that the data in a data warehouse is not completely static. This is especially true of dimension tables. Data in fact tables generally does not change. Once a row is added to a Sales fact table, for example, the values of the measures in that row don't generally change meaning over time.

However, the attribute fields in a dimension can and do change over time. A customer might acquire a new address. A product might be given a new description. The question naturally arises as to what to do with data that is already in the data warehouse, particularly in dimension tables, as values change.

This brings us to a discussion of primary keys in dimension tables. The first instinct of a designer is to use the same primary key found in the operational system for the data warehouse. If an operational database includes a CustomerID field for customers, that is a reasonable candidate for the primary key in a Customer dimension. However, several problems might arise from this practice. First, the CustomerID in the operational system might represent multiple customers if the value in the field is allowed to be reused. If the underlying process is not sound, the same problem will rear its head in a data warehouse. A second issue is that data moved into a data warehouse might come from multiple sources. The values of the CustomerID in the various systems may overlap.

In a desire to keep data in a data warehouse completely independent of data in the underlying operational data source, it's often suggested that *surrogate keys* be employed as the primary keys for dimensions. Surrogate keys are defined as a value not related to the primary key (sometimes called the *natural key*) of the underlying operational data. There are many reasons given for the necessity of surrogate keys. In addition to the two problems noted previously, there are other more general problems with changing dimensions, for which surrogate keys are sometimes an effective solution.

There are two basic ways of dealing with changes to dimensions over time. The two techniques are generally referred to as *Type 1* and *Type 2* changes. With Type 1 changes, the designer decides that any changes to attributes in the dimension are simply overwritten in the same record in the data warehouse. For example, if a customer changes their address, that new address is inserted into their existing row in the Customers table. This would mean, in tracking prior sales for the customer, that we lose the address of the customer at the time that the sale was made.

With Type 2 changes, an entirely new row is added for the customer with the new address. Prior fact records for the customer continue to point to the old row. New facts for the customer will point to the new row. When using the Type 2 change technique, it becomes necessary to use surrogate keys for the dimension table. This is because the multiple records for the same customer in the dimension table must have different primary keys. We can't simply use the CustomerID from the operational system as the same primary key for multiple records in the data warehouse.

The problem, however, with using the Type 2 change technique, is that it greatly complicates the maintenance of a data warehouse. Additional logic must be put in place to assign new surrogate keys when dimension attributes change, and to keep track of the correct surrogate key for a customer at any given point in time. Data retrieval is also considerably more complex since we now have multiple records in a dimension that represent the same entity.

One simple solution to this conundrum is to add additional fields to the fact table for dimensional attributes that can change over time. In this scenario, the fact record has the correct value for the attribute without having to link to a dimension table to obtain the value. As an example, let's say that we have a situation in which the customer's state can change. Unlike other address fields, such as City, we decide that it is essential that we know the customer's state at the time of the sale. To accomplish this, we can simply add a State field to the fact table. This ensures that the state is stored at the time of the sale. Even if the State field is in the fact table, it can still exist in the Customer dimension table. Whereas the fact table has the value at the time of sale, the dimension table has the state in which the customer currently resides. This is usually all the information an analyst needs, since we have both the original and current state stored in the fact and dimension table, respectively. With this technique, there is no need to add additional rows to the dimension table for changes.

To sum up the need for surrogate keys, if all the fields in a dimension are Type 1 fields, then surrogate keys are not strictly required, unless the underlying operation system(s) demand it. This is also true when the technique of adding dimensional attributes to the fact table is utilized. If Type 2 fields are utilized in a dimension, surrogate keys become a necessity.

Another aspect of the Type 1 and 2 issues is a practical matter of how to maintain dimensions. Whereas fact rows are normally just added to the database, individual dimension rows can be either updated or replaced. The simplest practice is to replace all rows in a dimension when a data warehouse is updated. If all fields in all dimensions are Type 1 fields, then we simply delete, and then insert all dimension rows that contain current values for all fields. A more complex option is to update only those rows that have been modified. When the update approach is taken, surrogate keys become more of a necessity.

The problem of maintaining changing dimensions is one we'll leave for data warehouse books. We bring up the topic only to point out some of the real-world complexities that present themselves when maintaining a data warehouse.

Looking Ahead

This chapter presented the basics of dimensional modeling. This design technique is frequently used to build data warehouses, which is in turn a basic element of business intelligence software. Unlike the normalized techniques explored in Chapter 6, dimensional modeling emphasizes a denormalized structure. In addition to being helpful with data retrieval operations, the dimensional model tends to be more in line with the needs and vocabulary of analysts. Rather than retrieve data from dozens of tables, analysts often prefer a simpler structure with basic dimensional elements such as Time, Customers, and Products. Furthermore, the star schema design neatly places all additive fields in a central fact table for easy retrieval.

We discussed the basic design elements of fact tables: foreign keys, measures, and attributes. Whereas measures provide the main *raison d'être* for fact tables, attributes also play an important part. In discussing dimensions, we focused on the design element of hierarchies and the role that they play in a drill-down operation. We then turned to some of the considerations that relate to slowly changing dimensions, and some of the possibilities for dealing with this difficulty.

In our next chapter, we'll leave theory behind and rejoin the more practical world of what can be accomplished with Microsoft Access as a business intelligence tool. We'll work through a number of queries that will allow us to build a basic data warehouse, and we'll see how that data can be assembled, organized, and productively used within Access.

Chapter 15

The Data Warehouse

In Chapter 13, we talked about the data warehouse as a structure often used as the basis for business intelligence software. By placing all relevant data in a single database, the data warehouse greatly aids data retrieval in a format useful for analysis. In Chapter 14, we extended the discussion to explain the construct of dimensional modeling—a key element in efforts to create a useful data warehouse. By separating data into facts and dimensions, a dimensional design allows the analyst to easily find and retrieve any needed data. Unlike the traditional normalized relational database design, dimensional designs translate effectively to a business intelligence type of analysis.

In this chapter, we'll take all that we've learned about business intelligence and apply it to the capabilities of Microsoft Access. The goal is to create something resembling a data warehouse from underlying operational data. Keeping in mind the ability of Access to link to external tables, we'll focus on using Access as a tool for organizing data into a useful format, following the principles of dimensional design. In the real world, powerful servers are generally needed to store and maintain data in a data warehouse. However, with smaller volumes of data, it is possible to use Access to organize data, through use of linked tables and queries, to provide an equivalent structure. This is what we'll explore in this chapter.

To illustrate the process of building a data warehouse in Access, it's necessary to have some meaningful data to work with. To that end, we created a small data set that we'll use for the examples in this chapter. In the course of running through the scenario described in this chapter, we'll develop an Access database with a number of related tables and queries. Appendix B describes where you can obtain and download a working sample of the same database used in this chapter. The Appendix also summarizes the steps covered in this chapter, and lists the tables or queries relating to each step.

In this chapter, we'll work through an exercise to design and create a data warehouse within Access. In brief, the process will involve creating dimension and fact tables to hold the main elements needed for a data warehouse. We'll then develop queries that tie the dimension and fact tables together into a proper star schema structure. We'll essentially use Access as an organizing tool to link to production data, and then create a data warehouse structure based on that data. After the data warehouse queries are created, we'll then develop a number of queries that would allow users to retrieve and analyze data in the data warehouse. This exercise will be continued in the next chapter, where we'll connect to the data warehouse using an Excel pivot table and use that pivot table for further analysis.

To summarize, the steps in the process in this chapter are:

- Create tables linked to production data.
- Create tables to store the dimensions of a data warehouse.
- Create tables to store the facts of a data warehouse.
- Create a data warehouse via a query that joins the dimension and fact tables together.
- Create queries designed to retrieve data from the data warehouse.

In creating our data warehouse, we'll bypass the complexities noted in our last chapter regarding slowly changing dimensions. By ignoring the need for slowly changing dimensions, we'll create a data warehouse in which the dimensions always contain current data. Additionally, we will also ignore the need for maintaining surrogate keys in our data warehouse. Once the decision has been made to exclude slowly changing dimensions from a data warehouse, the need for surrogate keys becomes less of an absolute necessity. As such, we'll use the natural keys from the underlying production database as keys in our data warehouse.

The steps outlined in this chapter to create a data warehouse represent a somewhat daunting endeavor. However, the general process has value for Access analysts, even if one discounts the value or necessity of creating a data warehouse. A simplified version of the previous five-step process is: 1) create tables linked to production data, 2) reorganize that data via Access queries or tables into a more useful summarized structure, and 3) create queries designed to retrieve data from the summarized structure. The point is that Access can be used to reorganize production data into a more usable format for analysis. Once the data is transformed, whether to a dimensional design or any other summarized format, it can be used for subsequent queries. One does not need to develop an entire data warehouse to make productive use of Access in this regard. In the last section of this chapter, we'll provide an example of a simplified data structure that, while not a data warehouse, still has the feel of a dimensional model.

Designing the Star Schema

In our exercise, we'll access a production database with nine tables. Figure 15.1 depicts those tables and the relationships between them.

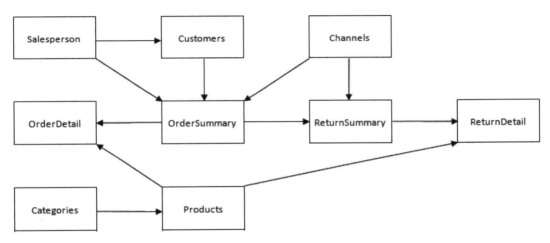

Figure 15.1
Production tables and their relationships.

All relationships in Figure 15.1 are depicted as outer joins, with the arrows indicting how the tables are related to each other. For example, the directions of the arrows show that customers can have many orders. Similarly, each OrderSummary row can have many associated OrderDetail rows. In brief:

- The Customers table has a row for every customer, and includes these attributes: FirstName, LastName, City, State, and Zip. The primary key is CustomerID. This table also has one foreign key, SalespersonID, which points to a row in the Salesperson table for this customer. This represents the salesperson currently assigned to the customer.

- The OrderSummary table has a row for every order placed, and includes this attribute: OrderDate. The primary key is OrderSummaryID. The table also has three foreign keys: CustomerID, ChannelID, and SalespersonID, pointing to rows in the Customer, Channel, and Salesperson tables for this order. In this scenario, the OrderSummaryID is not a completely meaningless number. This key represents a customer order number and is thus an important attribute of the order.

- The OrderDetail table has a row for every line item in an order, and includes these attributes: OrderQuantity, OrderPricePerUnit, and OrderCostPerUnit. The primary key is OrderDetailID. The table also has two foreign keys: OrderSummaryID and ProductID, pointing to rows in the OrderSummary and Product tables for this line item.

- The ReturnSummary table has a row for every return by a customer, and includes this attribute: ReturnDate. The primary key is ReturnSummaryID. The table also has two foreign keys, OrderSummaryID and ChannelID, pointing to rows in the OrderSummary and Channel tables for this return.

- The ReturnDetail table has a row for every line item in a return, and includes these attributes: ReturnQuantity, ReturnPricePerUnit, and ReturnCostPerUnit. The primary key is ReturnDetailID. The table also has two foreign keys, ReturnSummaryID and ProductID, pointing to rows in the ReturnSummary and Products tables for this line item.

- The Products table has a row for every product sold by the organization, and includes these attributes: Product, PricePerUnit, and CostPerUnit. The primary key is ProductID. The table also has one foreign key, CategoryID, pointing to the Categories table for this product.

- The Categories table has a row for every product category, and includes this attribute: Category. The primary key is CategoryID. This table has only three rows, representing these product categories: Coffee, Tea, and Spices.

- The Channels table has a row for each channel in which an order or return can be placed, and includes this attribute: Channel. The primary key is ChannelID. This table has only three rows, representing these channels: Internet, Mail, and Phone.

- The Salesperson table has a row for every salesperson, and includes this attribute: Salesperson. The primary key is SalespersonID.

Now that we have a sense of the data we're dealing with, the next question is how to apply the principles of dimension design discussed in the previous chapter to organize these tables and attributes into a star schema design. A good place to start is with the central fact table that forms the center of any star schema design. The candidates for this information lie in these four tables: OrderSummary, OrderDetail, ReturnSummary, and ReturnDetails.

In this situation, we have fact data at two different levels. First, we have some attributes at a summary level. The SalespersonID in the OrderSummary table applies to the entire order. However, the majority of data applies to the detail level. The quantity, price per unit, and cost per unit measures in both the OrderDetail and ReturnDetail tables applies to the detailed item line level. Generally speaking, it's desirable to have the facts in a data warehouse be at the most detailed level possible. As such, we'll create one fact table, named Sales. This table will contain information from both orders and returns, and will include certain bits of information at the summary level, such as SalespersonID.

At this time, we might ask how we can keep orders separate from returns if we are combining them in a single table. The answer to this question has to do with the magic of summation. If we store all order facts as positive numbers and all return facts as negative numbers, then we can simply sum all applicable rows and get a meaningful total amount. But what if we want to see only orders or only returns in a query? One solution is to create separate columns in the fact tables to store order and return data separately. That would allow us to select only order or return facts, as desired. However, another possibility, and the one we will follow, is to create a separate dimension that will allow us to retrieve order or return facts separately, based on a SalesTypeID code included in each fact row.

As for the dimension tables in our star schema design, there are four obvious candidates: Customer, Product, Channel, and Salesperson. The Customer dimension table is the most straightforward. All data for that dimension will come from the Customers table in the production database. The Product dimension table is a little less obvious. We have two tables that contain product information: Products and Categories. The Categories table is merely a code table that provides a description for the CategoryID column in the Products table. To avoid a snowflake schema design, we'll combine both tables into a single Product dimension table.

The Channel dimension table is simple and relates only to the Channels table. The Channels table has only three rows, representing sales by Internet, Mail, and Phone. This dimension relates to both orders and returns. In our scenario, it's possible for an order to be placed via the Internet, but an associated return for that order to come in on the phone.

Finally, the Salesperson dimension table has a code for each SalespersonID, along with the corresponding Salesperson name. Notice that we have a SalespersonID field in both the OrderSummary and Customers tables. The SalespersonID in OrderSummary identifies the salesperson who assisted with the order. We'll use the Salesperson dimension as a way to identify orders based on salesperson. In contrast, the SalespersonID in the Customers table represents the salesperson currently assigned to the customer. As such, we'll also store the Salesperson name in the Customer dimension itself.

As mentioned, we will also include a dimension that we'll call the SalesType dimension. This dimension will have only two rows, to indicate whether the associated fact is an order or a return.

In addition to Customer, Product, Channel, and SalesType, we will also want our star schema to contain a Time dimension. Since our production database doesn't contain a table specific to time, we'll need to create a table in Access to hold the elements necessary for this dimension.

Now that we've decided upon a general description of the star schema, we can lay it out on paper. Figure 15.2 depicts a dimensional database design with the previously-mentioned fact and dimension tables.

Figure 15.2
Dimensional design of the data warehouse.

Figure 15.2 depicts our fact table and six dimension tables. One final design question pertains to the Sales fact table. As noted, the OrderSummaryID field represents an order number, and is therefore something we'd like to store in the data warehouse. Why is there no Orders dimension that would allow users to look up sales by order number? The problem with an Orders dimension is that there would be simply too many orders to store. As discussed in Chapter 14, it's usually not a good idea to create dimensions with an inordinately large number of values in one level of a hierarchy. To resolve this problem, we'll store the order number as an attribute in the Sales fact table.

Creating Dimension Tables

With our star schema design in place, we will now begin to create the necessary dimension tables for the data warehouse. Before we can accomplish that, however, one necessary preliminary step is required. We'll first need to create tables that are linked to production data. In our scenario, we'll assume that we have production data stored in some other location. To create the links, we can utilize the techniques described in Chapter 3, "Tables and External Data." Linked tables can easily be established, whether the original source is an ODBC database, another Access database, or an Excel file.

A few words about naming conventions: To keep our queries and tables clear, we'll utilize prefixes for all queries and tables referenced in this chapter, to clarify the type of data they contain. All tables linked to a production source will be given the prefix "prod." Thus, the tables in Figure 15.1 will be shown as prodCustomers, prodProducts, and so on. The dimensions and fact tables shown in Figure 15.2 will be given the prefix "dim" or "fact," depending on whether it's a dimension or fact table.

Let's start with the easiest dimension: SalesType. As mentioned, the purpose of this dimension is to allow us to select rows from our fact tables that are only orders, only returns, or both. This table is unique to the data warehouse. As such, we will simply enter some values into a new table, which is shown in Figure 15.3.

Figure 15.3
Datasheet View of dimSalesType table.

The three rows in the dimSalesType table will be used to select orders or returns, as desired. The Channel dimension is also completely routine. This dimension is based solely on the prodChannel table. Figure 15.4 shows a Make Table query that creates the Channel dimension table. The resulting dimChannel table is shown in Figure 15.5.

Field:	ChannelID	Channel
Table:	prodChannels	prodChannels
Sort:		
Show:	✓	✓
Criteria:		
or:		

Figure 15.4
Design View of createChannel query.

dimChannel		
ChannelID ▾	Channel ▾
I	Internet
M	Mail
P	Phone

Figure 15.5
Datasheet View of dimChannel table.

The three rows in the Channel dimension will be used to drill into facts based on any of the indicated channels. Our next dimension, Salesperson, is similar in structure to the Channel dimension. The dimension is based on the prodSalesperson table. Figure 15.6 displays a Make Table query that creates the Salesperson dimension table, and Figure 15.7 shows some data in dimSalesperson after it is created.

Field:	SalespersonID	Salesperson
Table:	prodSalesperson	prodSalesperson
Sort:		
Show:	✓	✓
Criteria:		
or:		

Figure 15.6
Design View of createSalesperson query.

dimSalesperson	
Salesperson ▾	Salesperson ▾
1	George Kaplan
2	Christopher Newman
3	Connie Kandinsky

Figure 15.7
Datasheet View of dimSalesperson table.

The next dimension we'll tackle is the Customer dimension. This requires a slightly more complex query. In addition to prodCustomers, we'll also need to access the prod-Salesperson table to obtain the Salesperson name. Figure 15.8 shows the Make Table query used to create the table, and Figure 15.9 shows a few rows of data in the resulting table.

Figure 15.8
Design View of createCustomer query.

CustomerID ▾	CustomerName ▾	City ▾	State ▾	Zip ▾	Salesperson ▾
1	Sam Smith	Chicago	IL	60610	George Kaplan
2	Ralph Berry	Phoenix	AZ	85010	Christopher Newman
3	Lola Harvest	Seattle	WA	98104	Connie Kandinsky

Figure 15.9
Datasheet View of dimCustomer table.

Besides the join to the prodSalesperson table, the only other slight bit of complexity in the createCustomer query is the concatenation of the FirstName and LastName columns in the prodCustomers table into a single column. This nicely illustrates the ability of a data warehouse to transform data to a more appropriate format. The expression for the CustomerName column is:

- CustomerName: [prodCustomers].[FirstName] & " " & [LastName]

Like the Customer dimension, the Product dimension requires two tables as a source: prodProducts and prodCategories. Figures 15.10 and 15.11 show the Make Table query used to create the dimension, and a few rows in the resulting table.

Figure 15.10
Design View of createProduct query.

dimProduct		
ProductID ▾	Product ▾	ProductCate ▾
1	Cinnamon	Spices
2	Decaf	Coffee
3	Green Tea	Tea
4	Mustard	Spices

Figure 15.11
Datasheet View of dimProduct table.

The prodCategories table has only three rows, representing these product categories: Coffee, Tea, and Spices. Notice that we did not select the PricePerUnit or CostPer-Unit columns from prodProducts for the dimProduct dimension table. In our scenario, these two columns in the Products table give the current price and cost of each product. When an order is placed, this information is moved to the OrderDetail table, reflecting the details for orders when they are placed. The data warehouse, however, has no need for the price or cost in the Product dimension.

The Time dimension has no equivalent in the production tables. For purposes of this exercise, we'll create a table for the Time dimension with just two columns: SalesDate and FiscalQuarter. The SalesDate column will match with the OrderDate and Return-Date fields in the prodOrderSummary and prodReturnSummary tables. The

FiscalQuarter column will be used to translate this date into the correct fiscal quarter. Using the technique outlined in the Fiscal Calendars sidebar in Chapter 11, we'll create a table named dimTime. A few rows from that table are shown in Figure 15.12.

dimTime	
SalesDate	FiscalQuarter
6/1/2011	2011 Q2
6/2/2011	2011 Q2
6/3/2011	2011 Q2
6/4/2011	2011 Q2
6/5/2011	2011 Q2
6/6/2011	2011 Q2

Figure 15.12
Datasheet View of dimTime table.

Creating Fact Tables

Whereas the creation of dimension tables is relatively straightforward, the creation of fact tables is significantly more complex, for a number of reasons. First, fact table rows must contain foreign keys to every dimension table. Although these keys can be easily found, the situation is made more difficult by virtue of the fact that we're dealing with different aggregation levels. Some keys will be in the summary tables (prodOrderSummary and prodReturnSummary) and others will be in the detail tables (prodOrderDetail and prodReturnDetail). Additionally, we also have a situation in which we want to combine orders and returns together in a single table.

Another complication for fact tables is the requirement for maintenance. In our scenario for a working data warehouse, dimension tables would be refreshed daily. Other than the Time and SalesType dimensions, these tables are all created via Make Table queries that delete, and then rebuild the dimension tables with current data. However, as is normally the case with production systems, one would not want to completely refresh fact tables. By nature, fact tables are conducive to a process of adding rows to the table on a daily basis. An initial load of the table requires an insertion of rows for all available dates. After the initial load, we'll load the prior day orders and returns on a daily basis. This functionality is easily accomplished in Access by including parameters to specify a date range in our queries.

The process of appending data to our fact table, to be named factSales, will be broken down into three queries:

- As a one-time step, a createSales query will create the factSales table.

- An appendOrders query will append rows with information about orders to the factSales table.

- An appendReturns query will append rows with information about returns to the factSales table.

As mentioned in Chapter 11, an easy way to create a new table is to use a Make Table query. With the appropriate selection criteria, a table can be created without any rows in it. To accomplish this, we'll write the createSales query as if we were creating the appendOrders query to append order information to the factSales table. We'll save it as a Make Table query and then execute the query to create the table. After doing so, we'll copy the query and then change it to an Append query. Figures 15.13 and 15.14 show the createSales query.

Figure 15.13
Design View of createSales query (left side of screen).

Field:	SalesTypeID: "O"	LinePrice: [OrderQuar	LineCost: [OrderQuar	OrderNumber: OrderSummaryID
Table:				prodOrderSummary
Sort:				
Show:	✓	✓	✓	✓
Criteria:				
or:				

Figure 15.14
Design View of createSales query (right side of screen).

The nine columns in this query are described as follows:

- The SalesDate column comes from the prodOrderSummary table, and serves as a foreign key to the Time dimension.

- The CustomerID column comes from the prodOrderSummary table, and serves as a foreign key to the Customer dimension.

- The ChannelID column comes from the prodOrderSummary table, and serves as a foreign key to the Channel dimension.

- The SalespersonID column comes from the prodOrderSummary table, and serves as a foreign key to the Salesperson dimension.

- The ProductID column comes from the prodOrderDetail table, and serves as a foreign key to the Product dimension.

- The SalesTypeID column has a literal value of "O" and serves as a foreign key to the SalesType dimension. The "O" value identifies these rows as orders.

- The LinePrice column comes from the prodOrderDetail table, and contains this calculation: OrderQuantity * OrderPricePerUnit. This expression yields the total price paid by the customer for each line item in the order.

- The LineCost column is similar to the LinePrice column, but with this calculation: OrderQuantity * OrderCostPerUnit. This gives the total cost of the line item.

- The OrderNumber column comes from the prodOrderSummary table and has the value of the OrderSummaryID field. This column is provided so the user can relate the facts they are viewing to the order number.

The criteria for the SalesDate column selects rows with a date of 1/1/2000. Since this date doesn't exist in our database, this Make Table query writes no rows to the factSales table.

After the createSales query is executed, we can easily create the appendOrders query. As mentioned, we merely need to copy the createSales query, and save it with a new name. We can then change it to an Append query, specifying to append data to the factSales table. This will cause the values in the Append To line in the design grid to assume the proper column names. The final step is to modify the criteria for the SalesDate column to:

- Between [Begin Date] And [End Date]

The two parameters in this expression request the user to enter a date range for orders to be appended to the factSales table. When initiating the data warehouse, we can specify a broad date range for all data we wish to include. After the data warehouse is up and running, we can use this same query to append only the prior day's data to the data warehouse. Other than the name change and the modification to the SalesDate criteria, the appendOrders query appears exactly as in Figures 15.13 and 15.14.

With a few modifications, the appendReturns query is identical to appendOrders. The query is shown in Figures 15.15 and 15.16.

Figure 15.15
Design View of appendReturns query (left side of screen).

Field:	ProductID	SalesTypeID: "R"	LinePrice: [ReturnQ	LineCost: [ReturnQ	OrderNumber: OrderSummaryID
Table:	prodReturnDetail				prodReturnSummary
Sort:					
Append To:	ProductID	SalesType	LinePrice	LineCost	OrderNumber
Criteria:					
or:					

Figure 15.16
Design View of appendReturns query (right side of screen).

Like the appendOrders query, this is also an Append query that inserts rows into the factSales table. As such, this table has the same columns as the appendOrders query. There are, however, several differences. First, the source tables are prodOrder-Summary, prodReturnSummary, and prodReturnDetail. Second, the SalesTypeID column has a value of "R" to indicate that these rows are returns.

The third and more significant modification is that this query multiplies the Line-Price and LineCost columns by -1 to produce negative numbers. The calculation for the LinePrice column is: ReturnQuantity * ReturnUnitPrice * -1.

The fact that this number is always negative is a key feature of the dimensional design. When retrieving orders and returns together, the negative values of the returns will balance against the positive order values to produce a meaningful total sales amount.

After running the createSales query, and then the appendOrders and appendReturns queries, we can look at some data in the factSales table. Figures 15.17 and 15.18 show a few sample rows from the table.

factSales			
SalesDate ▾	CustomerID ▾	ChannelID ▾	SalespersonID ▾
6/15/2011	4	I	4
6/15/2011	7	I	5
6/15/2011	8	I	1
6/15/2011	8	I	1
6/10/2011	5	P	3
6/10/2011	6	I	2

Figure 15.17
Datasheet View of factSales table (left side of screen).

ProductID ▾	SalesType ▾	LinePrice ▾	LineCost ▾	OrderNumber ▾
8	O	10	8	18
8	O	20	16	19
8	O	40	32	20
9	O	24	18	20
9	R	-8	-6	5
9	R	-24	-18	6

Figure 15.18
Datasheet View of factSales table (right side of screen).

The SalesType column is key in that it specifies whether the row is an order or a return. Whereas all the order rows have positive numbers for the LinePrice and Line-Cost columns, the returns have negative numbers for these same columns. Some of the foreign keys, such as CustomerID and ProductID, appear useless as is, but will later be joined to dimension tables to provide meaningful information.

Creating the Data Warehouse

We have now created four Make Table queries to create four dimensions, and two Append queries to add data to the fact table. To review, these queries are:

- createChannel
- createSalesperson
- createCustomer
- createProduct
- appendOrders
- appendReturns

The first four queries create the dimChannel, dimSalesperson, dimCustomer, and dimProduct tables. The next two queries append data to the factSales table, which was initially created with the createSales query. The other two tables in our data warehouse, dimTime and dimSalesType, are created without the use of queries.

After running these queries and creating these tables, the next step in the process is to create a query that ties all the dimension and fact tables together. This query will utilize the joins shown in Figure 15.2. With a "dw" prefix to indicate data warehouse, we'll call this query dwSales.

Since the data warehouse data has already been transformed and stored in our Access database in dimension and fact tables, there is no need to store any additional data. The dwSales query can be a Select query. Creating the query is fairly routine. We merely need to connect the tables with the proper joins, and select the fields we want the user to see. There is no selection criteria involved. Figures 15.19, 15.20, and 15.21 show the design of the dwSales query.

The central fact table in this query is factSales. The six dimension tables joined to factSales are: dimTime, dimCustomer, dimProduct, dimChannel, dimSalesType, and dimSalesperson. Since the nature of our design dictates that all rows in our fact tables will join to a row in each of the associated dimension tables, we can utilize inner joins in this query. The columns we elected to display in this query are:

- From the dimTime table: SalesDate and FiscalQuarter
- From the dimSalesType table: SalesType
- From the dimChannel table: Channel
- From the dimCustomer table: CustomerName, City, State, Zip, and CustomerSalesperson

- From the dimSalesperson table: OrderSalesperson
- From the dimProduct table: Product, ProductCategory
- From the factSales table: LinePrice, LineCost, and OrderNumber

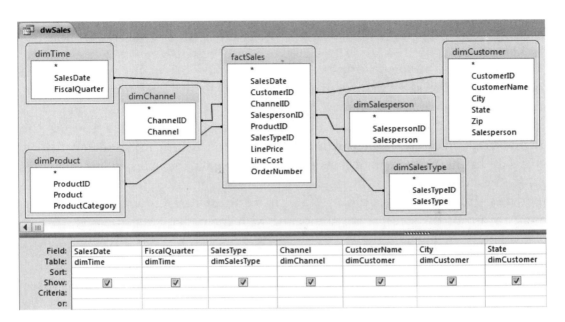

Figure 15.19
Design View of dwSales query (left side of screen).

Field:	Zip	CustomerSalesperson: Salesperson	OrderSalesperson: Salesperson
Table:	dimCustomer	dimCustomer	dimSalesperson
Sort:			
Show:	✔	✔	✔
Criteria:			
or:			

Figure 15.20
Design View of dwSales query (center of screen).

Field:	Product	ProductCategory	LinePrice	LineCost	OrderNumber
Table:	dimProduct	dimProduct	factSales	factSales	factSales
Sort:					
Show:	✔	✔	✔	✔	✔
Criteria:					
or:					

Figure 15.21
Design View of dwSales query (right side of screen).

With the exception of the SalesDate and OrderNumber fields, we haven't included any of the foreign keys that were used to join the tables, as these contain data unimportant to the end user.

The two salesperson fields in the data warehouse, CustomerSalesperson and Order-Salesperson bear a few words of explanation. As mentioned in the prior chapter, the problem of slowly changing dimensions is often a thorny one for data warehouse designs. Our implementation of two separate salesperson fields in this data warehouse addresses the issue by storing both the salesperson originally associated with the order, and also the salesperson currently assigned to the customer. The Order-Salesperson field is obtained by joining the SalespersonID in the factSales table with the dimSalesperson table that contains the salesperson name. Thus, this field has the name of the salesperson associated with the order. The CustomerSalesperson field is contained within the Customer dimension and represents the salesperson currently assigned to the customer. Since the Customer dimension is frequently updated, the CustomerSalesperson can change over time. In contrast, the OrderSalesperson is a permanent record of the salesperson associated with the order.

The dwSales query defines and represents our data warehouse. With this query, the data in the original production tables has been transformed into a different structure with relationships that conform to a dimensional database design. The query itself will not typically be used to retrieve data, but provides a useful starting point for the development of queries against the data warehouse.

Querying the Data Warehouse

The question now arises as to what can be done, from an analytical standpoint, with the dwSales query just developed. There are two basic options. In this section, we'll develop two queries that allow for reporting against the data warehouse. Thus far, all the queries in this chapter have been developed to organize and build a data warehouse. At this point, we want to proceed to use Access as a means to retrieve information from the data that has been organized into a data warehouse. In our next chapter, Excel Pivot Tables, we'll look at a way to connect an Excel pivot table to the dwSales query, to allow a more interactive way to view the data.

Using dwSales as a source, our first objective is to develop a new query that employs a few parameters to make data selection easier and more intuitive. A pervasive element in any data warehouse is the time dimension. Time always dictates the manner in which data is explored and retrieved. With this in mind, we want to allow for data retrieval for a specific date range. In addition, we also want to provide a few parameters that allow the user to select data based on dimensional attributes.

Using the "rpt" prefix for these reporting queries, we'll first develop a query named rptSales. This query will contain these five parameters:

- Begin Date: a required parameter to specify a date range
- End Date: a required parameter to specify a date range
- Sales Type: an optional parameter to specify Orders Only or Returns Only
- Customer Name: an optional parameter to specify a customer name
- Product Category: an optional parameter to specify a product category

Additionally, for the Customer Name and Product Category parameters, we want to allow the user to enter any portion of the name or category to obtain matches for that phrase, even if incomplete. Figures 15.22 and 15.23 show the design of this query.

Figure 15.22
Design View of rptSales query (left side of screen).

Figure 15.23
Design View of rptSales query (right side of screen).

Notice that the only data source for this query is the dwSales query. Since the dwSales query already contains all the necessary data, derived from the underlying dimension and fact tables, it isn't necessary to recreate the joins in this query a second time.

The Criteria values for the SalesDate, SalesType, CustomerName, and Product-Category columns are, respectively:

- Between [Begin Date] And [End Date]
- Like Switch ([Sales Type (optional): O = Orders Only, R = Returns Only] = "O","Orders", [Sales Type (optional): O = Orders Only, R = Returns Only] = "R", "Returns", 1=1, "*")
- Like IIf (IsNull ([Customer Name (optional)]), "*", "*" & [Customer Name (optional)] & "*")
- Like IIf (IsNull ([Product Category (optional)]), "*", "*" & [Product Category (optional)] & "*")

The parameters for the SalesDate columns utilize the BETWEEN operator to capture begin and end dates for the date range. The SalesType parameter uses the SWITCH function discussed in Chapter 8, and allows the user to enter "O" for Orders Only or "R" for Returns Only. If left blank, the parameter will return all orders and returns. When the query is run, the parameter selection window for Sales Type appears as in Figure 15.24.

Figure 15.24
Enter Parameter Value window for Sales Type.

The CustomerName and ProductCategory parameters both employ the same logic, using tests for NULL values, as well as pattern matching with the LIKE operator. The parameter selection window for the Customer Name appears as in Figure 15.25. The Product Category parameter selection window is similar.

Figure 15.25
Enter Parameter Value window for Customer Name.

The ability to enter both required and optional parameters in this query is a nice enhancement, but far from ideal. There are two main problems. First, although this query includes three optional parameters, the query should really have many more parameters to be useful. One would like to be able to select on just about any column. From a user interface perspective, however, it would be incredibly awkward to require a user to respond to a dozen different Parameter Value windows while running a query. The second issue is even more troublesome. For certain parameters, such as Product Category, it would be desirable to select one or more items from a list of allowable values, rather than having to know these values in advance.

Unfortunately, simple parameter queries in Access, such as the one we've just demonstrated, do not allow for the selection of values from a list. The solution to this situation is to employ Access Forms and Macros to create a form that provides all the parameter values for a given query. Such a form would have text boxes for the entry of known values such as dates, and list or combo boxes for the selection of values from a list. With such a setup, one could select one or more product categories from a populated list and have the query select only those values.

At this point, however, we have to state that these techniques, involving forms and macros, are far from simple to implement. As such, this technique is generally beyond the scope of this book. Additionally, the introduction of complex controls such as list boxes complicates selection logic in the underlying query. In truth, Access falls short of the full-featured reporting tools like Microsoft Reporting Services when it comes to designing reports with complex parameter requirements.

For anyone desiring a taste of this type of development, Appendix A of this book provides a brief tutorial on the use of forms and macros to allow for query parameters tied to selection in a form.

With these limitations in mind, let's press on to develop one more reporting query. This query will utilize aggregation, by grouping data by Product, ProductCategory, and SalesType. It will then sum the total sales and cost for each combination. As before, the only data source for this report query is dwSales. The design is shown in Figure 15.26, and a few rows of output appear in Figure 15.27.

Field:	Product	ProductCategory	SalesType	Total Sales: LinePrice	Total Cost: LineCost	SalesDate
Table:	dwSales	dwSales	dwSales	dwSales	dwSales	dwSales
Total:	Group By	Group By	Group By	Sum	Sum	Where
Sort:						
Show:	✓	✓	✓	✓	✓	☐
Criteria:						Between [Begin Dat
or:						

Figure 15.26
Design View of rptProductAnalysis query.

rptProductAnalysis				
Product ▾	ProductCategory ▾	SalesType ▾	Total Sales ▾	Total Cost ▾
Breakfast Blend	Coffee	Orders	104	78
Breakfast Blend	Coffee	Returns	-32	-24
Cinnamon	Spices	Orders	78	60
Curry	Spices	Orders	19	14
Decaf	Coffee	Orders	120	90
Earl Grey	Tea	Orders	15	12
French Roast	Coffee	Orders	150	120

Figure 15.27
Datasheet View of rptProductAnalysis query.

Note the simplicity of the query. The dimensional design of the data warehouse is particularly conducive to aggregation. In most cases, any dimension attribute can be used to group data, and any fact can be summed, averaged, or counted. In this query, we grouped data by three dimension attributes (Product, ProductCategory, and Sales-Type) and summed two facts (LinePrice and LineCost). We also applied the following parameter-based criteria to the SalesDate to select a desired range of orders:

■ Between [Begin Date] And [End Date]

As a result, this query shows every unique combination of products, product categories, and sales types for the specified date range, along with the total sales and cost for each group.

The reporting queries shown in this section are just two of many possibilities. Data can be aggregated in many ways, and parameters can be designed to retrieve data along numerous lines. To give two more examples, it would probably be helpful to add a query that aggregates the dwSales query by OrderNumber and SalesType. That would produce one row per order or return, allowing one to see useful summary information at this higher level. Similarly, one could develop a query that aggregates by CustomerNumber and Month, to provide summary information on total customer purchases per month.

Migrating to SQL Server

The exercise in this chapter has led us through a scenario that resulted in the creation of a data warehouse in Access. Principles of dimensional design were applied to create dimension and fact tables, and then to create a query that ties the data together into a star schema design. The end user is then free to utilize the data warehouse query as a source for further Access reports or, as will be demonstrated in the next chapter, as a source for an Excel pivot table.

Although the processes we have followed have created something resembling a data warehouse, the obvious needs to be stated: Few developers would choose Access as a tool to develop a data warehouse. There are several difficulties. The main problem is that Access is not a sufficiently robust tool for the storage of production data. In our scenario, we linked to production data, and used Access to organize that data and store redesigned tables in Access. In a real-world situation, one would want to keep all production data, even derived data such as a data warehouse, in a server database such as Microsoft SQL Server. Fortunately, Access provides a way to create SQL Server databases directly from tables stored in Access. This allows you to use Access as a design tool and then convert that design to SQL Server later.

Let's explore the steps involved in migrating an Access database to SQL Server. The process begins by clicking the SQL Server command in the Move Data section of the Ribbon, under the Database Tools tab. This initiates an Upsizing Wizard window that asks you to specify the following:

- Whether you want to use an existing database or create a new database. We'll assume a response of creating a new database.
- The name of an existing SQL Server.
- A name for the new SQL Server database. We'll specify the name "Data Warehouse."
- The tables you want to export to the new database. This window is shown in Figure 15.28. We've selected all of the dimension and fact tables in our Access database.
- Various table attributes to include, such as indexes and table relationships.
- Whether you want to create table structures only or also include data.
- Whether you want the new SQL tables to be linked to your current application.

Figure 15.28
Upsizing Wizard table selection window.

After completing the wizard, Access creates the specified tables in SQL Server. A portion of the SQL Server Management Studio screen is shown in Figure 15.29.

Once your data structure is in SQL Server, a plethora of additional functionality is available. The various Append and Make Table queries designed in Access can be easily converted into stored procedures in SQL Server. You just need to copy the SQL in each of the queries and tweak the syntax to conform to SQL Server specifications. One can then create jobs in SQL Server to execute the stored procedures to maintain the data in the data warehouse. The specifics of using SQL Server are beyond the scope of this book, but the main point is that any development effort undertaken in Access can be transferred to SQL Server without too much difficulty. As seen in the Upsizing Wizard, the transfer of tables is fairly automatic. However, the translation of other queries into SQL Server-stored procedures requires a manual effort.

It should also be noted that after a data warehouse database is migrated to SQL Server, reporting tools such as Reporting Services, as seen in Chapter 13, can be used to develop sophisticated reporting queries. For example, the two sample queries we developed in this chapter to query the data warehouse, rptSales and rptProduct-Analysis, could be easily transferred to Reporting Services. This can be done by simply copying the underlying SQL in the Access query to a report in Reporting Services, while adding a few minor tweaks for syntax differences.

Figure 15.29
SQL Server Management Studio Object Explorer.

Simplified Dimensional Models

At the beginning of this chapter, we mentioned that the arduous process of creating a data warehouse can be simplified and still prove to be an advantageous endeavor. In this chapter, we created a data warehouse that was more complex than would normally be attempted with Access. Simpler variants of the process we followed can certainly be utilized. For example, one might want to create a small data set for a narrow period of time, with just orders, customers, and product information. By ignoring returns, one can streamline the process and create everything with just one or two queries. With smaller amounts of data, it may not even be necessary to store data within Access. Because Access is able to turn any table into a query, most data can be defined via a Select query.

Additionally, the concept of a dimensional model can be stretched to cover other types of structures. We'll illustrate this notion with a brief example. Working from the production tables seen in this chapter, let's say we want to create a summary of customer buying habits, focusing on whether or not each customer has ever made purchases from each of the three product categories: coffee, tea, and spices. To accomplish this, we'll create a single Select query that captures this information. Figures 15.30 and 15.31 show the design of such a query and a few rows of data.

Figure 15.30
Design View of a query with indicator fields.

CustomerID	CustomerCount	HasPurchasedCoffee	HasPurchasedTea	HasPurchasedSpices
1 1		0	0	1
2 1		1	0	1
3 1		1	0	1
4 1		1	1	1
5 1		1	0	0

Figure 15.31
Datasheet View of a query with indicator fields.

Let's first discuss how this query works. The expression in the HasPurchasedCoffee field is:

■ HasPurchasedCoffee: Max (IIf ([CategoryID] = 'C', 1, 0))

The function in this column uses the IIF function to analyze the CategoryID field. If the value equals "C", a 1 is placed in the field. Otherwise, a 0 is put in the field. The query is grouped by the CustomerID. A MAX aggregation is applied to each group of customers, so the maximum value is selected. This means that if the customer had any purchase of coffee, the individual row with that purchase would have a 1. When grouping is applied, the entire customer group would also have a 1. Thus, a

1 means that the customer had at least one purchase that included coffee. The other two indicator fields have similar logic.

Let's now look at the output shown in Figure 15.31. The query produces one row per customer. Each row has the CustomerID, a field named CustomerCount with a literal value of 1, and three 0/1 indicator fields: HasPurchasedCoffee, HasPurchasedTea, and HasPurchasedSpices. Each of the indicator fields has a 0 or 1 value that indicates whether the customer has ever purchased from these categories. For example, this data indicates that customer number 3 has purchased coffee and spices, but not tea.

As it stands, the output is difficult to interpret and use. However, these types of indicator fields lend themselves perfectly to use in pivot tables. Using the technique explained in Chapter 12, "Crosstab Queries and Pivot Tables," we'll change the query to a PivotTable query, and then export it to Excel. Once the Excel pivot table opens, we can move the HasPurchasedCoffee field to the Rows area, the HasPurchasedTea to the Columns area, and the CustomerCount to the Values area. The resulting pivot table is shown in Figure 15.32.

	A	B	C	D
1		Drop Page Fields Here		
2				
3	Count of CustomerCount	HasPurchasedTea ▾		
4	HasPurchasedCoffee ▾	0	1	Grand Total
5	0	2		2
6	1	5	3	8
7	Grand Total	7	3	10

Figure 15.32
Excel Pivot Table with data from a query with indicator fields.

The pivot table shows that of our 10 customers, 8 people have purchased coffee. Of those 8 people, 3 have purchased tea. The flexibility of the pivot table allows for a similar analysis between any or all of the three groups of people captured in this data.

How does this data make use of the dimensional model? If you think about it, the three indicator fields are like dimensional attributes, and can therefore be placed in the Row or Column areas of the pivot table. The value of 1 in the CustomerCount field allows it to function like a summable fact. We'll explore pivot table functionality in the next chapter, but this provides an early taste of what is possible when one combines data organized in Access with the pivot table capabilities of Excel. In essence, the pivot table complements the dimensional structure of the data, and allows for interactive analysis of the data.

Looking Ahead

This chapter covered a lot of ground. Applying our knowledge of business intelligence and dimensional modeling gained in Chapters 13 and 14, we developed a database in Access that simulates the design and creation of a working data warehouse. With the ability of Access to link to external tables, we first established links to production, and then used Access to reorganize this data into a dimensional model. In our exercise, we stored our dimensions and facts in Access tables. The dimension and fact tables represent the core of the data warehouse. We then took the additional step of creating a single query that ties the dimension and fact tables together into a single construct. That query can then be used as a source for any number of reporting queries.

In our next chapter, we'll use the dwSales query developed in this chapter as a source for an Excel pivot table. The ability to use pivot tables with the dwSales query should make the power of dimensional models much more obvious. In essence, dimensional models and pivot tables complement each other nicely. The structure of pivot tables allows one to take full advantage of the separation of data into dimensions and facts in the dimensional model.

Chapter 16

Excel Pivot Tables

In the previous chapter, we used Access to reorganize data into a dimensional design, and stored that data within Access. This created a miniature data warehouse, with dimension and fact tables connected with a single query. After creating the data warehouse, we proceeded to design a few reporting queries to extract data from the new design. It is here that some of the limitations of Access became apparent. As a reporting tool, Access lacks the power and ease of use of more sophisticated reporting software, such as Microsoft Reporting Services.

In this chapter, we'll illustrate procedures to access the data warehouse built in Chapter 15 in an entirely different manner. By connecting to the data warehouse via an Excel pivot table, the real benefits of the dimensional design will become more apparent. In many ways, the ability to use Excel pivot tables with data created in Access represents the culmination of our goal of using Access as a business intelligence tool. The structure of Excel pivot tables perfectly matches and complements the dimensional design, and allows the analyst to exploit the relationships in the data warehouse to great advantage. We've already pointed out the striking similarities in structure between a dimensional design and pivot tables. Fact table attributes can be placed in the central Values area of a pivot table, whereas dimension attributes can be placed in the Row, Column, or Filter areas of the pivot table. After showing how to connect to data in Access, we'll explore the basics and nuances of pivot table functionality.

Although the examples in this chapter will be drawn solely against the dwSales query developed in Chapter 15, it should also be emphasized that Excel pivot tables are not only relevant to data in a data warehouse format. Whether your source data is normalized or in a dimensional design, the pivot table is an extremely useful tool for the analyst.

Connecting to Access

In Chapter 3, "Tables and External Data," we explained how to export Access data to Excel spreadsheets. This data was placed in normal Excel worksheets and had nothing to do with pivot tables. Later in Chapter 12, "Crosstab Queries and Pivot Tables," we showed how to use the PivotTable View of Access to export data to Excel pivot tables. As mentioned in that chapter, Excel pivot tables hold a number of distinct advantages over Access pivot tables. In summary, relative to the PivotTable View in Access, the pivot table interface in Excel is substantially easier to understand and work with.

Now we'll tackle the problem in reverse. We'll assume that you're working in Excel and would like to connect to data in Access. More specifically, we'll show how to connect to Access data within an Excel pivot table. In our sample scenario, we'll begin with the assumption that the dwSales query created in the previous chapter is available as a data source. If you would like to recreate these steps for yourself, the database with this query is available on the companion website for this book. Appendix B explains how to obtain that database.

The process of connecting to Access data via an Excel pivot table begins by opening a new Excel file or worksheet, and then navigating to the PivotTable command in the Tables section of the Ribbon, under the Insert tab. These steps should be followed:

1. Click the PivotTable command. The Create Pivot Table window appears.

2. Select the Use an External Data Source option. The window now appears as in Figure 16.1.

3. Click the Choose Connection button.

4. Click the Browse for More button. A Select Data Source window will pop up.

5. Click the New Source button. A Data Connection Wizard window will pop up. This is shown in Figure 16.2.

6. Select ODBC DSN, and then click the Next button. ODBC DSN stands for Open Database Connectivity Data Source Name. A Connect to ODBC Data Source heading will appear in the Data Connection Wizard window.

7. Select MS Access Database, and then click the Next button. A Select Database window will pop up.

8. Browse until you find the Access database, and then click the OK button. In our example, the name of the database is DataWarehouse.accdb.

9. In the Data Connection Wizard window, a Select Database and Table heading appears. This is shown in Figure 16.3.

10. Make sure the "Connect to a Specific Table" checkbox is checked, then select the dwSales View, and then click the Next button. In the Data Connection Wizard window, a Save Data Connection File and Finish heading appears. If you choose not to select a specific table at this point, you will be asked for a specific table later.

11. The window shows a file name with an ODC suffix in the File Name box. Click the Browse button to browse to a desired location to save this file. The file name can be changed. In this example, we'll shorten the file name to dwSales and enter a Friendly Name and description. This is shown in Figure 16.4.

12. Click the Finish button to complete and close the Data Connection Wizard.

13. The Create PivotTable window will still be open. Click the Choose Connection button and find the file you just created. It will be listed with the friendly name you had entered. Click the Open button, and then the OK button

Figure 16.1
Create PivotTable window.

With this sequence completed, you have a new pivot table in your Excel worksheet, connected to the dwSales query in the DataWarehouse.accdb database. As long as the location of the Access database doesn't change, the pivot table will stay connected. Furthermore, you have the ability to maintain the connection as an active connection in two different ways. First, you can select the Connection Properties command in the Data section of the Ribbon under the PivotTable Tools Options tab and check the box that states "Refresh the data when opening the file." This guarantees that the data in your pivot table is refreshed whenever you open the file. Also, you can click the Refresh command in the same section of the Ribbon to refresh the data at any other time.

Figure 16.2
Data Connection Wizard Welcome.

Figure 16.3
Select Database and Table.

Figure 16.4
Save Data Connection File.

Once the connection file is created, as outlined previously, the process to connect again in a new Excel worksheet is much simpler. The only steps required are:

1. Click the PivotTable command.

2. Select the Use an External Data Source option.

3. Click the Choose Connection button.

4. Find the connection file you created previously. Click Open, and then click OK.

The PivotTable Field List

Let's now examine the various aspects of the pivot table user interface. After the connection to the Access database has been made, the pivot table appears in Excel. The main portion of the Excel worksheet will display an empty pivot table, as shown in Figure 16.5.

When the focus is on any cell in the pivot table, a special PivotTable Field List pane appears, as shown in Figure 16.6.

The Field List is the key element of the pivot table user interface. It's comprised of two sections: the Field section and the Areas section. In Figure 16.6, the Field section appears on the left, listing all available fields in the pivot table. These fields are taken from the Access query that this pivot table is connected to. The Areas section is on the right of the Field List and shows the four areas of a pivot table.

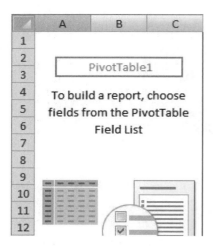

Figure 16.5
Empty pivot table.

Figure 16.6
PivotTable Field List.

The Field List can be formatted in four different ways. This is accomplished by clicking the icon in the upper right of the Field List and selecting one of the four options from the drop-down menu. In Figure 16.6, we have chosen to display it in the "Field Section and Areas Section Side-By-Side" format. Another useful option is the "Field Section and Areas Section Stacked" format, which places the Field section above the Areas section.

The Field List can be positioned on the left or right of your screen, or it can be detached from the sides and viewed as a floating pane in any other location. Positioning is accomplished by grabbing and dragging the top of the pane.

The main idea of the Field List is that you can drag any field in the Field section to any of the four areas in the Areas section. When you do this, the pivot table is instantly updated with values corresponding to the new layout. Or, if you don't want an immediate display of results, the Defer Layout Update checkbox in the Field List allows you to defer instantaneous updates of the pivot table.

Let's illustrate with a simple example. We'll drag the LinePrice field to the Values area, the ProductCategory to the Row Labels area, the Channel to the Column Labels area, and the SalesDate to the Report Filter area. After changing the format of the Field List to the "Field Section and Areas Section Stacked" format, the Areas section of the Field List appears as in Figure 16.7. The corresponding pivot table is shown in Figure 16.8.

Figure 16.7
Areas section of Field List.

	A	B	C	D	E
1	SalesDate	(All)			
2					
3	**Sum of LinePrice**	**Column Labels**			
4	**Row Labels**	Internet	**Mail**	**Phone**	**Grand Total**
5	Coffee	120	40	238	398
6	Spices	73	19	207	299
7	Tea	199			199
8	**Grand Total**	392	59	445	896

Figure 16.8
Pivot table with fields in all four areas.

Let's talk about the areas of the pivot table in greater detail. As Figure 16.7 indicates, there are four main areas: Filters, Columns, Rows, and Values. The Values area is meant for fields with quantitative values that can be summarized in various ways. The default aggregation applied to fields in the Values area is Sum. However, this can be changed. By clicking any cell in the Values area, and then selecting the Field Settings command in the Active Field section of the Ribbon, under the PivotTable Tools Options tab, one can change the summarization type from Sum to any of ten other types, including Count and Average. If, for example, the summarization type is changed to Count, then the Values area will display the number of rows for each combination, rather than a sum of the values.

Before discussing the other three areas of the pivot table, let's briefly mention how the pivot table commands are arranged in the Ribbon. When a pivot table is active, two new sets of commands become available in the Ribbon under a PivotTable Tools heading. One tab is named Options and the other is called Design. The Design tab under PivotTable Tools has most of the commands applicable to pivot table operations. These commands fall into these sections of the Ribbon: PivotTable, Active Field, Group, Sort, Data, Actions, Tools, and Show/Hide. The Design tab pertains to physical layout and design, and includes commands in these sections: Layout, PivotTable Style Options, and PivotTable Styles.

The Row and Column areas of the pivot table are meant for placement of non-quantitative attribute fields. It should be emphasized that, no matter what field is placed in a row or column, the pivot table automatically searches for all values of that field and displays only those values that exist. In other words, pivot tables are dynamic structures that find values and aggregate corresponding values in the Values area as appropriate. Depending on the values present in the rows or columns, the intersecting cells in the Values area give the corresponding results. For example, Figure 16.8 indicates that there was $238 of coffee sales via the phone.

Placement of a field in the Row or Column area is purely a matter of personal preference. In our example, we could have easily switched the row and column fields, placing the CustomerName in the Columns and ProductCategory in the rows. That would have resulted in a display of the same data, but laid out in a different format.

An important aspect of the pivot table interface is the ability to place more than one field in the Row or Column areas. Let's alter the pivot table of Figure 16.8 by adding the Product field to the Rows area. The new Field List is shown in Figure 16.9 and the resulting pivot table in Figure 16.10.

In adding the Product field to the Rows area, we added it *below* the ProductCategory in the areas section of the Field List. This caused a grouping to appear, with Products contained within the ProductCategory. The result is an intuitive layout of data with products grouped by category.

Figure 16.9
Areas section of Field List with two fields in Row area.

	A	B	C	D	E
1	SalesDate	(All)			
2					
3	Sum of LinePrice	Column Labels			
4	Row Labels	Internet	Mail	Phone	Grand Total
5	Coffee	120	40	238	398
6	Breakfast Blend	40	32	0	72
7	Decaf			120	120
8	French Roast	80		70	150
9	Hazelnut		8	48	56
10	Spices	73	19	207	299
11	Cinnamon	39		39	78
12	Curry		19		19
13	Ginger	20		70	90
14	Mustard	14		14	28
15	Oregano			84	84
16	Tea	199			199
17	Earl Grey	15			15
18	Green Tea	160			160
19	Oolong Tea	24			24
20	Grand Total	392	59	445	896

Figure 16.10
Pivot table with two fields in Row area.

In presenting data in a pivot table, much depends on an understanding of the relationships between the various fields. In the prior example, it made sense to place products within product categories. If we had reversed the order and placed product categories within products, the display would not be understandable. In essence, when two related fields are arranged in a natural order, they create what is commonly referred to as a *hierarchy*. However, in addition to placing two related fields together, one can also do the same with unrelated data. As an example, let's change the Row area to contain the ProductCategory and the SalesType fields. The result is shown in Figure 16.11.

	A	B	C	D	E
1	SalesDate	(All) ▼			
2					
3	Sum of LinePrice	Column Labels ▼			
4	Row Labels ▼	Internet	Mail	Phone	Grand Total
5	Coffee	120	40	238	398
6	Orders	144	40	246	430
7	Returns	-24		-8	-32
8	Spices	73	19	207	299
9	Orders	110	19	207	336
10	Returns	-37			-37
11	Tea	199			199
12	Orders	199			199
13	Grand Total	392	59	445	896

Figure 16.11
Pivot table with two unrelated fields in Row area.

Even though the ProductCategory and SalesType fields are unrelated, this still makes for a nice presentation. There is no natural hierarchy between ProductCategory and SalesType, but that's all right. We're simply introducing a new element in the analysis. In summary, if you have more than one field in the Row or Column area of a pivot table, and if those rows are related, it's important to make sure that they are presented in the correct order, according to the natural hierarchy that exists between them.

Layout Options

Pivot tables allow numerous ways of presenting their data. The Layout section of the Ribbon under the PivotTable Tools Design tab is shown in Figure 16.12.

Figure 16.12
Pivot table Layout commands.

Let's focus first on the Report Layout command. When this command is selected, one is presented with three options:

- Show in Compact Form
- Show in Outline Form
- Show in Tabular Form

The default is Compact Form. Thus, the pivot tables shown in Figures 16.8, 16.10, and 16.11 are all in Compact Form. Figure 16.13 shows the same pivot table from Figure 16.11 in Outline Form. Figure 16.14 shows it in Tabular Form.

	A	B	C	D	E	F
1	SalesDate	(All) ▾				
2						
3	Sum of LinePrice		Channel ▾			
4	ProductCategory ▾	SalesType ▾	Internet	Mail	Phone	Grand Total
5	Coffee		120	40	238	398
6		Orders	144	40	246	430
7		Returns	-24		-8	-32
8	Spices		73	19	207	299
9		Orders	110	19	207	336
10		Returns	-37			-37
11	Tea		199			199
12		Orders	199			199
13	Grand Total		392	59	445	896

Figure 16.13
Pivot table in Outline Form.

	A	B	C	D	E	F
1	SalesDate	(All) ▾				
2						
3	Sum of LinePrice		Channel ▾			
4	ProductCategory ▾	SalesType ▾	Internet	Mail	Phone	Grand Total
5	Coffee	Orders	144	40	246	430
6		Returns	-24		-8	-32
7	Coffee Total		120	40	238	398
8	Spices	Orders	110	19	207	336
9		Returns	-37			-37
10	Spices Total		73	19	207	299
11	Tea	Orders	199			199
12	Tea Total		199			199
13	Grand Total		392	59	445	896

Figure 16.14
Pivot table in Tabular Form.

The first thing to notice is that, in contrast to the Compact Form, both the Outline and Tabular Forms have an extra column. In the Compact Form, shown in Figure 16.11, the ProductCategory and Product fields are both contained within column A. In the Outline and Tabular Forms, these fields are separated into columns A and B. The main benefit of this is that it allows for a display of the field names in the header rows. The Compact Form merely states "Row Labels" in cell A4. The Outline and Compact Forms show the field names in cells A4 and B4.

The main difference between the Outline and Tabular Forms is that the Outline Form places subtotals above each group. The Tabular Form places the subtotals below each group.

In addition to changing the Form, you also have the option to include or exclude subtotals or grand totals. This is done by using the Subtotals and Grand Totals commands shown in Figure 16.12. When both subtotals and grand totals are turned off, the pivot table appears as in Figure 16.15 when in Tabular Form.

	A	B	C	D	E
1	SalesDate	(All)			
2					
3	Sum of LinePrice		Channel		
4	ProductCategory	SalesType	Internet	Mail	Phone
5	Coffee	Orders	144	40	246
6		Returns	-24		-8
7	Spices	Orders	110	19	207
8		Returns	-37		
9	Tea	Orders	199		

Figure 16.15
Pivot table in Tabular Form with no Subtotals or Grand Totals.

When subtotals are turned off, the layout makes a difference in terms of the number of rows displayed. Figure 16.16 shows the pivot table of Figure 16.15 in Outline Form. Note that this layout requires additional rows to display the ProductCategory groups.

The layout of a pivot table is of particular importance when sharing pivot table data with others. If a colleague wants to view a pivot table you've been working with, they need to have the same access to underlying data. Plus, since pivot tables are interactive devices, the state of any given pivot table changes frequently over time. Because of this, the easiest way to share pivot table data with others is to save it as a normal Excel worksheet. As a worksheet, it's generally best to save data without subtotals and in the Tabular Form.

	A	B	C	D	E
1	SalesDate	(All) ▾			
2					
3	Sum of LinePrice		Channel ▾		
4	ProductCategory ▾	SalesType ▾	Internet	Mail	Phone
5	Coffee				
6		Orders	144	40	246
7		Returns	-24		-8
8	Spices				
9		Orders	110	19	207
10		Returns	-37		
11	Tea				
12		Orders	199		

Figure 16.16
Pivot table in Outline Form with no Subtotals or Grand Totals.

Here's the procedure to save a pivot table as a worksheet that can be shared with others:

1. Select all cells in the pivot table.
2. Copy those cells using the Copy command or Ctrl-C.
3. Open a new Excel Workbook.
4. Select the top item shown in the clipboard.

When you select the top item in the clipboard, Excel automatically pastes all the values that were in your pivot table, along with all special formatting, to your new worksheet. This allows the viewer of that worksheet to see the data and formatting exactly as it appeared in the pivot table.

Filtering Data

So far, all the data we've viewed in pivot tables has involved a selection of individual fields and the subsequent formatting of that data. We now want to see how additional selection criteria can be applied to fields that have been moved to a pivot table from the Field List. In pivot table terminology, this is referred to as *filtering*. Filtering criteria can be specified in two basic ways. First, the Filter area of the pivot table can be used to filter all data in the pivot table. Second, filtering can be applied to individual fields in the Row or Column area of the pivot table.

Let's first demonstrate usage of the Filter area. Continuing with the pivot table shown in Figure 16.15, you'll notice that the Filter area of the pivot table contains the Sales-Date field. The current value of the field displays as "(All)". This means that all dates are allowed. Even though this field is in the Filter area, there is essentially no filtering being applied. We now want to utilize the SalesDate field to select only certain individual dates. To do this, we merely click the drop-down icon next to "(All)". When this is done, we see the filter pane shown in Figure 16.17.

Figure 16.17
Filtering options for a field in the Filter area.

To filter on SalesDate, we can select any particular date. Figure 16.18 shows the pivot table that results after the date 6/10/2011 is chosen in the filter.

	A	B	C	D
1	SalesDate	6/10/2011		
2				
3	Sum of LinePrice		Channel	
4	ProductCategory	SalesType	Internet	Phone
5	Coffee	Orders		50
6		Returns	-24	-8
7	Tea	Orders	24	

Figure 16.18
Pivot table with one item chosen in the Filter area.

With this filter in place, we now see only sales that took place on 6/10/2011. The value of the filter is shown in the Filter area. The values in the rest of the pivot table are adjusted accordingly. When the Select Multiple Items checkbox is checked, one can select multiple values for the SalesDate. After checking this and then selecting dates in the range 6/10/2011 to 6/15/2011, we see the pivot table shown in Figure 16.19.

	A	B	C	D	E
1	SalesDate	(Multiple Items)			
2					
3	**Sum of LinePrice**		Channel		
4	**ProductCategory**	SalesType	Internet	Mail	Phone
5	Coffee	Orders	104	40	90
6		Returns	-24		-8
7	Spices	Orders	10		72
8		Returns	-37		
9	Tea	Orders	159		

Figure 16.19
Pivot table with multiple items chosen in the Filter area.

We now see the expression "(Multiple Items)" in the Filter area, indicating that multiple SalesDate values are in the filter. Just as multiple fields can be moved to the Row, Column, or Values area of the pivot table, multiple fields can also be moved to the Filter area. For example, a filter on both SalesDate and State can be accomplished by adding State to the Filter and then specifying the states to be viewed.

In addition to using the Filter area, filtering can be applied to individual fields in the Row or Column area of the pivot table. Figure 16.19 shows drop-down icons next to the ProductCategory, SalesType, and Channel fields. When the drop-down menu for the ProductCategory field is selected, a pane with filtering options is displayed, as in Figure 16.20.

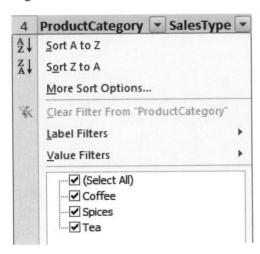

Figure 16.20
Filtering options for a field in the Row area.

The top section of the filter pane allows you to sort the values in the specified order. The bottom section allows filtering by any specified value. The middle section allows you to select a filter on the field based on either the field name or the aggregated values for that field shown in the Values area of the pivot table. The Label Filter is particularly useful for wildcard searches. For example, this can be used to search for all customers with a name containing "Smith." The Value Filter can be used, for example, to search for all products that have combined sales of over $500 in the date range under consideration.

Grouping and Formulas

By filtering on fields in the Row or Column areas, you can prevent individual values from displaying in the pivot table. This, in effect, creates a smaller group of data, based on values in that field. In addition to filtering, Excel also provides the ability to explicitly combine multiple values into a single group. This is accomplished via the Group Selection command in the Group section of the Ribbon under the PivotTable Tools Options tab.

Let's start with the pivot table shown in Figure 16.21. This shows sales by Product-Category. The LinePrice has been placed in the Values area. Nothing is in the Columns area.

	A	B
1	SalesDate	(All)
2		
3	ProductCategory	Sum of LinePrice
4	Coffee	398
5	Spices	299
6	Tea	199

Figure 16.21
Pivot table showing sales by ProductCategory.

To illustrate the grouping process, we'll combine Coffee and Tea into one group. To do this, we select one of the cells that says Coffee, and then hold down the Ctrl key while selecting the Tea cell. We then click the Group Selection command in the Group section of the Ribbon under the PivotTable Tools Options tab. The Pivot table is then transformed to the display shown in Figure 16.22.

Notice that a new group named Group1 was created under a ProductCategory2 label. Since we're using the Tabular Form layout, an extra column was added to hold the new group. The logical next step would be to add subtotals, so the total for the new group can be seen.

	A	B	C
1	SalesDate	(All)	
2			
3	ProductCategory2	ProductCategory	Sum of LinePrice
4	Group1	Coffee	398
5		Tea	199
6	Spices	Spices	299

Figure 16.22
Pivot table with grouping.

Another feature of pivot tables related to grouping is the ability to create custom formulas. Two types of formulas can be created within pivot tables: Calculated Items and Calculated Fields. Both of these can be generated from the Formulas command in the Tools section of the Ribbon under the PivotTable Tools Options tab.

Calculated Items create functionality similar to grouping. To illustrate, we'll create a new item within the existing ProductCategory field that represents Coffee and Tea together. To do this, we select a cell in the ProductCategory group, and then select the Calculated Item command under the Formulas command. This causes an Insert Calculated Item window to appear. Within this window, we'll use the Insert Item button to add Coffee and Tea as items in the Formula. The result is shown in Figure 16.23.

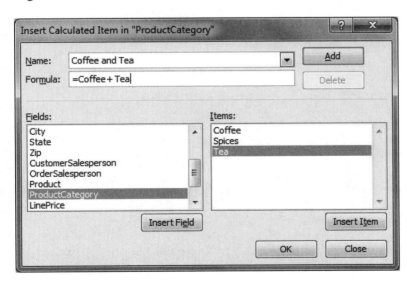

Figure 16.23
Insert Calculated Item window.

After adding this new item, the pivot table originally shown in Figure 16.21 now appears as in Figure 16.24.

	A	B
1	SalesDate	(All)
2		
3	ProductCategory	Sum of LinePrice
4	Coffee	398
5	Spices	299
6	Tea	199
7	Coffee and Tea	597

Figure 16.24
Pivot table with a Calculated Item.

The presentation in Figure 16.24 is slightly awkward in that it displays values for coffee and tea twice, but this can be cleaned up by altering filtering on the Product-Category field to exclude the individual Coffee and Tea items.

The other type of formula that can be created is called a Calculated Field. To illustrate, let's first expand on the pivot table in Figure 16.21 by adding the LineCost field. This is shown in Figure 16.25.

	A	B	C
1	SalesDate	(All)	
2			
3		Values	
4	ProductCategory	Sum of LinePrice	Sum of LineCost
5	Coffee	398	306
6	Spices	299	217
7	Tea	199	148

Figure 16.25
Pivot table with LinePrice and LineCost.

Using the Calculated Field command, we can create a GrossProfit field based on LinePrice and LineCost. Figure 16.26 shows the Insert Calculated Field window used to create the new field.

The new GrossProfit field can now be added to the pivot table, which appears as in Figure 16.27.

The custom items and fields created in the prior examples remain as permanent attributes of the pivot table. If you should want to delete a calculated item or field, the Insert Calculated Item and Insert Calculated Field windows can be used to delete those previously added items or fields.

Figure 16.26
Insert Calculated Field window.

	A	B	C	D
1	SalesDate	(All)		
2				
3		**Values**		
4	**ProductCategory**	**Sum of LinePrice**	**Sum of LineCost**	**Sum of GrossProfit**
5	Coffee	398	306	92
6	Spices	299	217	82
7	Tea	199	148	51

Figure 16.27
Pivot table with a Calculated Field.

Drill Down and Drillthrough

Perhaps the most exciting aspect of using pivot tables has not yet been mentioned. This is the ability to perform *drill-down* operations on data. Another operation somewhat related to the drill down is the *drillthrough*.

The drill-down operation works on related fields that have been placed into a pivot table. More specifically, the related fields are those that form a natural hierarchy. In our sample data, one example of related fields that form a natural hierarchy is ProductCategory and Product. A second example is State, City, and CustomerName. With these fields, one would like to be able to drill down from State to City to CustomerName, or from ProductCategory to Category.

Let's illustrate the process with State, City, and Zip. Although it's true that a zip code can be associated with more than one city, there's no such situation in our data. Our sample data happens to include three customers from Arizona, so we'll focus on that state. Figure 16.28 shows a pivot table with the State, City, and Zip fields in the Rows area. We've added a filter to the State to display only the states of Arizona and New Mexico.

	A	B
1	SalesDate	(All)
2		
3	Row Labels	Sum of LinePrice
4	AZ	
5	Phoenix	
6	85006	20
7	85010	114
8	Tucson	
9	85708	48
10	NM	
11	Albuquerque	
12	87106	145

Figure 16.28
Pivot table with a natural hierarchy of fields.

So far, this is a routine display of data. Note that we've chosen to use the Compact Form layout, which is particularly conducive to drill-down operations. However, before we can drill down, we must first drill up. This is accomplished in one of two ways. The manual method is to double-click both the Arizona (AZ) and New Mexico (NM) cells. The second and simpler method is to select either state, and then click the Collapse Entire Field command in the Active Field section of the Ribbon under the PivotTable Tools Options tab. When either of these methods is employed, the result is as shown in Figure 16.29.

At this point, it appears that we have only the State field in our pivot table, but that isn't true. Since we're viewing data in the Compact Form, we only see one column for the Rows section. If we were in the Outline or Tabular Form, we'd see three separate columns for State, City, and Zip. We can now perform the drill-down operation. To do this, we can double-click on either state, or else use the Expand Entire Field command to show values in all hidden fields. We'll just double-click the Arizona cell. The result is shown in Figure 16.30.

⬚	A	B	
1	SalesDate	(All)	▾
2			
3	Row Labels ⬚	Sum of LinePrice	
4	AZ	182	
5	NM	145	

Figure 16.29
Pivot table after executing the Collapse Entire Field command.

⬚	A	B	
1	SalesDate	(All)	▾
2			
3	Row Labels ⬚	Sum of LinePrice	
4	AZ		
5	Phoenix		
6	85006	20	
7	85010	114	
8	Tucson		
9	85708	48	
10	NM	145	

Figure 16.30
Pivot table after drilling down on one cell.

After doing the drill down, all the hidden information for Arizona magically appears. The data for New Mexico doesn't appear, because we only drilled down on Arizona. It needs to be emphasized that drill-down and drill-up operations have nothing to do with filtering. These functions only determine what data is visible at a particular moment in time.

If we wanted to add the CustomerName field as a fourth level to our hierarchy, this can be accomplished by double-clicking on any zip code cell. When that is done, a Show Detail window pops up, as shown in Figure 16.31.

After selecting the CustomerName field, the name will appear for the Zip field that was selected. Then, to show the CustomerName for all data, we can do an Expand Entire Field command on any State cell. The pivot table, shown in the Tabular Form layout, is shown in Figure 16.32.

Figure 16.32 also illustrates another device that helps with drill-down operations. By selecting the Buttons command in the Show/Hide section of the Ribbon under the PivotTable Tools Options tab, small plus and minus buttons appear in each drillable cell. The minus indicates that no more drilling is possible. The plus indicates that one can drill down further on that cell.

Figure 16.31
Show Detail window.

	A	B	C	D	E
1	SalesDate	(All)			
2					
3	**State**	**City**	**Zip**	**CustomerName**	**Sum of LinePrice**
4	AZ	Phoenix	85006	Elaine Crane	20
5			85010	Ralph Berry	114
6		Tucson	85708	Diana Day	48
7	NM	Albuquerque	87106	Randy Smith	145

Figure 16.32
Pivot table with a four-level hierarchy and buttons.

An operation somewhat related to the drill-down is the drillthrough. Rather than clicking on a cell in the Row or Column area, the drillthrough allows you to double-click on a cell in the Values area. When this is done, a new Excel worksheet automatically opens, showing detail rows for all data that make the value in that cell. For example, if we were to double-click on the cell with a value of 114 in Figure 16.32, it will show all sales for Ralph Berry. Figure 16.33 shows a partial view of the new worksheet that opens up.

Figure 16.33 shows only five out of the 15 fields in the pivot table, but the idea is that all detail for all fields is displayed. In this example, four rows of data make up the number. If you examine the values of the LinePrice column, you can see that they add up to 114. This, in essence, validates and provides detail on exactly how the value of 114 ended up on the pivot table. In this example, another useful piece of information provided by the drillthrough is a listing of the order numbers that contributed to the sales.

K	L	M	N	O
Product	ProductCategory	LinePrice	LineCost	OrderNumber
Breakfast Blend	Coffee	32	24	16
Oregano	Spices	42	32	2
Ginger	Spices	40	28	2

Figure 16.33
Result of a drillthrough operation on a cell.

Using PowerPivot

With Excel 2010, Microsoft introduced a new add-in for Excel called PowerPivot. This add-in provides a new pivot table interface with three distinct advantages over the standard pivot table. First, unlike pivot tables that merely connect to external data, PowerPivot actually imports data into your Excel file, storing it in a highly compressed format that results in quick retrieval. After the data is imported, you can view the data in a special PowerPivot window dedicated to displaying the raw data.

The second and more significant advantage of PowerPivot is that it allows for a connection to multiple tables. In the prior pivot table example, we connected to the dwSales query in our Access database. Standard pivot tables allow you to connect to only one single table or view. In contrast, the PowerPivot interface allows you to connect to any number of tables or queries in multiple data sources. Additionally, PowerPivot will examine the data and automatically determine the relationships that exist between tables as you work on them.

The third main advantage of PowerPivot is that it includes a powerful language called DAX, or Data Analysis Expressions. In our prior example, we saw that pivot tables allow you to create custom fields and items that can be added to the Field List. In PowerPivot, this capability is extended to include a whole range of custom functions that take advantage of the unique data structures found in pivot tables. The functions available in PowerPivot include new Time Intelligence functions that allow you to compare and manipulate data over periods of time.

The PowerPivot add-in is currently available at this Microsoft website:

■ www.powerpivot.com

After the add-in has been installed, you have the option of using either the standard pivot table interface, or the PowerPivot interface. In the remainder of this chapter, we'll take a brief look at PowerPivot, to see how it applies to the data previously seen in this chapter. After the install, a new PowerPivot tab appears on the Excel Ribbon. This is shown in Figure 16.34.

Figure 16.34
The PowerPivot tab on the Ribbon.

To get started, the first step is to click on the PowerPivot Window command at the far left of the Ribbon, under the PowerPivot tab. When this is done, a new Power-Pivot for Excel window opens. The purpose of this window is to hold and display the raw data you want to work with. Initially, this window is completely blank except for the Ribbon.

We then click the From Database command in the Get External Data section of the Ribbon, and select From Access. This initiates a Table Import Wizard that takes us through a number of steps to obtain some data. We'll first browse for our DataWarehouse.accdb Access database, and then select any Tables or Views we want to import from that database. If we desired to make things easy, we'd select the same dwSales query used in our prior pivot table example. However, to illustrate the capabilities of PowerPivot, we'll instead select all the underlying dimension and fact tables in the database, and leave out the dwSales query. These tables are: dim-Channel, dimCustomer, dimProduct, dimSalesperson, dimSalesType, dimTime, and factSales. Excel then copies the data in these tables to the PowerPivot window, a partial view of which is shown in Figure 16.35.

The data in each table is shown on a separate worksheet, viewable via tabs on the bottom of the screen. The next step is to click the PivotTable command in the PowerPivot window. This causes a new pivot table to be created from the data we just imported, with the focus moved to a new worksheet with the pivot table. We then see the familiar Pivot Table interface, with a few new enhancements. In place of the Pivot Table Field List, a PowerPivot Field List appears, shown in Figure 16.36.

The first noticeable difference is that the fields are now organized by table. Second, we see two new areas in the pivot table: Slicers Vertical and Slicers Horizontal. As will be seen, these areas are similar to the Report Filter area. To begin the process of placing data into the pivot table, we'll move the LinePrice field of the factSales table to the Values area, and the ProductCategory field of the dimProducts table to the Row area. Our screen now looks like Figure 16.37.

Figure 16.35
The PowerPivot window after data has been imported.

Figure 16.36
The PowerPivot Field List.

Two problems are immediately apparent. First, the pivot table seems to be displaying invalid values. Clearly, Coffee, Spices, and Tea do not each have a total price of $896. Second, we see a warning in the Field List that states that relationships may be needed. This means that PowerPivot does not yet know how the ProductCategory and LinePrice fields are related to each other. The resolution to this problem is simply to click the Create button on the PowerPivot Field List. When this is done, a Relationship window pops up that examines the data and automatically detects the relationships between these two fields. When this process completes, the pivot table assumes the correct values.

Figure 16.37
The pivot table and PowerPivot Field List.

In this manner, as new fields are added to the pivot table, new relationships are discovered by PowerPivot and added to a list of known relationships. After adding a few more fields, we can look at the relationships that were created by PowerPivot. These can be seen by opening up the PowerPivot window, and then clicking the Manage Relationships command under the Design tab. This is shown in Figure 16.38.

Figure 16.38
The Manage Relationships window.

As shown, PowerPivot has created four sets of relationships between various tables. In addition to this automatic process, one can create relationships manually by selecting the Create button on this window.

Before we leave our quick tour of PowerPivot, we'll illustrate one more feature. Figure 16.39 shows the same data seen previously in Figure 16.32. However, this time we have placed the SalesDate field in the Slicers Vertical area rather than in the Report Filter.

SalesDate		State	City	Zip	CustomerName	Sum of LinePrice
6/6/2011		AZ	Phoenix	85006	Elaine Crane	20
6/7/2011				85010	Ralph Berry	114
6/9/2011			Tucson	85708	Diana Day	48
6/10/2011		NM	Albuquerque	87106	Randy Smith	145
6/13/2011						
6/14/2011						
6/15/2011						
6/8/2011						

Figure 16.39
Pivot table with the Slicers area.

The idea of the Slicers area is that one can click on one date at a time and immediately have the data in the pivot table reflect that change. This is somewhat easier and more intuitive than having to go into a filter to modify data selection.

We'll leave details on the numerous capabilities of PowerPivot to books specific to the topic. From a business intelligence perspective, this tool occupies an interesting middle ground between lower-end pivot tables and higher-end tools that create full-blown OLAP cubes. In essence, PowerPivot gives the end user the ability to create their own data structures with the power of OLAP cubes. Thus, by using Access as a tool to organize data, and PowerPivot as a tool to access that data in a meaningful way, one has the ability to create business intelligence on the desktop.

Looking Ahead

In this chapter, we examined the ability of Excel pivot tables to attach to Access and further manipulate that data. In Chapter 15, we created a single query, named dwSales, that had reorganized production data into a dimensional structure, such as is typically done in data warehouses. Starting with this query, we showed how to connect to that data via an Excel pivot table, allowing us to view and manipulate relationships in an interactive manner.

After the connection was established, we explored the various aspects of the pivot table user interface, including field lists, layout options, filtering, grouping, formulas, drill-down, and drillthrough. This plethora of functionality assists the data analysis process by making it simple to summarize data in almost any desired level of aggregation, utilizing any or all dimensions in the underlying query.

We finished the chapter with a brief look at PowerPivot—a new tool that provides a few key capabilities over standard pivot tables. The most significant of the new features of PowerPivot is its ability to connect to multiple data sources and automatically detect relationships between data elements. Additional benefits are its array of new functions that take full advantage of the pivot table structure, and its ability to store data in a highly compressed cube-like structure that allows for efficient and quick data access.

With this book nearly concluded, a few additional thoughts are in order. We've taken a long and hopefully fruitful journey through the world of Access, from beginning chapters that covered the basics of the user interface to topics dealing with the details of data selection. We've learned how to utilize functions, summarize data, and utilize subqueries. Chapter 12, on Crosstab queries and pivot tables, led into the business intelligence topics of Chapters 13 through 16. Through all of this, the emphasis has been on topics useful for data analysis. The business intelligence construct covered in the final chapters was presented as a means of extending data analysis to a more structured way to organize data. The basic assumption was that reorganizing data into a dimensional design allows for further analysis possibilities that take advantage of this simpler structure. We illustrated how Excel pivot tables can work in conjunction with Access data, whether that data is in a normalized or dimensional structure.

The world of Access is an interesting one, because it requires and involves three overlapping concepts: logic, data, and analysis. The logic of Access is intimately related to the underlying SQL language that drives data retrieval. In fact, one can't truly understand the virtues and limitations of the Access graphical user interface without some knowledge of SQL. Hopefully, the "See the SQL" sidebars in this book have whetted your appetite to learn more about this language. In some ways, the logic involved in Access queries is more complex than the pure Boolean logic taught in university logic classes. This is because it needs to deal with the practical reality of data. The challenge of dealing with data as it is designed and stored in the real world definitely adds to the challenge and excitement of working with Access. The other component to this puzzle is analysis, which relates to the need to actually learn something useful from all this data. No easy formulas can be offered in that endeavor, since everyone's organization is different. The peculiarities of the data found within each organization is a world unto itself and can't be easily generalized. We can only hope to offer the basic tools that allow you to accomplish your goals, whatever they may be. It is my sincerest hope that this book assisted in that pursuit.

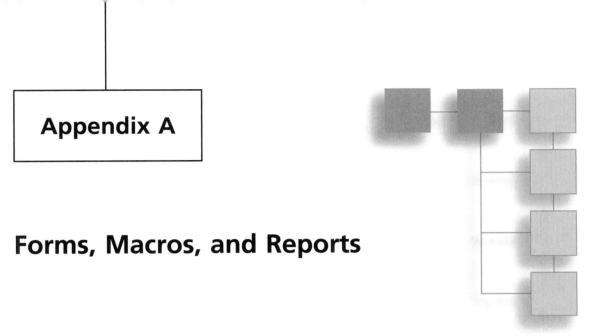

Appendix A

Forms, Macros, and Reports

The primary emphasis in this book has been on Access queries, and to a lesser extent, tables. The topics of forms, macros, and reports have barely been mentioned.

To rectify this shortcoming, this appendix provides a brief tutorial on this material. These topics are too complex and broad to provide even an overview of what can be done. Instead, we'll discuss a scenario in which we develop a small database with a few components involving forms, macros, and reports. This will hopefully provide a taste of what can be done in this area. You can find this database on the Cengage Learning companion website at:

- **www.courseptr.com/downloads**

The name of the database file is SalesDatabase.accdb.

The objective of this database will be to provide these two capabilities:

- A form that allows the user to select parameter values for a query, and then execute that query.
- A report that has been designed to aggregate data.

In Chapter 15, "The Data Warehouse," we mentioned that one shortcoming of standard Access parameters is the inability to provide a drop-down list of allowable values. The form in this database will show how this can be done.

We have not previously covered the ability to create reports in this book. Reports in Access can be based on any table or query, and allow the designer to format the data as it would appear on paper. In addition, the report can be designed to aggregate and summarize data, even if that summarization isn't part of the underlying query.

To accomplish these objectives, we'll create seven objects in this Access database:

- A table that holds information about sales by state and region.
- A query that selects data from the table, with selection criteria by region. This query will be tied to a form that's used to select parameter values and execute the query.
- A query that selects unique values of the Region field. This query will be used by the form to display the allowable values for region.
- A report that selects data from the table, summarizing data by region.
- A form used to select parameter values for the query and execute it.
- A form that serves as the main form for the database. This form will open automatically when the Access file is opened, and allow users to run either the query or the report.
- A macro that allows the user to view a message box with instructions on how to use the database.

Let's start with the table. Figure A.1 shows the data in a GeographicSales table.

Region	State	Sales
New England	VT	20000
New England	NH	25000
New England	ME	15000
Midwest	IL	40000
Midwest	IN	20000
Midwest	IA	15000
Southeast	FL	35000
Southeast	Georgia	20000
Southeast	Louisiana	15000

Figure A.1
Datasheet View of GeographicSales table.

The main query we want to write will select values from this table, based on the Region. The query is simple except for the parameter criteria value. The design of the query is shown in Figure A.2.

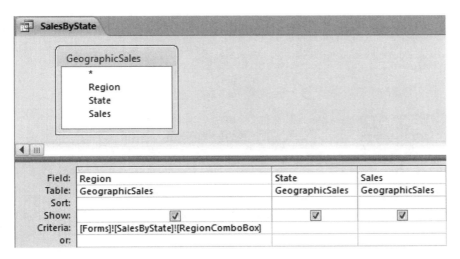

Figure A.2
Design View of SalesByState query.

The value in the Criteria line under the Region column is an expression with three components. The [Forms] component specifies that this expression comes from a form. The [SalesByState] portion is the name of the form. The [RegionComboBox] part is the name of the combo box object located on the SalesByState form. We can specify this value even though the form does not yet exist. This query will take the value specified in the combo box on the form and use that value to select the Region.

We now need to create a second query that will return a list of allowable values for the parameter. The design for this query is simple. We select the Region column from the GeographicSales table, and then set the UniqueValues for the query to Yes. As a result, this query will return the three regions in the table: New England, Midwest, and Southeast. We'll name this query UniqueRegions.

Now let's create a main form for the application. To begin the process of creating a form, we select the Form Design command in the Form section of the Ribbon under the Create tab. This places a blank form on the screen. We'll first place a label on this form, stating the title of the form for the user. To do this, we simply select the Label icon from the Controls section of the Ribbon under the Form Design Tools Design tab. We then drag a label onto the form, and then enter a value in the newly created Label box. We'll call it "Sales Database."

We now want to add a button that will close the form. To do this, we'll select the Button icon from the Control section, and place a button on the form. This causes a Command Button Wizard to pop up, asking a number of questions about the content of the button. After selecting the Form Operations category, the wizard appears as in Figure A.3.

Figure A.3
Command Button Wizard.

We'll then proceed to select the Close Form action. The next screen asks if we want text or a picture on the button. We'll select Text and specify the value "Close Form." Finally, when the wizard asks for a name for this command, we'll accept the default value. The result is the placement of a button with the name "Close Form" on the form.

We'll follow a similar process to add another button to the form to quit Access completely. We'll select the Application category, then the Quit Application action, and name the button "Quit Access."

We'll save this form with the name MainMenu and then go into the Access Options in the Backstage View to specify this form as the startup form. This is done by clicking the Current Database tab and specifying the value MainMenu as the Display Form. The form just created appears as in Figure A.4.

Figure A.4
MainMenu form.

We'll now move on to the form used to execute the SalesByState query. As before, we'll create a new form and add a label for the title. On this form, we want a button that will execute the query. To do this, we select the Miscellaneous category on the Command Button Wizard, and then the Run Query action. The next screen asks the name of the query to run. We then finish up with the button wizard as before.

Let's also add a button to return to the MainMenu form. To do this we'll again add a button, and select the category Form Operators and the Close Form action. We'll specify text for the button as "Return to Main Menu."

Finally, let's add a combo box control to this form. This will allow the user to select a parameter value. After adding a combo box control to the form, a Combo Box Wizard will appear. The first screen asks whether you want the combo box to get values from another table or query, or if you'll supply the values yourself. We'll reply to get the values from a table or query. The next screen asks for the name of the table or query. We'll specify the UniqueRegions query we created. The next screen asks for the field that contains the values to be listed in the combo box. We'll select the Region field. We'll then specify to sort the values in ascending order, and then specify a label for the combo box of "Select a Region."

For this combo box to work, two additional adjustments are necessary. First, the name of the combo box needs to be changed to "RegionComboBox". This is the name used in the parameter in the SalesByState query. This is done by changing the Name property for the combo box. Second, the form needs to be saved with the name "SalesByState". This is the name of the form in the parameter of the SalesBy-State query.

After all this is done, the SalesByState form will look like Figure A.5.

Figure A.5
SalesByState form.

The procedure for the user is to select a region in the combo box. Figure A.5 shows the selected value of "Midwest," but by clicking the down arrow, any of the other valid values can be chosen. After the selection is made, the user clicks the Run Query button, and the query is run and displayed.

Let's now turn to reports. In this exercise, we will create a report based on the GeographicSales table. To initiate the report, we'll click the Report Wizard command in the Reports section of the Ribbon, under the Create tab. This causes a Report Wizard window to appear, as shown in Figure A.6.

Figure A.6
Report Wizard table and field selection.

We'll select the GeographicSales table and all available fields. The next screen lets you specify grouping for the report. After selecting grouping by Region, the screen appears as in Figure A.7.

Figure A.7
Report Wizard grouping selection.

The next screen, shown in Figure A.8, asks for the sort order.

Figure A.8
Report Wizard table sort selection.

On this screen, we'll click the Summary Options button. This causes a Summary Options window to pop up. As shown in Figure A.9, we'll specify Sum values to be calculated, and that we want summary values only.

Figure A.9
Report Wizard Summary Options.

We then proceed to a screen that asks whether the layout should be Stepped, Block, or Outline. We'll select the Stepped layout. The final screen asks for a report name, which we'll provide as Sales By State. The report is now complete, and appears as in Figure A.10.

Figure A.10
Sales By State report.

The report groups the data by region and provides summary totals for each region. It's important to remember that this report was created from the table, which did not include any summary information. In effect, the report created grouping and aggregation without us having to write a query.

Now that the report is created, we can return to the MainMenu form and add a button to execute the report. We'll also want to add a button to allow the user to go to the SalesByState form that executes the SalesByState query. To add a button to execute the report, we'll select the Report Operations category, and then the Open Report action. To add a button to go to the SalesByState form, we'll select the Form Operations category, then the Open Form action, and then supply a text value of "View Query" for the button. After doing this, the form should look like Figure A.11.

Figure A.11
MainMenu form.

To recap, we created the following six objects:

- MainMenu form: the main entry point for the application
- SalesByState form: selects parameters for and executes the SalesByState query
- GeographicSales table: holds data
- SalesByState query: selects data from GeographicSales by a region parameter
- UniqueRegions query: supplies values for the allowable values for the parameter
- Sales By State report: selects data from GeographicSales, summarizing by region

As a final topic in this appendix, let's discuss macros. Macros can be used in numerous ways and for a multitude of purposes. In this tutorial, we'll provide just one example of what can be done. To get started, we'll click the Macros command in the Macros & Code section of the Ribbon, under the Create tab. The main portion of the screen appears as in Figure A.12.

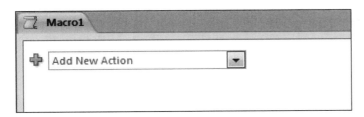

Figure A.12
DesignView of a new macro.

Macros can consist of any number of steps. This screen shows the first step of the macro, which at this point has not yet been assigned an action. When clicking the drop-down arrow for the step, one is presented with a list of 70 actions from which to select. In this exercise, we'll select the MessageBox action. The screen then appears as in Figure A.13.

At this point, we need to enter the required information for the MessageBox. After filling in the text boxes, the screen appears as in Figure A.14.

If desired, we can now add another action. However, we will choose to end it here, as this will be a simple one-step macro. After saving the macro with the name Message-Box, we'll return to the MainMenu form and add a button to execute this macro. The button will be created with the Miscellaneous category and Run Macro action. We'll select the Instructions macro and specify "View Instructions" as the text for the button. After clicking the new View Instructions button, the MainMenu form appears as in Figure A.15.

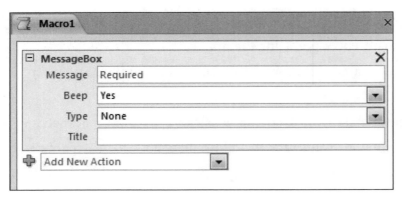

Figure A.13
DesignView of a macro with a selected MessageBox action.

Figure A.14
DesignView of a macro with a completed MessageBox action.

Figure A.15
MainMenu form with a message box generated from a macro.

This demonstration of macros barely touches the subject. In addition to the numerous actions that can be employed, there is also the option of specifying logical flow for those actions. For example, one can specify that certain steps in a macro be executed only if a specified expression evaluates to true.

Appendix B

A Sample Business Intelligence Database

The Access database described in Chapter 15, "The Data Warehouse," is available at this Cengage Learning companion website:

- **www.courseptr.com/downloads**

The name of the database file is: DataWarehouse.accdb.

This database illustrates the process of building a data warehouse that can be used for business intelligence analysis. At the beginning of Chapter 15, the process of building a data warehouse is described as being composed of these steps:

1. Create tables linked to production data.
2. Create tables to store the dimensions of a data warehouse.
3. Create tables to store the facts of a data warehouse.
4. Create a data warehouse via a query that joins the dimension and fact tables.
5. Create queries designed to retrieve data from the data warehouse.

The database on the companion website conforms to the discussion in Chapter 15, with one exception. In step 1, rather than create tables linked to production data, we have supplied tables that already contain data. These are the tables with the "prod" prefix.

The following is a listing of the tables and queries contained in the provided Access database, corresponding to the above-mentioned steps:

- Step 1: Create tables linked to production data.

This first step involves providing tables that contain production data. See Figure 15.1 for a diagram that shows the relationships between these tables. In a real-world situation, one would want to link tables linked to production data. As a matter of convenience, these tables in our Access database are not linked. They already contain the sample data.

The tables with production data are:

> prodCategories
>
> prodChannels
>
> prodCustomers
>
> prodOrderDetail
>
> prodOrderSummary
>
> prodProducts
>
> prodReturnDetail
>
> prodReturnSummary
>
> prodSalesperson

■ Step 2: Create tables to store the dimensions of a data warehouse.

In this step, Make Table queries are executed to create the required dimension tables. The queries that accomplish this are:

> createChannel
>
> createCustomer
>
> createProduct
>
> createSalesperson

The tables created by these queries are:

> dimChannel
>
> dimCustomer
>
> dimProduct
>
> dimSalesperson

Two additional dimension tables are provided in the database:

> dimSalesType
>
> dimTime

- Step 3: Create a table to store the facts of a data warehouse.

In this step, Append queries are run to create a fact table for the data warehouse. The queries that accomplish this are:

appendOrders

appendReturns

The table created by these queries is:

factSales

In addition, a query is provided to initially create the factSales table:

createSales

- Step 4: Create a data warehouse via a query that joins the dimension and fact tables.

In this step, a Select query is provided that relates the dimension and fact tables. This query creates the data warehouse. See Figure 15.2 for a diagram of the relationships between these tables. This query is:

dwSales

- Step 5: Create queries designed to retrieve data from the data warehouse.

In this step, Select queries are provided that report on data in the dwSales query. These queries are:

rptSales

rptProductAnalysis

INDEX